NURSLINGS OF

IMMORTALITY

William A. Bentley devoted his life to the study of snow crystals. He lived in the mountains of New England. It is estimated that he took over four hundred thousand micro-photographs of which a selection of about two thousand have been published in a book entitled *Snow Crystals* by W. A. Bentley and W. J. Humphreys, Copyright 1931 by McGraw-Hill Book Company, Inc. Six of these are reproduced here by permission. Although all snow crystals have the hexagonal ground-plan, Bentley says that he never found two crystals exactly alike.

NURSLINGS OF IMMORTALITY

by

RAYNOR C. JOHNSON
M.A. (Oxon), Ph.D., D.Sc. (Lond)
Master of Queen's College, University of Melbourne
author of
"The Imprisoned Splendour"

" But from these create he can
Forms more real than living Man,
Nurslings of Immortality."
P. B. SHELLEY

HARPER ⚛ COLOPHON BOOKS
Harper & Row, Publishers
New York, Evanston, San Francisco, London

First HARPER COLOPHON edition published 1972

LIBRARY OF CONGRESS CATALOG CARD NUMBER: 74-186141

STANDARD BOOK NUMBER: 06-090262-0

To MARY
With gratitude and affection
also to
MAUREEN, BERYL AND TREVOR, LESLIE, AND DAVID
good companions on the Way of Return
and last but not least
to my friend for long ages
AMBROSE

FOREWORD

by The Rev. Leslie D. Weatherhead, M.A., Ph.D., D.D.

My friend Dr. Raynor Johnson, questing for a reasonable philosophy of life, has written what is to me a wonderful book, thought-provoking, challenging, and a book which opens up new vistas of speculation. The term epoch-making may be too lightly used, but I believe his last book, *The Imprisoned Splendour*, deserved that description and, in my opinion, this does too.

Inasmuch as this book is in part an exposition of Mr. Douglas Fawcett's philosophy of "Imaginism", I am not competent to make any useful comment on it. But I am glad to comment on the sections concerning religion.

I have frequently stated my own beliefs, and they seem in harmony with those of the author.

1. Man's perception of truth should be a constantly growing thing, and in each generation man should claim freedom to restate truth as he sees it in the light of new knowledge and clearer insight. St. Paul exerted his right to state, in the thought-forms of his day, the truth as he saw it. We should do the same and refuse to be imprisoned by the language and outlook of a devout and brilliant Jew of the first century, just as we refuse to be bound by the thought-forms and outlook of, say, Newton, however brilliant he may have been. The light of truth moves on, and as soon as it authenticates itself in our minds as truth, we must follow it wherever it leads and be held back by no one, however brilliant or devout. A *mental* image such as a creed provides, inspiring though it is in many ways, can also inhibit the development of thought and worship, much as a *metal* image arrests the growth of ideas. Both can produce idolatry. No one today, trying to write down the truth about God, would do so in the unaltered language of the creeds. Why, then, does a thinking Church cling to their language when the truth calls for re-statement?

2. Where truth is relevant to man's personality, we should realise that it has no value for that personality until it is *seen and felt to be true* by intuitive insight and response. When this happens, truth should be accepted, not as though a terminus had been reached, but as a stage forward in a long journey. Clearly, then, we must not be told what it is compulsory to believe, for compulsion and real belief never go together. I may "*assent*" in order to please, or for fear of one kind or another, but "*belief*" means that truth has possessed my mind and obtained the sanction of my inner self. That possession cannot be

denied without insincerity. Jesus never imposed belief, but He did say that the first commandment was to love God with all one's mind.

3. From this it follows that the Christian must never turn away when new ideas are offered him. The heresy of one age is sometimes the orthodoxy of the next. New ideas are not to be gulped down because they are new, any more than old ideas are to be retained because they are old. The new ideas are to be examined. Old ideas are to be treated with reverence since so many scholars have held them and so many saints have lived by them, but reverence should never mean insincerity. Only perceived truth has authority and power in our lives. Let us by all means leave many new ideas *sub judice* until we can meditate on them and examine them, neither rejecting nor accepting, but waiting that guidance into the truth which is promised, remembering that no one can be guided anywhere if he refuses to move!

4. We shall never win for Christianity the thoughtful people of today while our religion is imprisoned in the superstitions of the fundamentalists, or those who escape from all subsequent adventurous thinking in the supposedly secure harbour called orthodoxy. In my view, creeds are to a large extent prisons. I admire them and their authors as one admires those who hammered out statements of scientific truth, such as Dalton and his atomic theory. But creeds were written down not to be imposed on men for ever, but to clarify the thought and to meet the challenge of their day. They represented what men believed at the time they were written. But why chant every Sunday, "I believe in the resurrection of the body", and then have to explain that you do not mean "resurrection" or "body" in the sense in which their author used the words? It is like chanting Dalton's atomic theory that the atom is the smallest conceivable part of an element, adding that by "atom" you mean "electron", or whatever the latest theory may substantiate as the truth so far perceived.

5. It is this refusal to move on in our thinking, still clinging to outmoded words, this using of words which say one thing and meaning by them something quite different, which is losing respect for religion amongst thoughtful people. This authority scientists now have. They are not slaves to tradition. They do not ask, "Is this view venerable"? They ask, "Is it true"? and they discard it at once if it is not. They do not ask for "belief". They offer evidence, and always they are ready to MOVE ON, while admitting, as religious people should, how little is known, how vast the area of mystery. For example, the dogma of the blessed Trinity may be the least erroneous way of thinking about the nature of God, and was written down to answer the charge that Christians worshipped three Gods, but who today would seriously say with the creed, "He that doth not believe this shall be damned"?

How can man imprison in a form of words devised fourteen hundred years ago, the entire nature of the Eternal and Infinite God?

6. This point of view has more than academic importance. Many thoughtful men are hungry for what religion can offer. They know that its essentials are a fundamental need, but they are like hungry men who arrive at the baker's shop and find it closed. They can see the loaves through the windows, but they cannot get at them. The truth is that the churches are not offering men the food they need. Men are put off by many things, but mostly by archaic language and imposed credal demands. As Froude the historian said, "If medicine had been regulated three hundred years ago by Act of Parliament; if there had been thirty-nine articles of Physic and every licensed practitioner had been compelled under pains and penalties to compound his drugs by the prescriptions of Henry the Eighth's physician, Dr. Butts, it is easy to conjecture in what state of health the people of this country would at present be found." The spiritual state of our health can be partly accounted for by similar obscurantism in sincere religious thinking. The unintelligent effort has been made, not to find out the truth, but to preserve Christianity unchanged. "The churches", said the late Clutton Brock, "are not taken seriously because they think officially, because they seem tied by the leg to certain dogmas, however long their tether may be. Their apologetics, when most liberal and intelligent, remain apologetics, having for their aim, not the discovery of truth, but the proof that there is still some truth in Christianity." Certain basal facts are true for ever, of course, but the theologian has been more concerned to defend tradition than to discover truth, and the consequence is that in this modern world *he is left hugging words to his heart when the strength of the truth is no longer in them*. Only when truth becomes our own, born again for us in the silence of our own hearts, has it power and beauty. I welcome this book. It makes me ask questions about what I really do believe. It stimulates my mind to *move on*. It unlocks locked doors. It opens up new vistas. Some ideas may be mistaken. One wonders how far we are all trying to rest in mistaken ideas, and whether that is why so many of us are restless. How many of us try to feel a thing is true by repeating it every week, when honest examination would show us our mistake and lead us to *move on*. Says Browning in "A Death in the Desert":

> "God's gift was that man should conceive of truth
> And yearn to gain it, catching at mistake
> As midway help till he reach fact indeed."

7. This book deserves close study rather than casual reading. In my opinion, it helps us move on towards truth. We need not be con-

cerned about new speculations, views and ideas. The truth is mighty and will prevail. But it will prevail more quickly if its temporary expressions are constantly re-examined and challenged. He who seeks the truth is always near to God, for God inspires the seeker's quest, sustains his enquiries, and is Himself the end of all our journeying.

FOREWORD

by Douglas Fawcett

What is the basic hypothesis of the philosophy called Imaginism? Well, when contrasted with the fundamental Hegelian attitude, its meaning stands out in high relief. Ignoring here a wealth of minor hypotheses, I exploit this illuminative contrast as follows:

Plato, upholder of "the divine principle of Reason", laid the foundations of the rationalism which Hegel, using and developing Kant's categories, was to complete. Hegel, exploring his own mind, declined to regard the reason showing therein as merely "one among a crowd of other faculties". He exalted this phase of mind into "the basis of everything", into the "energy" and "sovereignty" of the universe. Reason's stress, with its cosmic logic universal and irresistible, became for him "the all-animating spirit of all the sciences". The real is the rational and the rational is the real. The task of philosophy is to descry the energising notions (ideas, concepts) under the shapes which these assume in phenomena, that is to say, in appearances in Nature and the history of sentient life. Only "particular modes of expression", not reason "in its proper form", show in human experience. In this way Hegel, transcending "the field of the external and internal sense", lures us into his Neverland of abstract thought. The notion is the "secret of the mind", neither seen nor heard. But it and its mode of expression are rooted in the Divine Idea, in the rational "Truth-Whole", complete, perfect, and finished, which is named God or the Absolute. No subjective idealism is implied; cosmic appearances are established on God.

I pass now to the contrast by which we are to profit. Imaginism differs radically from Hegel's adventure of thought. It insists that his experiment was made at the cost of ignoring very much which human knowledge includes. In *selecting* reason as "sovereign" of the world, Hegel incurred a risk—could this phase of the human mind, promoted to the glory of the Absolute, provide a basis for everything else? Failure in this regard has proved decisive.

Imaginism contends that ultimate reality, the *Fons et Origo* of Being, God as World-Ground or World-Principle, that completely concrete and flexible activity from which all phenomena proceed, resembles, not the abstraction—reason—but the private imagining or fancy so richly exemplified in ourselves. Imagining, urged J. S. Mackenzie, has been too long "the Cinderella of philosophy", though "all existing things are, in an intelligible sense, imaginary".[1] Divine intuitive imagining is

[1] *Elements of Constructive Philosophy*, p. 440.

II

that radiance beyond reason which, present to itself, has no need of abstract thought. Reason is just a name for reasonings; reasonings, their notions (concepts), propositions, and logic are features only of the lives of finite sentients such as ourselves, features generated slowly in the time-process in connection with organisms. The evolution of inference, inductive and deductive, can be indicated. Its beginning is in fancy and at first has only practical value. Logic, as Professor Montague holds, emerges as the censor of this fancy. I have dealt with this topic more fully elsewhere.

The critic, however, may ask—is imagining so pervasive as to be all-embracing? Selection was the reef on which Hegelianism was wrecked. Perhaps the activity now selected may be merely a phase of my mind, not the basis of all aspects of the universe. The objection is timely, but an answer is made in the words of Professor Ribot: imagining "is everywhere" in my mind, not merely a phase among phases devoid of it. It operates in the simple and the most complex mental happenings alike, e.g. "underneath all the reasonings, inductions, deductions, calculations, demonstrations, methods, and logical apparatus of every sort" [1] this activity constructs. Considering the cosmos at large, F. C. S. Schiller held that Imaginism "can really afford to be what other metaphysical hypotheses falsely claim to be, viz. all-embracing. It can be represented as including not only all reality but all unreality". It can include all that we suppose to exist, but is source also of the novel, of phenomena as yet unborn—as none of the Indian, German, and British Absolutes, complete, perfect and finished, can be! The free man of the future, ignoring the herd-creeds but aware of this World-Principle, will unite religion and joy; religion meaning a "tie" (ligare=to bind), i.e. devotion to the noblest value in his outlook.[2] He will solve also long-standing philosophical and theological problems. Thus he will dethrone the changeless Deities or Absolutes of different types; dispel the mystery investing time-sequence which Bosanquet and others have regarded as the "central crux" of philosophy; surmise plausibly how the particular world-process called ours came to exist, stressing the underlying factors of creative evolution. He will have come to understand the actual origin of evil and the sources of the abominations which pollute so much of Nature and human history, having accepted a causation compatible with freedom and chance. He will forecast also a purgation of reality denied to thought-systems which posit changeless Absolutes. Lastly he will dwell to great profit on the riddles of the origin, standing, and prospects of the human individual; riddles which, solved unsatisfactorily, generate contempt for life and demoralise.

[1] *Essay on the Creative Imagination.*
[2] Cf. *Oberland Dialogues*, Chap. VII, "A Chat about Religion."

Well, the main hypothesis of Imaginism has been stated with just a glimpse of its range. Patient verification in the fields of science, art, and religion is called for. The reader is fortunate in being able to profit by the guidance of an eminent physicist, who is also a philosopher and expert in psychical research, Dr. Raynor Johnson. We two inquirers have never met in the flesh. Enjoyment of *The Imprisoned Splendour* led me to write to its author, who in this way was to know of my *Zermatt* and *Oberland* Dialogues. We are now fellow-soldiers in the war against materialism which today seems to be fighting in its last ditch.

AUTHOR'S PREFACE

EVERY thoughtful person recognises the need for finding a "philosophy of life". Such finding is really a life-long task except for those who have closed their minds to new ideas. To all of us there come hours when we hunger to understand the riddle of life, why we are here and for what goal we are bound. Is life just "a tale told by an idiot, full of sound and fury, signifying nothing", or is it full of meaning of which at present we can only grasp a little? Is it a succession of chance events turned perhaps by the fortunate and determined person to advantage, or is it shot through with benevolent purpose even though we are too close to it to see the pattern? We may hold tentative answers to these questions, yet they remain to haunt our thinking.

A philosophy of life has not necessarily any close relationship with academic philosophy, although some philosophers have important things to say to us—if we could understand them. I have done my best in this respect. I may perhaps claim without immodesty to have a reasonably wide knowledge of certain other fields which interest me, psychical research, mysticism, and religious experience, but I want to make it clear that I write primarily as a scientist. My concern first and last has been with truth, so far as I can see it. I do not expect many readers to agree with all the views I have expressed; I only ask that they weigh them carefully, for I believe that they illumine a little the essential mystery of life.

Some two years ago, by a strange series of events, my attention was first directed to the relatively little-known philosophical works of Mr. Douglas Fawcett, and as I read and meditated upon his thought, I came to the conclusion that he had, by a stroke of genius, found a clue to the great Mystery. By his appreciation of the real nature of Imagining he has thrown a flood of light on those ultimate questions which challenge thoughtful people afresh in each generation. His views have implications for scientific and for religious thought which I have endeavoured to present as simply as I could.

I want to emphasise, however, that my task has been only that of an interpreter: the original creative thought has been wholly that of Mr. Fawcett. Full of years, he is happily still with us as I write, and he has honoured me by writing a Foreword to this book. I venture to make one prediction, and this I shall not live to see fulfilled: this outlook will slowly but profoundly influence thought, and Mr. Fawcett's name will be better known a century hence than it is today.

My task, as an interpreter, has been to bring Mr. Fawcett's philosophical ideas and outlook within the grasp of the ordinary person untrained in special academic disciplines but seeking a philosophy of life. The long reign of scientific materialism is drawing to a close, and philosophically minded scientists are groping around to see what outlook will replace it. Ordinary men and women are looking with much wistfulness and concern to find meaning in their world, and frequently do not find answers which satisfy them in the modern presentations of religion. In the outlook presented in this book there is something to meet both these needs. It is an outlook in which both East and West should be able to meet together in understanding: and this is one of the great needs of the Age. If the book helps some who read it to see themselves and their environment *sub specie aeternitatis*, I shall be well content.

May I make a few suggestions to the reader, who I shall assume is not trained in philosophy. The philosopher should of course study Mr. Fawcett's own works, the *Zermatt Dialogues* and the *Oberland Dialogues*, as indeed I hope some of my readers will afterwards do. Chapter II cannot by its very nature be simple reading: I advise my readers not to struggle with it, but to absorb its "atmosphere", pass on, and return to it later if they wish. The non-scientific reader could omit any passages in Chapter III which present difficulty to him: they are not essential to the main theme of the book.

I do not claim that the following chapters are solely an exposition of Imaginism, but rather that this outlook has been the source of inspiration in my own thinking.

It is a pleasure to thank many authors and publishers who have allowed me to quote from their works, and thus to enrich or clarify my own. These kindnesses I have acknowledged separately. For help in typing the manuscript I wish to thank Mrs. Kroese and Mrs. Dunwoody. For the unique help which she has given to me I desire to thank Miss Geraldine Cummins. Finally, my old friend Dr. Leslie Weatherhead has honoured me by writing a Foreword to the book, and I am grateful to him for this kindness.

R. C. JOHNSON.

QUEEN'S COLLEGE,
UNIVERSITY OF MELBOURNE.
February 1956.

CONTENTS

ACKNOWLEDGMENTS

I DESIRE to thank the following authors, publishers, or owners of copyright for permission to quote extracts from the works which are mentioned below: Messrs. George Allen and Unwin Ltd. for extracts from *Letters to a Friend* by C. F. Andrews, from *The Nature of Human Personality* by G. N. M. Tyrrell, and from *The Facts of Life* by C. D. Darlington, and from an article in *The Hibbert Journal* by Professor H. H. Price; Messrs. Burns, Oates, and Washbourne Ltd. and Sir Francis Meynell for extracts from *The Works of Francis Thompson*; Cambridge University Press Ltd. for extracts from *Science and the Modern World* by A. N. Whitehead, and from *Honest Religion* by John Oman; Messrs. Jonathan Cape Ltd. for extracts from *Diagnosis of Man* and *The Circle of Life* by Kenneth Walker; Messrs. William Collins Sons and Co. Ltd. for an extract from *Thirty Years of Psychical Research* by Charles Richet; Crown Publishers Inc. N.Y. for extracts from *There is a Psychic World* by Horace Westwood; Miss Geraldine Cummins for extracts from three of her books, *The Road to Immortality*, *Beyond Human Personality*, and *Travellers in Eternity*; Lord Glenconner for a poem from *The White Wallet* by Pamela Grey; Messrs. Faber and Faber Ltd. for an extract from *This World and That* by Payne and Bendit; Mr. de la Mare for the poem *Vain Questioning*; John Farquharson, Esq., for an extract from *The Will to Believe* by William James; Good Housekeeping for a poem by Harry Lee; Messrs. Hamish Hamilton Ltd. for a passage from *Progress and Catastrophe* by Stanley Casson; The Houghton-Mifflin Co. for extracts from a poem *So far, so near* by C. P. Cranch; Messrs. Macmillan and Co. Ltd. for extracts from *Nature, Man and God* by William Temple, *Creative Unity* by Rabindranath Tagore, and with Mr. Diarmuid Russell for three poems of A. E. (George Russell) from *Collected Poems*. A number of passages are quoted also with Mr. E. D. Fawcett's permission from his books *Zermatt Dialogues* and *Oberland Dialogues*. The McGraw-Hill Book Co. Inc. for the plate of snow crystals from the book of Bentley and Humphreys with this title; Sir Francis Meynell for the last three verses of Alice Meynell's poem *Christ in the Universe*; Messrs. A. P. Watt and Son for part of a sonnet of Henry Newbolt *When I remember* from *Poems New and Old* (John Murray Ltd.); James Nisbet and Co. Ltd. for extracts from *God in Christian Thought and Experience* by W. R. Matthews; Oxford University Press for passages from *The Problem of Christ in the Twentieth Century* by W. R. Matthews, and the Clarendon Press, Oxford, for the verse of a poem by Robert S. Bridges from *The Yattendon Hymnal*; Messrs. Rider and Co. Ltd. for extracts from *The Country Beyond* by Jane Sherwood, from *Grades of Significance* by G. N. M. Tyrrell, and from *The Nameless Faith* by Lawrence Hyde; Messrs. Routledge and Kegan Paul Ltd. for extracts from *New Model of the Universe* by P. D. Ouspensky, and from *Religion, Philosophy and Psychical Research* by C. D. Broad; the S.C.M. Press Ltd. for extracts from *Life is Commitment* by J. H. Oldham; Messrs. A. P. Watt and Son on behalf of the Tweedsmuir Trustees and Messrs. Cassell and Co. Ltd. for an extract from *Sir Walter Scott* by John Buchan; also for lines from the *Countess Cathleen* by W. B. Yeats by permission of Mrs. Yeats and Messrs. Macmillan and Co. Ltd.; Messrs. Methuen and Co. Ltd. for extracts from *Body and Mind* by William McDougall, and from *Supernormal Faculties in Man* by Eugene Osty; The Hon. Secretary of the Society for Psychical Research for numerous extracts from the Proceedings and Journal cited; Messrs. George G. Harrap and Co. Ltd. for a verse from *The Poems of Sir William Watson* 1878-1935; Messrs. Sidgwick and Jackson Ltd. for an extract from a poem of Rupert Brooke entitled *Safety*.

THE NEED FOR A PHILOSOPHY OF LIFE

In my youth I regarded the universe as an open book, printed in the language of physical equations and social determinants, whereas now it appears to me as a text written in invisible ink, of which, in our rare moments of grace, we are able to decipher a small fragment.

ARTHUR KOESTLER (*The Invisible Writing*)

Men need not be envied who, in the voyage of their lives, are not silently conscious in meditative moments of their working days of some High Figure who first placed chart and compass in their hands.

LORD MORLEY

AN AGE OF INSECURITY

IT is probably unwise to anticipate the verdict of future historians upon the age in which we live. To some, looking back, it may seem the great Age of Science and Technology. When we reflect upon nuclear research and its applications, upon supersonic flight, radar, radio-astronomy, television, and electronic computing devices, such a judgment might not be ill-founded. To others, looking back, it may seem to have been the Age of the last great World Wars. But if the future historian could look within the mind of the common man today, he might well decide to name it the Age of Insecurity.

In an interesting book[1] written in 1937, Stanley Casson has analysed the conditions which have led to progress and decline in civilisations. He quotes from the letters of Sidonius, who was a Roman nobleman living the life of a country squire near Clermont in Southern France about the middle of the fifth century. We are able to see through his eyes the life of pleasant culture, hunting, and dinner parties enjoyed by himself and his friends. There was no serious expectation with them that things would ever change. Had he but known it, outside his curtained windows the sunset of the great Roman Empire was providing the last gleams of day. Thereafter, dark night descended upon Europe for a thousand years. When at last signs of the oncoming night could no longer be ignored, poor Sidonius—with some reluctance—entered the Church, where, as Casson says, "the shadows were more obvious than the beams of light" and where "as so often before, men fled in terror of the unknown to the comforts of the unknowable". There he lived, as

[1] Stanley Casson, *Progress and Catastrophe.* (Hamish Hamilton Ltd., 1937.)

the words of his own epitaph inform us, "tranquil amid the swelling seas on the world".

Writing before the Second World War seemed inevitable. Casson drew a parallel between the conditions then existing and those heralding the Dark Ages of Europe. Now, ten years after the close of that war, it is not generally felt that the outlook is much brighter for mankind. When the ordinary man hears that hydrogen bombs are being stockpiled, each of which has explosive power equal to a million tons of T.N.T., and will cover with deadly radio-active dust a circle of fifty miles radius, he decides that he can do nothing about it and switches on his television set or goes into his garden to hoe the weeds. Both Sidonius and modern man have thus contrived to make tolerable a situation heavy with destiny which they could neither control nor understand. Sidonius became an ornament of the Church. Perhaps from his monastic retreat he heard rumours of Vandals and Goths at the gates of Rome, and turning, with a trembling hand to celebrate the Mass, wondered if life here and now had any enduring values. Modern man, in a more secular age, has made his retreat largely into the worlds of sport and entertainment, and in the intervals between he has adopted the war-time formula "Business as Usual". It cannot be denied, however, that he is suffering from much repressed anxiety. The prevalence of neurosis in our day is one of the clearest indications of this.

I shall have many things to say to modern man in this book, but I want to express this conviction immediately: that there is no security in escape—the only security is in courage. Courage is at least possible when a man has found a satisfying philosophy of life. In the light of this he can judge and meet with confidence all that may come to him. Real security is not found in the absence of external danger, but in attaining a certain inner knowledge and awareness. Such a man is then able to say with Rupert Brooke

> Safe shall be my going,
> Secretly armed against all death's endeavour;
> Safe though all safety's lost; safe where men fall;
> And if these poor limbs die, safest of all.

A philosophy of life is something that each man has to discover for himself. No truth that another may express is of any value until it becomes alive in his own thinking and experience. I shall try to present an outlook on man and his destiny which is alive for me, and which is true so far as I can see at present. I hope it may be a stimulus to the thought of others, and that it may point the way to that courage which flows from tranquillity "amid the swelling seas of the world".

IS HUMAN LIFE MEANINGFUL?

We tend to assume too easily that the age in which we live is one of unique difficulty, danger, and uncertainty. Every age may well have thought the same, for human nature craves for a background of security as a setting in which it may pursue its search for happiness. It is probably when bereavement, suffering, and loss break suddenly into this personal quest that most people ask themselves what, if any, is the meaning and purpose of life. Floods in China may render hundreds of thousands homeless, famine in India may cause suffering of a physical and mental kind beyond computation—and we may murmur our regret. But it is when we look at the features, still and unresponsive in death, of someone we have loved, that the real questioning of the heart and mind begins.

We live between the mysteries of birth and death. We come from the unknown and we pass into it again, as do all our fellow-mortals. Our own choice determines neither event, so far as we know. The more we ponder on the salient events between, the less we appear to be the architects of our lives. The given-ness of things is increasingly evident. It is as though we stand at the door of the theatre of life and the Great Producer hands to us a part, saying, "See what you can make of that!" Our freedom is substantially not to alter the part, but to play it well or indifferently. There appears to be so much of good that we have not earned and so much of ill that we have not deserved that the problem of the meaningfulness of life is fundamental. We like to take experience and link it all together in chains of cause and effect so that we can see both how and why things have arisen. We find in practice that the extent to which we can do this is very small. It might indeed be suggested that the play in which we are acting is a play of several Acts and that the riddle of events is determined by Acts which have gone before (which we do not remember) and Acts which will follow after (of which the script is not yet given to us). It might also be suggested that the Great Producer hands us each Act a page at a time and interweaves change and novelty as the play proceeds. We are all abundantly aware of the mystery of life, and none of us can read the Great Producer's mind.

The play is full of laughter and tears, but the tears puzzle us more than the laughter, for we have that strange unquenchable sense that we are born for happiness as the sparks fly upward. We look backwards and think what might have been, and what we might have done, forgetful for the moment of the given-ness of things.

Nothing is perhaps more poignant, to us the players, than the passing away of things we have valued and people we have loved. Perhaps we may meet them in a later Act or in the intervals between the Acts; but who can speak with authority on these things? Behind every philosophy of life lies the unsolved riddle of Time, whose

> moving waters at their priest-like task
> Of pure ablution round Earth's human shores

we certainly could not do without. Yet, what precious cargoes Time also carries away from our sight! On these occasions we ask questions about the meaningfulness of life. Science makes no claim to answer such questions, and the answers that Religion gives are not generally acceptable in this scientific age. The mystical insights of religion doubtless hold the clues to our most perplexing problems, but unless the answers are in terms which the questioner can understand, and to which he can make an intuitive response, he gains nothing. The fact is that all living truth springs from a perennial fountain within ourselves, and when some truth of religion becomes alive for us, it is because we already know it. All that outward formulations of truth can ever do is to express in a limited idiom the spirit's unlimited perceptions. Moreover, all the higher religions, which in their beginnings expressed the mystical insights of some great illuminated Soul, gather accretions through their interpreters and distortions through their zealots. The minds of men have an incorrigible tendency to create systems of thought. When this process is applied to the mystical insights of spiritual genius, the results are similar to those which an artist might achieve if, having some vision of surpassing delicacy, he endeavoured to portray it on a small canvas, using coarse brushes and inferior colours. In the case of Christianity the original Vision was timeless and universal but the first canvas was Jewish in its conception. This has always been considered to have particular authority, and it is perhaps this historic emphasis, in colours which do not attract modern man, which is one of the prime causes of Christianity's limited appeal. Perhaps some day we shall bow before the living vision rather than the static picture, and realise that this vision, in its timeless quality, is accessible to every age with equal authority. At present much of religion is "belief in believing". I shall say no more about religion at present, but I shall return to it in a later chapter of the present book.

Nor is modern man likely to find the answers to his heart-searching questions in present-day philosophy. Like the sciences, philosophy has found it necessary to create an exact language of its own, which is difficult to understand without a special training. Moreover, there are fashions in philosophy as there are in science, medicine, and art, and today the trend is towards the analysis of terms rather than an attempt to answer metaphysical questions.

It has been customary to describe certain epochs as "ages of faith", and others as "ages of scepticism". For my part, I think the urge of man to understand something of the meaning of his pilgrimage is in-eradicable and is found in every age alike. When the more orthodox avenues of enquiry do not satisfy, we find the quest pursued in other directions. I shall mention some of these and comment briefly on them.

MAN'S SEARCH FOR TRUTH

(1) I can think of no question to which a clear and unequivocal answer is more important for human beings than the one "Do the 'dead' live?" A widespread *conviction* of this truth, as distinct from faith, hope, or agnosticism about it, would do more in my opinion to raise standards of conduct, to check materialism, and to lighten the valley of the shadow than the answer to any other single question. Professor C. D. Broad has written:[1]

"It seemed to Sidgwick, and it seems to me, that unless some men survive the death of their bodies, the life of the individual and of the human race is 'a tale told by an idiot, full of sound and fury, signifying nothing'. I cannot understand how anyone with an adequate knowledge of physics, biology, psychology, and history can believe that mankind as a whole can reach and maintain indefinitely, an earthly paradise. Such a belief is a sign of amiability in the young; but of imbecility, ignorance, or wilful blindness in the mature. . . . All that I maintain is that it (survival) is a necessary condition, if the life of humanity is to be more than a rather second-rate farce."

Most people move in grooves of thought, and find it difficult to summon the courage and energy to investigate without prejudice a system of unfamiliar enquiry and belief. It is always uncomfortable and disconcerting to have the presuppositions of one's thinking disturbed. This weakness of human nature, perhaps more than any other single factor, has operated to discount and indeed to deride the investigation by psychical research of mediumship. Undoubtedly the second factor is that fraud and dishonesty have sometimes occurred at the expense of the credulous element in human nature, and these are anathema to the scientific spirit. Thanks however to the painstaking work of psychical research, covering now some seventy years and marked by careful experiment and critical judgment, the equal of that in any other field of enquiry, we can now make some reliable statements about the phenomena of mediumship. Where every possibility of fraud is elimin-ated, there have occurred many phenomena which are best understood if they are regarded as para-normal phenomena of the medium's own

[1] *Religion, Philosophy and Psychical Research*, p. 114. (Routledge and Kegan Paul Ltd., 1953.)

mind, exercised to an unusual degree in the trance state. But when the fullest allowance is made for these, there remains a substantial body of data, of which by far the simplest explanation is that it derives from the surviving discarnate beings of deceased persons. I, personally, give it as my considered judgment that certain deceased persons have, beyond any reasonable doubt, demonstrated their survival in the fullness of their powers of the change we call death. From such a conviction, of course, flow consequences in thought of the most far-reaching kind. All the values of life are conserved, not for the race merely, but for the individual. The camp of materialism has broken up. We are on the mainland—not on an ice-floe doomed to melt in the end. A whole continent of adventure is in front of us. We can greet our more cautious scientific friends with the knowledge that there are high lands to be explored beyond the foot-hills, even though we are not qualified as yet to reach them.

(2) Rudolf Steiner (1861-1925) originated a system of thought which is known as Anthroposophy or Spiritual Science, and it has won the interest and appreciation of many intelligent people. To pass from the writings of H. P. Blavatsky to those of Steiner is to pass from a twilight atmosphere of esotericism, magic, and mystery into the fresh air and revealing light of a penetrating mind. Judging him even by high standards, he was a very unusual boy, for we are told that at eight years of age he discovered in a book of geometry which was lent to him a fascinating new world. At fifteen years of age he saved his small earnings to buy Kant's *Critique of Pure Reason*, and this he studied when he felt other lessons were worthless. He was university-trained, and in the best sense a well-educated man moving with freedom and confidence in the fields of science, philosophy, and literature. While less than thirty, he was invited to join other scholars of the first rank in editing a new edition of the works of Goethe.

The most remarkable feature about Steiner was that apparently from his earliest years he possessed active and well-developed para-normal faculty. He was equally aware of two worlds, the familiar sensory one, and a "spiritual" world, and through many years of lonely searching he endeavoured to make sense of his experience and explore as far as he could these different levels of reality. He acquired a great deal of super-sensible knowledge and came to realise that the attainment of higher levels of consciousness through development of the mind's latent powers was essential to any discovery of the deeper truths about the world. He described the disciplines by which others could undertake this development and verify the observations he had made himself. These observations included the nature of man and of his various principles or vehicles, the method and story of man's evolution, and generally they provided answers to those profound questions about man's place in the universe which have always haunted seekers after truth.

Steiner was no friend or advocate of other-worldly mysticism, but maintained his devotion to the spirit of scientific enquiry throughout his life. He expressed his conviction that the search for hidden knowledge and wisdom must be related to the sensory world and not a flight from it. The system of knowledge which he left behind has in fact borne fruit in many practical fields such as those of healing, education, agriculture, and religion.

Steiner's legacy to the world is, I think, valuable in itself, stimulating in its character, and a pointer to vast fields of knowledge upon which Western man has scarcely yet focussed his attention. He claims to have set down nothing which was not based upon observations he had made himself. It has the great merit of being presented by a man well-versed in Western science and philosophy so that it is shown to us in its relation to what we believe and know.[1] Much of what he has recorded may well stand the test of others' observation in coming years: so far, however, he has had no successor. We must bear constantly in mind that no one else's experience can ever be an adequate substitute for our own. Steiner would have heartily endorsed the truth of this, for on higher levels of the world, "to know is to experience, and to experience is to know".

(3) There is an interesting system of thought linked with the name of G. I. Gurdjieff, which would probably not have been known outside a small circle of intellectuals had it not captured the interest of a number of able writers. P. D. Ouspensky was for eight years a pupil of Gurdjieff, and subsequently between 1923 and 1947 (when he died) taught small groups of people in London. Dr. Kenneth Walker, a Harley Street surgeon, himself a pupil of Ouspensky, has expressed a sense of the great importance of the teaching, and the late Dr. Maurice Nicoll has expounded the psychological principles behind it at great length.

Briefly expressed, it is a theory about man and the universe, fragmentary and esoteric in its character. Man is a machine. He believes that he acts, but in fact things merely happen. Man is a sleeper who can only be awakened by the exceptional man (who is awake). He is a prisoner who does not realise he is in prison, and failing to be aware of this he has no chance of escape. It is maintained that immortality is not something inherent in man, but that it has to be won. It is an essential part of this system to provide a psychological technique, or system of "work" on one's self, by which these things can be achieved. This is

---

[1] An excellent introduction to Steiner's thought is found in *A Scientist of the Invisible*, by A. P. Shepherd, D.D. (Hodder and Stoughton Ltd., 1954.)

described as a fourth way to the achievement of immortality, in contrast with the way of the fakir (in which the will is developed through physical austerities); the way of the monk (in which the will is developed through the subjection of the emotions); and the way of the yogi (which consists of work on the mind). Those who have followed this psychological practice for some years are probably the only ones who can assess its value. Of the teachings, I should be disposed to comment that they will remain with a small circle, and that stimulating as they are to thought, their fragmentary character and unrelatedness to the main stream of philosophic enquiry will not lead to their further development. From time to time such occult fragments of teaching appear above the surface, refresh the ground for a little space for a few people, and disappear as mysteriously as they have come.

(4) One of the significant features of our time is the growing interest of the Western world in the religious philosophy of Hinduism—especially in its best and most popular form of Vedanta. For intellectuals there are translations of René Guénon's books and expositions by Indian scholars such as Sri Aurobindo and Radhakrishnan. For the ordinary person there are the symposia edited by Isherwood and a number of fascinating biographies of Indian saints and holy men. This growing interest in the life and thought of the East may perhaps be traced to the widespread appreciation in the West of two figures of modern India, Gandhi and Rabindranath Tagore. Its deeper roots are probably to be found in a half-conscious sense of incompleteness and dissatisfaction which broods like a cloud over our highly developed materialistic civilisation, and a craving to discover whether in this ancient land there is not to be found some secret of the good life which we have missed.

In his characteristically poetic prose Tagore has reminded us

"The East has its seat in the vast plains watched over by snow-peaked mountains and fertilised by rivers carrying mighty volumes of water to the sea. There under the blaze of a tropical sun, physical life has bedimmed the light of its vigour and lessened its claims. There man has had the repose of mind which has ever tried to set itself in harmony with the inner notes of existence. In the silence of sunrise and sunset, and on star-crowded nights, he has sat face to face with the Infinite, waiting for the revelation that opens up the heart of all that there is."

The *Upanishads* are for the serious student, but the *Bhagavad Gita* in its profundity and simplicity is one of the world's great books and we should all, in both East and West, be the gainers in meditating on its wisdom. G. W. Russell (A. E.), the Irish poet and mystic, said of it, "I feel the authors must have looked with calm remembrance back through a thousand passionate lives, full of feverish strife for and with shadows, ere they could have written with such certainty of things which the soul feels to be sure."

The essence of Vedanta is monistic, i.e. it accepts one supreme principle *Brahman*, from which everything has issued. The essence of man, called the *Atman*, is one with the *Brahman*. *That thou art* is the supreme concept of Indian thought: the spirit of man is one in its nature with the supreme Spirit. We only think that other things have some reality because we have not known our true nature. We are ignorant of this: the reality is obscured from us by veils of *maya*. Re-incarnation, a continual cycle of births and deaths, is man's destiny until he achieves freedom and enlightenment by the realisation of his own true nature. The great law of Karma, of justice working through chains of cause and effect, secures that the conditions of man's living are those which he has created for himself in his long past. By the long process of upward striving or aspiration, and by progressive detachment from the unreal, the veils of maya are ultimately pierced, the karmic debts are ultimately discharged and the great returning home takes place.

In the briefest of summaries, this is the core of Vedanta, and the seeker after truth will be the richer in his outlook for pondering deeply upon it. It is at once a blend of religion and metaphysics, and in part a science of man.

(5) It would be possible to extend almost indefinitely an account of the ways in which men have sought the truth about life. They range from the philosophies of the higher religions such as Buddhism and Taoism to occult systems of the greatest variety. The latter usually blend in different proportions fragments of ancient wisdom of considerable generality with psychological practices akin to yoga designed to provide access to the para-normal powers of mind. These flourish because of two instinctive elements in human nature—the element of curiosity and the love of power. The data of psychical research—or para-psychology as it is sometimes now called—provide adequate evidence of many unusual powers inherent in the human mind, which can doubtless be harnessed to the task of widening the bounds of our knowledge both of this world and the next. As we know only too well in our day, wider knowledge and greater powers may be used for good or ill, and in themselves they do not lead to wisdom. Some may consider that in the spirit of scientific enquiry they should pursue these powers, and in this spirit it is all to the good. But I am quite sure that those who are seeking wisdom—insight about ultimate things—will not find it along this road. There are many significant worlds or levels of appearance behind the physical awaiting man's exploration and understanding: but Wisdom is far different from knowledge.

AIM OF THE PRESENT BOOK

The question "Is human life meaningful?" might well have been the title of this book, but having myself a conviction of the sublimity of man's destiny I prefer to use a phrase of Shelley[1] to convey this. The meaning of our human pilgrimage is avidly sought by man in the extremity of personal need and against a background of insecurity. The only answers that can ultimately be satisfying take us into deep waters. They involve the nature and activity of God Himself, what if any is man's relation to this mighty Being, the purpose of the vast universe in which our planet Earth is such a tiny speck, how and why man came to exist, whence comes the Evil in the world, and what is the nature of this strange river of Time which carries us along whether we wish it or not. I attempted in a previous book[2] to open a few doors and explore a little way, and here I return to the task with, I venture to think, a master-key which may unlock many of the others. I found this master-key in a very strange way of which sometime I may feel free to write. This key to understanding is the philosophical work and outlook of Edward Douglas Fawcett, more particularly as it is expressed in his two volumes *Zermatt Dialogues* (1931) and *Oberland Dialogues*[3] (1939). Mr. Fawcett is a professional philosopher and his works demand more concentrated application than the ordinary person is able to give. Unfortunately, even in academic circles his work has received little attention and the brilliant and far-reaching character of his intuitions arouse no serious interest today. It is my hope in this book to expound Fawcett's viewpoint in terms which are clearly intelligible to the ordinary person. It seems to me that it illuminates the major mysteries in a way which no other philosophy does. I shall try to illustrate its relevance to a deeper understanding of the data of natural science and also to the data of psychical research which are likely to be of increasing importance to the science of the future. I shall endeavour also to present a constructive picture of the life after death in order that so far as possible our human life here may be viewed in a cosmic setting.

It would be absurd to claim for Imaginism—which is the descriptive label attached to Fawcett's outlook—that it is a completely rounded system of philosophical thought. I am content to claim that in its broad outlines it is a cosmic outlook bearing the authentic stamp of truth, and I found, after studying it closely, both illumination of mind and inspiration in the thought that humanity is bound on so great an enterprise. I hope I can convey this to my readers.

[1] Used by Shelley in *The Poet's Dream* to describe the vitality of poetic imagining.
[2] *The Imprisoned Splendour.* (Hodder and Stoughton Ltd., 1953.)
[3] Published by Macmillan and Co. Ltd. See also *The World as Imagination* (1916) and *Divine Imagining* (1921).

I have decided to proceed with an introduction to Imaginism in the next chapter so that in the light of this we may then examine the scientific picture of the world. The wider issues are discussed in detail in later chapters.

Chapter

2

INTRODUCING IMAGINISM

THE BASIC CHARACTER OF IMAGINING

MOST people think of imagination or fancy as a subjective activity of the mind in which it creates spontaneously a flow of imagery. It is usually considered to be a faculty of little importance in practical life, but one which is an advantage in the artistic temperament. The artist is commonly supposed to escape in his art from the hard realities of life, and present to us the products of his fancy or inspiration in music, drama, painting, and literature. In those of us whose imagination lacks originality, or who have acquired no special skill in expressing it, the faculty is called day-dreaming. The common reaction to it is one of depreciation, and the psychologist is anxious to remind us that it is often compensatory to that which real life offers to us. The term "imaginary" is, indeed, popularly equated with "unreal".

The term "imagination" is rather ill-defined. It includes in its ordinary usage that *activity* of the mind which is imagining, and it often includes also in its meaning the *products* of imagining—those things which are imagined. We are interested in the faculty itself, and shall therefore use the term imagining.

We are going to suggest that this spontaneous uncontrolled activity of the relaxed mind, which in future we shall call fancy, is an overflow or bubbling-up in its least disguised form of a fundamental dynamic activity of the mind which is best termed imagining. We shall hope to show that all other activities of the mind are more or less transformed products of the basic imagining. When we recall some of the characteristic activities of the mind—memory, anticipation, wit, perception, reason, etc.—this may seem a large claim. Our first task is therefore to justify the claim.

Psychologists have been interested in the *products* of imagining, for purposes of psychiatry and psychotherapy, but the activity itself has received scant attention. It has been too lightly assumed that the association of old memories in new ways is an adequate explanation of its nature, much as in a kaleidoscope a few pieces of coloured glass may be arranged by chance to give a large variety of patterns.

Such a view could at most account for a few special cases—some dreams, delirium, and states of mild dissociation—while overlooking the profound character of creative novelty and inspiration. It is like assuming that a new work of art could be accounted for by bringing fragments of old canvases together, a Beethoven symphony accounted for by fragments of other musical compositions, or an ode of Wordsworth by phrases gleaned from other writing. The world contains now what it did not contain before these artists lived. It is not disputed that they created their works out of colours, musical notes, or words already present in the world. Human creation certainly implies the use of raw material. The point is that something new is added in the process, and this is the activity of imagining.

In a very rambling miscellany,[1] Samuel Taylor Coleridge discussed the subject of imagining in relation to literary creation. He does not deny that by the laws of association the raw material of creation is brought up into consciousness, but he rejects with scorn the idea that automatic machine-like activity can give rise to the most complicated literary structures without any creative "I" to shape them. He writes of imagining as an "esemplastic" power—shaping things into one. I shall here quote a passage of which the full significance will be clear later to the reader.

"The Imagination then, I consider as either primary, or secondary. The primary Imagination I hold to be the living power and prime agent of all human perception, and as a repetition in the finite mind of the eternal act of creation in the infinite I AM. The secondary Imagination I consider as the echo of the former, coexisting with the conscious will, yet still as identical with the primary in the *kind* of its agency, and differing only in *degree*, and in the *mode* of its operation. It dissolves, diffuses, dissipates in order to re-create: or where this process is rendered impossible, yet still at all events it struggles to idealize and unify. It is essentially *vital*, even as all objects (as objects) are fixed and dead."

If, as we claim, Imagining is the psychical spring within the mind, from which all other faculties derive, we must examine these carefully for evidence of their origin. Fancy, as we have said, is an upsurge of the fundamental creative power in its natural undisguised form. In the mind's other faculties we shall sometimes have to dig below the surface of techniques and accepted processes to discover it at work. Imagining is found to be always there, and Fawcett in a picturesque phrase[2] compares it with "a lava stream hidden under the slaggy crust of its own making and yet ever and anon sighted through clefts in the crust, or when white-hot at the growing point of its advance".

We shall later have occasion to dwell on the fact that Imagining, regarded as the fundamental power (not only within ourselves but in God), has two aspects. One of these is conservative, and it is in virtue of this activity continuously exercised that things continue in being. The

---

[1] *Biographia Literaria* (1817), Chapter XIII.
[2] *Oberland Dialogues*, p. 45.

other aspect is additive and therefore rich in creative novelty. In the fancy of the poet, the inventor, or the day-dreamer, it is the latter aspect which is the more prominent. We are now in a position to look at some of the mind's faculties, and we take memory first. It is interesting to find that Professor William McDougall thought of this as a form of imagining. In Chapter 9 we discuss it in some detail: all we need say now is that the conservative aspect of our fundamental power maintains memory in being, and that when we remember something, it is a new reconstruction which we make, based on this faint pattern.

Consider the faculty of anticipation. We have a simple illustration in everyday life when, before stepping off the pavement to cross a busy street, we look carefully, and form a judgment of the wisdom of doing so. This exercise of practical reason is sustained by the imaginative faculty although this may never rise into consciousness. Conservatively, it maintains the memory of accidents that we have seen, experienced, or read about; it maintains also the memory of our past experience in crossing streets so that we know what we can do again; and creatively we anticipate our safe arrival on the other side. The imaginative power behind anticipation is there in all human beings, and it is so strong that where, as we say, there is "nothing to look forward to", one of two things usually happens. Either it breaks through to the surface in uncontrolled anxiety states, and such a person lives in a state of misery wondering what he will do if such-and-such happens. Alternatively, the energy may be bottled up and a state of depression follows. Sometimes it may create an inner world of fantasy unrelated to life.

Wit is another of the mind's faculties found in very varying degrees in different people. Behind wit is imagining, scintillating like a fountain and creating verbal surprises, novel contrasts, and unusual juxtapositions of ideas which are of its essence.

In all forms of Desire we can trace the imaginative faculty at work both sustaining and elaborating it. The psychology of salesmanship is to stimulate desire by stimulating imagining of the many advantages or joys of possession. The exile comes back from the ends of the earth with great anticipation to see once more his boyhood's home. How often he returns to discover that the fairy fingers of fancy have painted his memories far different from the reality! Imagining sustains and creates between a lover and his beloved: it often sustains and creates a great deal which other people cannot see.

IMAGINING AND REASON

Perception is a difficult subject and will be deferred until Chapter 5. Perhaps what we have said may be tentatively acceptable to the reader, but he may be in revolt at the idea that reason owes anything to imagining. Has not reason given to us our finest intellectual achievements: the idea of Natural Law in science, the orderly system of mathematical thought, the realms of logic and philosophy? These are in striking contrast surely with the fairyland of imagination where artists and poets dream their dreams? Did not Hegel, seeking the sublimest faculty of man through which to form a conception of God, come to the conclusion that God was best described as Cosmic Reason?

But when we look behind the process of reasoning we find it is a process of experimenting. We reason about concepts: these are the raw material of experiment. Mathematics has its operational methods, so has logic: these are reason's tried and trusted weapons. When we reflect upon their origins, we discover that they were themselves once the products of imaginal experiment. All that is now taken for granted and used confidently was once imagined, tried tentatively, and came to be trusted because of experience. What are concepts but, in the first instance, fancies which we have created imaginatively as substitutes for facts? Such fancies have always to be tested against reality and are regarded as true concepts if they represent the facts sufficiently well to be satisfactory substitutes when we think about these realities.

We may of course have many fancies which do not stand the test of experiment, i.e. they are neither true nor useful. We may, on the other hand, have fancies which are useful but not true in the sense that there is nothing in Nature corresponding to them. The mathematician, for example, fancies imaginary numbers, infinite numbers, and queer kinds of space. These are useful concepts, but not true in the above sense. It is the business of every learned discipline to test fancies, converting some into true concepts and incorporating these into wider concepts or systems, while rejecting others as neither true nor useful. Every science is constantly doing this. The function of reason is to be—in a happy phrase of Professor Montague—a "censor of fancy", its job being to test what imagining has originated.

It may be of value to the reader to hear the opinions of some eminent thinkers in a variety of fields. Professor W. P. Montague[1] writes:

" Imagination is the main source of all new ideas and of all variations, not only in the life of art, but in the life of science. . . . [It is] the business of comparing the newly born hypothesis of imagination with the established community of older principles which constitutes the work of reason. The function of reason is, in other words, not so much to originate as to prove. Reason is the censor of fancy, selecting from the wealth of new ideas those which can successfully stand comparison with the old and be made harmonious with them."

[1] *Ways of Knowing*, pp. 64-5.

Professor Ribot writes in his *Essay on the Creative Imagination*:

"Underneath all the reasoning, inductions, deductions, calculations, demonstrations, methods, and logical apparatus of every sort, there is something animating them that is not understood, that is the work of that complex operation, the constructive imagination."

Earl Russell, who has no love for mysticism, speaking of the field of pure mathematics, recognises that where normal techniques can go no further, progress is by a "new effort of logical imagination". Professor A. N. Whitehead says that mathematics consists "in the organisation of a series of aids to the imagination in the process of reasoning".

In philosophy, Hume[1] spoke of imagination as "a kind of magical faculty in the soul which, though it be always most perfect in the greatest geniuses, and it is properly what we call genius, is however inexplicable by the greatest efforts of human understanding". Kant,[2] puzzling over the variety of faculties attributed to the human mind and seeking a common unifying source or "fundamental power", says:

"We have to enquire whether imagination combined with consciousness may not be the same thing as memory, wit, power of discrimination, and perhaps even identical with understanding and reason."

Professor Wildon Carr,[3] in an article on *Imagining and Reasoning* agreeing with Kant, wrote:

"Popularly, imagination is held to be a subjective activity depending on the passive power of receiving and retaining sense impressions, recalling them as memories, hence of recombining them more or less fantastically."

But he gives as his conclusion:

"Imagination is more original, more fundamental, and more essential a factor in the mental life than sensation or understanding or reason."

Karl Pearson speaks of the Laws of Science as "products of the creative imagination", and the poet-philosopher Blake wrote: "What is now proved was once only imagined."

Enough has been said to support the view that Reason itself is one of the transformed products of the fundamental power of Imagining. Reason was doubtless first created in a very simple form, viz. to be a practical tool to aid us in the struggle for existence. In this elementary form of Reasoning the part played by Imagining is but thinly veiled. In Reason's development as a complex instrument to handle concepts such as are abundant in science, mathematics, and philosophy, the

---

[1] *Treatise*, Vol. I, Section 7.
[2] Professor N. K. Smith, *Commentary to Kant's Critique of Pure Reason*, p. 265.
[3] *Philosophy*, April 1931.

fundamental power has been over-laid and obscured by its products: but it is still there. Imagining retains the creative initiative, and Reason's function is to curb and sift its endless products.

We shall at this point leave the consideration of our finite human minds and take a leap into the infinite. In the light of this adventure in thought we shall then return to look once more at our finite selves.

GOD AS DIVINE IMAGINING

When the philosopher Hegel sought to represent as adequately as he could the nature of the Supreme Being, the World-Ground, or God, he took the faculty of Reason as the highest thing he knew, and described Him as Cosmic Reason. He thought of Cosmic Reason as on the throne of the Universe. For him reason was not merely a faculty of mind which aids us in our search for truth: it was in its most exalted form "the very pulse of cosmic life". "The real is the rational, and the rational is the real", said Hegel with enthusiasm. In plain language this means that everything which proceeds from Cosmic Reason must be eminently reasonable. In the end Hegel was himself driven to admit that "Nature is too weak to exhibit reason everywhere", that "much is accidental and wholly without meaning". Philosophers who followed him were compelled to retreat more and more from the view that the merely Rational can be ultimate.

We can briefly summarise the grounds for rejecting Hegel's view of God, as follows:

(1) There is much that is noxious and evil in the world which it is absurd to attribute to Cosmic Reason. We may enumerate sharks, vipers, and mosquitoes, cancer, hereditary disease and insanity, appalling cruelty, bestial lust, and all the delusions and errors of every kind which have stained the pages of human history. There is so much which by no stretch of the imagination can be called applied Reason.

(2) There are many existents in the world, things like Will, Intuition, Feeling and Beauty, which cannot be derived from Reason.

(3) Hegel spoke of "types of rational thought" as comprising all that exists in the world. But types of thought are concepts: they are symbols which *stand for* reality, not reality itself.

(4) From our human standpoint, Reason appears to have arisen as an aid in our struggle for survival, and in its higher phases it developed as an instrument for understanding the world by testing fancies about it. Its use can provide us only with probabilities, not with certainties. As Fawcett remarks, "To attribute supreme rationality to the Divine is certainly not to flatter Him."

The philosopher Schopenhauer, after rejecting Hegel's Cosmic

Reason, advanced a view of God as Cosmic Will, which was supposed to be above Time, unconscious and blind, in the sense that such Will was not guided by ideas. Such a view need not detain us. We shall later show that it is logically untenable. The suggestion that the Supreme Power is unconscious arose from the need to account for the evil and suffering which afflict the world. We shall find that these dark problems are capable of another solution.

We shall not pursue these thoughts further, but present what Professor Mackenzie called "the only fighting alternative".

The activity of Ultimate Reality, the Supreme Power, resembles most closely the human experience which we call imagining.

When God imagines He creates. Nothing can exist outside of Divine Imagining. In so far as the drop can declare the nature of the ocean, Fawcett[1] says:

"The ocean is like pure imagining in myself, the imagining which amazed Hume and therefore his critic Kant. . . . Kant's 'fundamental power', as we saw, works in the depths of the human soul, underlying all its so-called faculties, including perception, but it streams into our surface life least disguised in the form of productive fancy. And what Kant supposed to work only in the depths of the human soul is held to be also the 'fundamental power' of the universe."

Reasoning is a useful creation of human imagining, but on the Divine level it is inconceivable and would be a defect. It is in any case "about" reality: it can only attend to abstracted aspects and concepts. But the higher Imagining is essentially concrete.

"Pure imagining, which is not *about* Reality, but Reality itself, shining in its own light, is all in all. What is before it is posited by it, conservatively or additively; the past as 'made' reality is conserved; the future is the imagining in its creative march. Every aspect of every content and of all the related contents is intuited through and through."[2]

Such a world-principle fulfils the basic condition of being all-inclusive, for there is nothing which we can imagine, perceived or unperceived, which could not be found in Divine Imagining. Dr. F. C. S. Schiller indeed remarked that Imagining provides not only for all reality but "for all unreality"—for those things which are not, but which may be. It would be impossible to reason imagining into being, but it is possible to imagine reason into being. It has in fact been done.

THE NATURE OF CONSCIRING

We foreshadowed the need for more exact terms in the development of the subject, and at this point we shall pause to introduce them. We

---

[1] *Oberland Dialogues*, p. 58.   [2] *Zermatt Dialogues*, p. 115.

shall in future regard the term Divine Imagining as synonymous with the Supreme Power and inclusive of both the activity of creating and the things created. When we wish to refer to the creative activity itself we shall speak of Divine Consciring[1]; when of the things created, which are the products of consciring, we shall speak of conscita or contents. It is important not to view consciring and its conscita as separate or independent, for conscita are not only created by consciring, they are sustained in existence by it. Divine Consciring may be regarded as the spiritual activity which is creating and sustaining the universe. It is Fichte's "infinite activity" fully aware of and grasping all its conscita. It is Keyserling's "ultimate, essentially non-objective Reality from which objects are poured forth like sudden fancies". It is God ineffable, the supreme Mystery towards which the highest mystics soar, perhaps in vain. Yet it is prolonged into God immanent who

> wields the world with never-wearied love,
> Sustains it from beneath and kindles it above.

As we shall see later, Divine Consciring is prolonged into ourselves where it acquires a certain independence. We are aware of the finite consciring in ourselves where it is usually referred to as "consciousness" or in a focussed form as "attention". We cannot of course observe our consciring as we do objects in our environment, but we have immediate knowledge of it and live by it. "Consciousness" is not a very good word for our purpose. In the first place it has a rather ambiguous connotation; secondly, there is no derived term equivalent to "consciousing", and thirdly, it suggests a kind of neutral light of awareness or what William James called "inert diaphaneity". Consciring, however, connotes a power which in varying degrees—depending on the status of the finite centre—creates, sustains, and grasps into a whole. Although human centres have attained to that intensity of consciring which is commonly called "self-consciousness", most of their activity is submerged or veiled from them. The activity of the waking mind is no more than the tip or spearhead of the total consciring, which easily falls below a critical threshold in anaesthesia or sleep. In our terminology the waking state will be called a level of "reflective"[2] consciring, and the unconscious state one of "irreflective" consciring of the human soul. A great deal of our past experience is of course stored on irreflective levels of the soul.

Proceeding downwards from man we have a vast range of levels of consciring in Nature, of diminishing intensity and creativity, from the higher animals where it is in some degree reflective down to electrons

---

[1] *con*=together with ; *scire*=to know or to be aware of.

[2] "Reflective" suggests "bent back" on the self. Thus there is awareness not only of contents or conscita, but also of the self as being aware of them.

and protons[1] on the lowest of irreflective levels. A lump of rock or earth is an aggregate of innumerable centres of irreflective consciring, although it has no integrated centre of consciring of its own as has an organism.

Our human reflective consciring is at its best very limited. Note how our past experience slips away from us into the depths of memory. Note how habit, which has been described as the "enemy of consciousness", encroaches constantly on our area of reflective consciring. Note also how small an area of conscita we can attend to. "Attention", which is focussed reflective consciring, is necessary if we are going to attempt anything creative, and even then much of our activity is not radically creative ("inspired") but remoulding given conscita. Note particularly how attention or concentration has to select from the total field presented to us and in so doing excludes almost everything else. In contrast with this Fawcett[2] says:

"Divine Imagining . . . sires and drives all the world-steeds abreast. It does not concentrate selectively; it 'attends to' centre and circumference at once. It creates entire the roots of being and it creates in every aspect, conservative and additive of an Infinite field."

What a contrast there is between man's focal consciring which like a spot of phosphorescence quickly fades into the darkness, and the Divine imagining which encompasses the whole Universe with its radiance, so that it has been said,[3] "The world-systems are balls that dance on the jets of consciring!"

Before we look at the evolutionary process which created Nature and ourselves we shall look at some of the many facets of Divine Imagining.

MORE ABOUT DIVINE IMAGINING

(1) God is fully conscious, enjoying an intensity of consciring over an infinite field at which we can only faintly guess. Such a statement would not commend itself to Schopenhauer, von Hartmann, and others, who, faced with the evil of the world, regard the world-principle as blind and purposeless, having risen, so far as they can see, by chance, to a flickering consciousness only in ourselves. Thus Thomas Hardy could write:

Like a knitter drowsed
Whose fingers play in skilled unmindfulness
The Will has woven with an absent heed
Since life first was; and ever will so weave.

[1] We shall deal with issues raised by this in Chapter 3.
[2] *O.D.*, p. 90.
[3] *Z.D.*, pp. 87, 170.

We shall later see that Evil is susceptible of another explanation. In any case an unconscious world-principle (composed of conscita only) raises insoluble problems such as:

"how fruitful change occurs at all in such contents buried in blackest night; how these contents are in part continuous and hold together, in part discrete and loose; and how above all the *conscious* centre or finite centre, e.g. man himself, arises in time. The usual device is to say that the conscious finite centre 'emerges', but it cannot 'emerge' from a realm in which it did not exist. Proteus was said to 'emerge' from the sea, but to do so he had first to be under it."[1]

In such a field of enquiry as this, we cannot do other than extrapolate upwards from the insights we have of ourselves, accepting with gratitude the further and fuller insights of high Mystics, and testing all of these views continually for their self-consistency and their congruity with the truth we know.

Let us return to our first statement that God is fully conscious and consider if we have any evidence to support it. We observe in ourselves that we do many things, as we say, "without noticing". They are habitual and familiar actions. If, however, I have to walk on a narrow and dangerous path, or understand a philosophical view, or solve a problem, I can only do so by concentrated attention. Such has been called the "spearhead of finite consciring". The distributable consciring in man is limited and has to be focussed to be creative. Now, God does in fact create conservatively and additively in what may well be an infinite field. From this we can properly infer that His range and intensity of consciring are indefinitely great compared to ours. He has no need to ignore other things to conscire one thing intensely. Divine consciring may be described as fully reflective and indeed "radiant" over the whole universe.

(2) Divine Imagining creates both conservatively and additively. This statement calls for amplification. By "creating conservatively" we mean a process of maintaining in being or preserving in existence. We often overlook this important fact, that the very existence of things implies a continually sustained act of Divine consciring. Bear in mind that there are no conscita ("objects") which are not related to consciring, and it will be obvious that if its aspect of conservation ceased for a moment to operate then,

> the great globe itself,
> Yea, all which it inherit, shall dissolve,
> And, like this insubstantial pageant faded,
> Leave not a rack behind.

[1] *Z.D.*, p. 90.

By additive creation we mean of course the introduction of what is new. The conditions under which this takes place lead us to the riddle of causation and then on into the story of the evolution of Nature and man. At this stage we shall only remark that additive creation implies change and this involves Time. Divine Imagining is changeless only in this sense, that it retains for ever its own nature. But because it is *Imagining* it is forever the source of change: it could not be imagining if it were not. *Time-succcession is the form or manner in which novelty is introduced into existence. Time-succession is therefore real and fundamental, for it has its origin in Divine Imagining itself.* It has not to be explained away as an "appearance" or "unreal", as believers in a changeless Absolute have to do.

What we affirm of Divine Imagining—that it creates conservatively and additively—we can discern alsò in ourselves as finite centres of consciring. Our creativity is small indeed, but its conservative sustaining aspect is obvious as our personal memory (which is for the large part on irreflective levels). Its additive or novel aspect is most marked in the creative genius, Beethoven, Michelangelo, Newton and Shakespeare, while in most of us creativity rises little above the rearrangement of presented data. It is well, however, to remember that some fragment of the new probably enters into every situation and event, into every act of perception or feeling or doing. History, whether personal or general, can never quite repeat itself.

(3) As we have just indicated, Divine Imagining as a world-principle cannot be equated with the "Absolute" of some philosophers, which is also the Brahman of Indian thought, and the "One" of Plato and Plotinus. The common concept involved in all these views is that the Absolute is spiritual Reality "complete, perfect and finished" and therefore above change. For believers in an Absolute the two outstanding problems are Time and Evil.

What is the status of History, and what is the nature of the changing experiences in which we finite beings are all immersed? The answer of the Absolutists follows a common line. In its most clear-cut form it says that human experience is illusion; it is a dream from which men may awaken to know the Real. In its less clear-cut form it says that the passing show has only empirical reality, i.e. we must give it a limited status for practical purposes, and say that it belongs to a "phenomenal" world. For McTaggart, the Cambridge philosopher, an exponent of Hegel, Time is unreal. F. H. Bradley also says plainly that if time-succession and change are real, the Absolute is a delusion. Hence he regarded change as a self-contradictory idea! In complete disagreement with these views, Imaginism regards time-succession and change as real, since they proceed from the very nature of Divine Imagining.

As for the problem of Evil, since change cannot be ascribed to the Absolute, it follows that all the abominations of history: its tortures, persecutions, massacres and cruelty, and all the little pettiness and filthiness and jealousies of men are a revelation in the phenomenal world of what is eternally in existence in the Absolute. This is an incredible and wholly unacceptable position. To talk with Bradley of the "transformation" of Evil is to explain nothing, and in any case transformation implies time-succession. The Imaginist explanation of Evil will be presented later. Here we shall only say that there is no inevitable permanence in Evil. Both past and present only continue to exist because they are sustained by Divine Imagining—and a radical purification of any world-system is always possible by Divine consciring ceasing to sustain the offensive part of it.

(4) The term "perfection" is used of the Absolute: how far can it be applied to Divine Imagining? The literal meaning of "perfect" is "thoroughly made" and the implication of a thing being perfect is that it would not be improved by any change. Fawcett very wisely says that we should reserve the term for finite things such as a perfect rose, a perfect poem or a perfect work of art. In so far as "perfect" is applied to the world-principle, this inevitably suggests that it must comprise all imaginable forms and varieties of finite perfection already complete. We therefore prefer to describe Divine Imagining as "perficient" rather than perfect. It creates in the end the best imaginable things, but its very nature is constantly to be creating the new.

This view of God removes many otherwise insoluble problems which the idea of an Absolute leaves untouched. These difficulties are always being put forward in a variety of ways. Thus Socrates asked whether God being "perfect" could be dissatisfied. Is there any good which He could desire which He does not possess? On this view He could not have created the world, for this implies time and change and the fulfilment in doing so of some need and desire. All such difficulties are swept away by the nature of Divine Imagining. Says Fawcett[1]:

"Divine Imagining . . . includes and compels change; is not a perfect reality but a perficient power which is not 'finished' but creates additively. It is not merely transcendent but immanent in change. And time-succession is not false appearance but a mode of ultimate reality, the form of additive creation itself."

Another expression of the same Absolutist difficulty says that since God is infinite He cannot conceive anything new as He already contains it. Another person might argue that the inability to create novelty is a limitation on His nature which shows that God cannot be infinite. It is

[1] *Z.D.*, p. 210.

clear that we need to define the term infinite. To say that what is infinite is not limited by an "other" is insufficient, for it might have self-imposed limitations. For example, we conceive Divine Imagining as having imposed on itself a type of limitation in relation to man's freedom. We conceive that it has also limited itself in any particular world-system to certain types of imaginal activity, or else diverse and inconsistent forms of it might produce a chaos incapable of evolution. Divine Imagining is rather to be regarded as infinite in *potency*. This according to the Neo-Platonists is the true sense of the word. "The real infinity of that which truly is, is neither of multitude or magnitude, but of potency alone."[1] Divine Imagining is infinite because there is no limit to its power to create both additively and conservatively. Where we are thinking in numerical terms, as for example of galaxies or starry hosts, we should interpret "infinite" as meaning indefinitely many. We should not claim more than this.

(5) God does not think: He imagines. By imagining He creates, and this is essentially objective reality on every significant level. Thought is *about* reality, it is abstract when compared with the concrete reality itself. Thought is a makeshift valuable to finite beings like ourselves, but left behind by gods who intuit the real. Observe that in ourselves imagining ranges from the concrete type of the good artist, sculptor, or novelist, to the abstract type which becomes thought, as in mathematician and philosopher. All our concepts are substitutes for facts.

Here, perhaps, we may say what we understand by truth. Truth has to do with thought—which is *about* Reality—and with statements which express that thought. These are "true" if they sufficiently correspond to the Reality to be adequate substitutes for it in our thinking.

(6) Divine Imagining has its "feeling" aspect, perhaps best described as supreme Delight, Love and Beauty. We shall discuss later the problems associated with Evil, which It provisionally tolerates in the world-systems. The solution which we shall present in no way vitiates the affirmation which we now make about Divine Imagining. We know how, in ourselves, there are moments of delight which accompany harmonious consciring. Our times of heightened awareness increase such joy, whereas when habit has dulled the intensity of consciring, pleasant feeling falls away. We have seen that the nature of Divine Imagining is radiant and fully reflective, to an extent which we can only faintly guess. It must therefore have present in Itself the "glory of feeling on its highest level"—the best imaginable—and this Imagining is Divine in scope, not human. It is significant to observe that the Mystics who in rare moments have been granted some vision of Reality

[1] T. Whittaker, *The Neo-Platonists*, 2nd Ed., p. 170.

speak with one voice of this supreme Delight—Love—Beauty, to tell more of which all words fail them.[1]

THE NATURE OF THE WORLD AROUND US

Having looked briefly at imagining on both the Divine and human levels we shall consider the status of the world around us of which we are informed through our senses. We shall not digress to talk about perception, i.e. of how our senses convey impressions to us. This is briefly discussed in Chapter 5.

All things exist because of Divine Imagining. The world which is around us and includes us is a psychical continuum, and being of this nature no conscita are insulated from each other. Co-mingling or inter-penetration occurs throughout the whole of a given world system. Every existing entity has a field of influence in virtue of which it may affect in varying degrees all others. We are accustomed in everyday life to think of physical objects as clear-cut and isolated, forgetful of the fact that the physical level is only one significant level of the world obscuring much more than it reveals. The insights of poets are to be taken literally. Thus Shelley says:

> All things by a law divine
> In one another's being mingle

and Francis Thompson echoes this:

> All things, by immortal power,
> Near or far,
> Hiddenly
> To each other linkéd are
> That thou canst not stir a flower
> Without troubling of a star.

The tree out there, seen by four observers A, B, C, and D, is called by Fawcett a "common tentacular fact"[2] spreading its tentacles in all directions. Four of these are present to the viewpoints of A, B, C, and D. The tree-fact is of the same nature as the facts present to A, B, C, and D. A tree out there, a tree perceived, and a tree recollected in memory, are of the same mind-like or psychoid nature—even though conscired with different intensity.

Such a view may seem strange to the plain man, and we must look into it further. He says, "I thought a tree was made of matter". By this, he means that a tree occupies space, possesses a characteristic shape, and offers resistance to touch. Certainly like all other natural objects a

---

[1] See R. C. Johnson, *The Imprisoned Splendour*, Chapters XIV-XV. (Hodder and Stoughton Ltd., 1953.)

[2] *Divine Imagining*, p. 21.

tree possesses these qualities, but "matter" is a concept of ours which we postulate as the stuff exhibiting these qualities. It is a useful *concept* in so far as it facilitates reasoning and scientific research. In words of Whitehead it veils "the extremely abstract character of scientific generalisation under a myth which enables our imaginations to work more freely". We certainly perceive objects rich in qualities, but we only conceive "matter". As Fawcett says: "We must decline to equate a way of thinking about Nature with Nature herself."

So also concepts such as mass, energy, and force, which are useful in physics, are of no value to metaphysical thought with which we try to understand the real nature of the world. When the physicist is desirous of measuring how much resistance or inertia objects show, he conceives the idea of "Mass", but the nature of what is actually symbolised by this term is not known. Another concept of similar value in the quantitative analysis of physical change is "Energy". But this also is a symbol for an unknown something, and throws no light on the nature of the world in its infinite variety. There are, however, two features associated with "Energy" which may be significant for us: (1) the conservation aspect, which is that the sum total of energy in the whole system remains the same, and (2) that associated with energy transformations there is a mysterious vanishing and appearing of qualities. These two aspects, one concerned with conservation and the other concerned with qualitative novelty, are the two fundamental aspects of consciring. We suggest that Consciring is the Reality of which only certain quantitative aspects are symbolised by the physicist's concept of energy. Energy is a useful mathematical concept, but it has no power to account for the changing qualitative richness of the world. Consciring has this power.

The terms electron and proton which stand for entities variously imagined as being particles or waves (and in certain circumstances capable of changing into radiation) are symbols with which "human imagining chases elusive fact". They are what Bain calls "representative fiction", of value for certain limited purposes. Certainly there is nothing in these, or in any arrangements of them, to account for colour, sound, scent. We suggest that they may be the most primitive organisms that we know, and that they are elementary centres of irreflective consciring. Whitehead regards the atom as a minor society of these organisms, and Nature may perhaps be considered as a vast society of societies.

The features of Nature which cry aloud for understanding are not the specialised aspects abstracted from reality which have lent themselves so effectively to measurement by physicists. They are rather the qualitative richness and variety of the world, its colours, music, and scents. These are the very things which measurement has had to ignore, and yet they are the experience of the plain man and the joy of the poet.

They are what Tagore has called "not the anatomy of the world, but its countenance".

We suggest that Nature is a psychical continuum, though the part we see is only a fragment or aspect of a greater whole which is sustained by Divine Imagining. It consists of objects which exist independently of our perceiving them, and which are best regarded as more or less stable groupings of qualities. This content is all imaginal and the part of Nature which we sense is just its spearhead penetrating our minds and then conscired by us with sufficient intensity to lift a small part of it into our awareness. (Consider how little we know of the myriad processes in a single blade of grass.) In perceiving, we clothe this fraction of penetrating content with imaginal content drawn from our own memory. Note also that in any visible scene there is very much that we do not "take in". We pay attention to some particular object, and this act of perception has its creative aspect, for (1) it selects or carves it out of the psychical continuum and (2) it enriches it by personal content in the process of interpretation. We shall consider perception further in Chapter 5. Incidentally we note that none of the processes in nerve cells or fibres, which are involved in sensing, ever rise into awareness. In this respect they are like the myriad external processes which cannot be conscired by us with a sufficient intensity to raise them above the critical threshold.

CREATION AND THE METAPHYSICAL FALL

We have seen that Divine consciring has two aspects, conservative and additive. In virtue of the latter, new things are created; in virtue of the former, all things remain in existence or persist in their being. At the beginning of our world-system we suggest that only the conservative aspect of consciring was active in maintaining an archetypal system of perfect beauty and harmony which God imagined. Just as we may claim of a great poem or piece of music that it is perfect, that no imaginable improvement is possible, so we may conceive this archetypal world-system to be perfect after its kind as a Divine work of Art. It was not wholly outside Time, for it possessed the three characteristics of Time, duration, simultaneous aspects, and internally it contained time-successions. It did not, however, change *as a whole*. A sonata of Beethoven or a sonnet of Wordsworth is a finite whole which does not change, although within itself it contains successions, simultaneous aspects, and an enduring aspect. So of the Divine work of Art. But this perfect archetypal world had the limitation that it existed only for its Divine Author, just as a poem might exist only for its human author. A time came when Divine Imagining conceived that this world-system could exist in another manner—at a price. Finite sentients[1] could be generated within it, so that ultimately the world-system would exist *for them* and not merely as content for God. With this decision came the beginning of change, the descent into creative evolution, the initiation of the process of Becoming as distinct from that of Being.

Comparing the initial situation to a poem, Fawcett[2] says:

"The poem cannot be bettered, but, after all, it is a poem which exists only for God. It contains indefinitely many characters indeed, but these, like the little group of characters in *Hamlet*, exist originally only for the maker of the poem. The 'characters' are completely under central control; hence the harmony of the work of art remains stable. But with the passage of these 'characters' into centres of consciring, the more advanced of which exist *for themselves* and not only for the divine artist, the Initial Situation gives place to the Metaphysical Fall. The 'characters' are no longer docile, they have become relatively independent agents and take charge, as it were, of the poem throughout its extent; they alter it, add to it and can even mar it in part. The reign of chance and evil is inaugurated."

Yet because all this is tolerated we can be sure that the end result will justify all that has been entailed. Why? Because in a world-system sustained by Divine Imagining its changes will be subject always to that inexorable guiding pressure which will impel it to the best imaginable end. To say that Becoming is a corruption of Being is to look backwards, not forward to a more glorious state of Being. "The supreme artistic triumph of evolution," says Fawcett, "is the making of conscious individuals who, passing at long last into the divine life are to swell and diversify Joy."[3]

How do the myriad finite sentients arise? In the initial archetypal world which is complex and qualitatively rich there is profound interpenetration without conflict. Suppose the intensity of consciring to increase, and increase differentially, then certain regions of the field of content may become distinct primitive natural agents consciring at first irreflectively[4] on their own account, just as the wind blowing over

---

[1] By "finite sentients" are meant centres of consciring. They may range from the lowest forms of irreflective consciring (as electrons, protons, etc.) to centres of reflective consciring of different degrees as in animals, human beings, and gods. We cannot safely use the term "individual" as equivalent, for on the one hand electrons and protons may disappear, they have not won the permanence of individuality. On the other hand there may be superhuman beings where the concept of a Divine Society is truer than that of isolated individuality.

[2] *Z.D.*, p. 500.   [3] *Z.D.*, p. 287.

[4] Irreflective consciring—such as of a proton for an electron or of a worm for the soil is doubtless expressed in a primitive form of perception. Somewhere at the higher animal level a measure of reflective consciring is won, characterised by the awareness of the self as perceiving. Both the self and the object of awareness are illuminated: it perceives and knows that it perceives. But there is no permanent self below the level of man.

charcoal embers may kindle innumerable glowing points. At a later stage of evolution, a second step in the intensity of Divine consciring may raise certain centres over the threshold into reflective consciring. With each of these steps the activity of Divine Imagining partly immerses itself in the process of evolutionary change. These free centres now assert themselves, the interpenetration becomes an occasion of thwarting or invasion, and the process of self-assertive conflict sets in. As Heraclitus said, "Strife is the father of all things." The original harmony begins to be lost and the struggle for existence by finite sentients begins. The primitive centres may be called mentoid or psychoid, but they are not minds, only mind-like. Presumably their bodies are the small elements of the content-field which they conscire. The rills of Divine Consciring are prolonged into these quadrillons of natural agents, but there they acquire a certain apartness from their source. On the lowest levels (inorganic) the minor agents, electrons, protons, atoms, molecules, etc., remain very much under central control, but at the biological level the initiatives come into marked conflict and their limited consciring may run amok. In this situation of conflict, Divine Imagining is continually at work consciring creatively. It works through what we may call the Imaginal Dynamic, constantly innovating so as to harmonise conflicting elements, constantly injecting fresh reality into the time-process so as to keep a constant guiding pressure towards its goal.

"Inter-penetration, conflict, imaginal solution: these are the three aspects of the Imaginal Dynamic, the 'principle of movement' which rules the manifested world. Given a situation of inner discords, transformation is the resource which serves to reduce the discords, as much as is possible, to harmony. But this reduction, again, produces a new situation which becomes in its turn the seat of inner discords, which tend to increase, whereupon is created a fresh transformation equally provisional. The world-process is thus forced along the path of imaginal or creative evolution."[1]

We might illustrate this in every field, in physics and chemistry, in physiology and in the economy of Nature, in the field of morals and religious thought, in politics and economics. Everywhere the pendulum swings uneasily, but never too far. If one factor seriously threatens stability, another arises to counter the danger, so endeavouring to secure what the Greeks would have called the "divinity of measure".

We have spoken of an archetypal world of perfection of content and described the metaphysical fall into an order of change and conflict as the long road to a higher perfection. It may be asked what relationship this bears to the views of astronomers about the origin of our world-system or galaxy. It is interesting to note that they believe it had a

[1] *O.D.*, p. 181.

beginning which can be traced as far back as a diffuse nebula, and they believe that the availability of its energy is slowly disappearing so that some day it will have an end. In relating these viewpoints it seems probable that the *physical* aspect of the world-system was the last to be created and will be the first to be discarded in this vast evolutionary process. Behind the physical and nearer to the ultimately Real, as I have tried to show elsewhere,[1] are significant levels of existence on which more fundamental activities are taking place. The appearance of the spiral nebulae described by astronomers is therefore not to be taken as an early stage on the downward arc of Becoming.

THE IMAGINAL DYNAMIC

In his world-view Plato frequently contrasted the world of our present experience and its conflict, change, and multiplicity with the world of the Absolute, a harmonious unity above time and change. In this latter realm he placed Ideas—glorified concepts—the unchanging essences or prototypes of all those entities that manifest in myriad forms in our lower world. He conceived Ideas of "tree-ness", "rock-ness", courage, and so on. The Imaginist viewpoint distinguishes sharply between thought *about* reality and reality itself, and it is critical of all this exaltation of conceptual thought to the divine level. Schopenhauer also conceived of Ideas, not above time, but operative in time—as Unities falling into multiplicity. It is strange to think of these as products of Schopenhauer's blind Will, but setting this criticism aside, his "Ideas" are the nearest ancestors of what we call "Imaginals". The primary Imaginals are permanent basic forms of Divine Imagining. They are cosmic powers which contain within themselves by their selective action and co-operation the drive which has created all that exists. To enumerate them would be a task far beyond the power of the human mind, which in any case has a measure of conscious awareness of the physical level only.

The archetypal world-system of which we have written would be constructed from a certain group of primary Imaginals prior to its fall into the process of Becoming. The particular type of world-system and the possibilities inherent in it are doubtless determined by the particular group of Imaginals which co-operate, in much the same way as a game of chess or cricket is limited by the initial conditions or rules of the game. But within these limits there is enormous scope for freedom and for both destructive and constructive imagining by finite sentients, so that the potentialities gradually unfold. Secondary imaginals are built from the primary ones, and as evolution takes place such new imaginals

[1] R. C. Johnson, *The Imprisoned Splendour*. (Hodder and Stoughton Ltd., 1953.)

insert themselves as novelty into the developing system when conditions make it possible. The processes of conflict and reconciliation get into full swing and make the world as we know it.

The vista which unfolds before us when we contemplate the infinite possibilities of Divine Imagining is far beyond any capacity of ours to imagine or describe. Astronomers inform us that to their knowledge there are many millions of spiral nebulae (the so-called "island universes") in various stages of condensation into stars. These are presumably the physical levels of other world-systems substantially insulated from each other (on this level) by incredible depths of space. Each of them is an experiment in Divine Imagining possibly with different initial conditions, i.e. with a different group of primary Imaginals involved in its archetype. Just as a game cannot be played simultaneously with two different sets of rules, but separation of the games in space is essential if these are both to develop their possibilities, so the vista before us is of an unending creation of world-systems temporarily insulated on certain lower levels to permit the wealth of Divine Imagining to manifest.

"There is infinite variety native to Divine Imagining, though each particular world-system is finite throughout; a unique imaginal flower unlike all other flowers that blow. These incompatible finite world-systems, all equally present to God, are held provisionally apart, coming together at long last in a succession of harmonising Divine Events, each more glorious than its predecessor."[1]

Such is the possibility which must haunt our thought.

Let us return to consider further the nature of Imaginals. They correspond to the "eternal objects" of Whitehead's thought, and the "essences" of Santayana. The Imaginal of Light is used by Fawcett as an illustration[2]:

"I am in what is (for me) a dark room, and I draw a match along the surface of a box. What happens? Certain periodic processes in Nature are quickened, and there emerges quality, which, penetrating my retina and the cortex of my brain, is conscired as yellow light. Whence and wherefore this invasive quality? It is a portion of the light-Imaginal, in so far as it appears in our world-system. Conditions consequent on the rubbing of the match allow light, and light of a certain colour only, to be embodied in, and radiated from, a physical object which previously I was unable to see."

The light-imaginal is an inexhaustible source of all the appearances of light whenever and wherever they occur. It occurs in the physical world, constantly invading and withdrawing locally according to the suitability of conditions for its manifestation, and it is of course prolonged into the brain and mind of observers in the form of vision. The state-

---

[1] *Z.D.*, p. 312. [2] *Z.D.*, p. 361.

ments of science about light are in the form of symbolism describing these accompanying conditions.

The primary Imaginals (like Divine Imagining) do not change as a whole, i.e. they persist in being what they are, but they include within themselves time-successions as illustrated by the innumerable specific instances of change just mentioned. Moreover, through the interaction of primary imaginals and perhaps even the imagining of finite centres, secondary and tertiary imaginals, and indeed a whole hierarchy of imaginals, are created. The story of the evolution of living creatures on our planet is a notable illustration. We observe higher imaginals appearing and using bodies which are the products of subordinate imaginals in a creative manner. Thus as Fawcett remarks, "The organism of the fox has a long history before the fox-consciring lights it."[1] A famous book bears the title *The Descent of Man*. We shall find it illuminating to posit that the appearance of man on the Earth is the confluence of two streams of heredity: the heredity of the soul and the heredity of the body. It was the descent of a higher imaginal to the physical level made possible by the ascent of subordinate nature-imaginals to the necessary level of complexity. The manifestation of a soul-imaginal (if such we may call it) may well occur simultaneously in a number and variety of vehicles. To put it otherwise, the spiritual roots of a human being, if traced back, may share with many others an origin in a common imaginal or sub-imaginal. This view will be developed further in Chapter 13.

THE STATUS OF TIME AND SPACE

A poet speaking of the Divine artistry describes "Time as the lilt of His song and Space the breadth of His harmony". Kant, who wrote at great length on these themes, considered both Time and Space as known by us subjectively through direct intuition, not as concepts which we formulate because of sensory experience. From our standpoint they are perhaps most satisfactorily described as two ways in which contents can be regarded *together* for consciring.

We have previously referred to the three different aspects of Time: duration, simultaneity, and succession. Their meaning is illustrated by considering some colour patches. These endure unchanged for a considerable time since they are not instantaneous appearances. When they are conscired together they are simultaneous—and incidentally this possibility implies a spatial relationship between them. Finally, consciring them one after the other implies time-succession. The first two aspects of time are involved in the conservative aspects of Divine Imagining while the third aspect is most characteristic of the additive

[1] *Z.D.*, p. 321.

or creative aspect. We emphasise again that because of the nature of Imagining all these aspects of Time are real. The believers in a complete and perfect Absolute, above Time, exclude themselves automatically from any real understanding of time-succession which they have to explain away as an appearance. The significance of much of human life, the meaning of conflict and struggle, of suffering and pain, of freedom and moral choice is hard to find if all that happens is a sham succession only showing what is eternally present in an Absolute.

Time-succession, then, is the form or manner of additive creation. It becomes operative as soon as the archetypal world falls into the process of Becoming, i.e. as soon as consciring is locally intensified and finite sentients are created. We may ask what is the standing of "past", "present", and "future"? We all have a "specious present", a very small time-interval which for practical purposes is all *present*, and during this we are aware that reality is being made and that we ourselves can contribute to its making. The *past* is *made* reality, which so far as we know we can do nothing to influence, and which we can only conscire with a faintness which is in striking contrast with the vividness of perception. It is, however, possible that super-human beings exist who have an extended specious present, who may indeed conscire a considerable range of the past and future with the same vividness as we conscire the present. They may, for all we know, be able to act in that past. To such beings our lives may seem as small and insignificant as the lives of houseflies do to us; although here we must remember that the mark of a minor god will be not only in the breadth of time-range of his consciring, but also in its depth which may give him an awareness of micro-processes to which we are blind. Yet even this consciring may penetrate but a small part of any world-system, and is trifling compared with Divine Imagining which sustains all the world-systems, and the made reality which is being added to them every instant.

Our access to the past is only through memory except in so far as through retro-cognition we may conscire that with which we have not had personal acquaintance in our present life. To Divine Imagining the past must be equally available with the present. Since it is only sustained by this consciring, it is obvious that any part of it may drop out of existence for ever by His ceasing to conscire it—and for this we may be thankful. It may be asked in what sense the past is normally sustained by God: are all those finite sentients who toiled and fought and suffered still toiling, fighting, and suffering in some sense? Is Hannibal still crossing the Alps; are the hosts of Ghengis Khan still burning and plundering; is Julius Caesar still landing in Britain, and Mr. Gladstone still talking about Home Rule for Ireland? In the "Eternal Now" of an Absolute such must be the case, but with the clue of Imaginism in our hands we can deny this. The past "is deserted by the finite centres of consciring—reflective and irreflective—which were active at its making. It is conserved as mere content within God."[1] A god might still conscire the form of Julius Caesar landing on the coast of Britain as it was two thousand years ago, but the centre of consciring which was Julius Caesar is, we may suppose, active elsewhere *in the present*. The past may be compared to a coral reef which was once the scene of enormous activity but is now empty of life save where new reef is in the making.

Turning to the Future, we shall not at this point discuss the many aspects connected with pre-cognition and free-will which are linked with it. To a superhuman being or minor god able to conscire profoundly over a wide field, the outlines of the Future in the making may well be discerned. He may in any case be helping to direct the processes of Imaginal activity in given situations. One can conceive that even for such a one the distant future is vague and indistinct, but that with increasing nearness to the present, events find a growing clarity of form and definition. It may be regarded as a plastic future until we finite sentients make our contributions in the specious present—after which it becomes a frozen form and joins the unalterable past. The activity of the great Imaginals, and the consciring of many super-human sentients, co-operating to move the process of world-becoming onwards to a goal of perfection, must perforce result in something very far from a blank or unplanned future. At the same time, there can be no question of a fixed pre-determined future merely unfolding itself in Time. The future is at each stage being moulded and influenced, and from our human standpoint it is plastic and alterable until we finally make our own contribution in its passage through the chilling chamber of the present (see Chapter 11). As Fawcett says, "The Imaginal dynamic teems with free initiatives . . . and responds to every novel problem with a novel solution."

The existence of spatial relationships, as we previously suggested, is an invention of Divine Imagining which, by reducing the conflict of interpenetrating Imaginals, renders possible the simultaneous development of many different world-systems with incompatible initial conditions. Space is not to be regarded as an entity in itself but a manner of co-existence of very varied content, made by this form of separation "compossible". If we conscire several objects together, their relations *are space*.

We consider that the spatial exists in Nature itself: it is not, as some philosophers would have us believe, something created by our finite minds to make sense out of our experience of the world.

[1] *Z.D.*, p. 447.

"If space is a manner of existence characterising Nature—a phase of Divine Imagination—and Nature pours content into our souls, these souls must contain much of the spatial 'given immediately'. They are above it in part, but they stand in it like Titans in the deep sea. . . . I will go further and urge that, not only sense-contents, but other contents of our minds are spatial, and that consequently the prejudice against introducing 'extension' into the human mind has become absurd."[1]

It is reasonable to suppose that space and time had no beginnings: that they were existent even in the archetypal world-systems. It has been pointed out, however, that certain higher content of our souls such as Love, Beauty, and Joy are not essentially linked with space, although they are linked essentially with Time and the latter may therefore be primary. Penetrating behind the physical level into other more significant levels, as the mystic does, I can see no reason for supposing that the spatio-temporal becomes less real, but I can find much evidence to suggest that space is not to the same extent an isolating barrier.

It has often been pointed out that in the exercise of fancy and of visual memory (and in dream-experience) the visualiser has a private space-world of his own—for the things he visualises have their spatial relations within his mind. They do not usually exclude each other with the vigour characteristic of the physical order, but this may be due to the weakness of normal human consciring. We tend rather too easily to assume that the space-world of private imagining is different from that of the familiar external world, perhaps because we fail to grasp the psychoid character of the world and the fact of inter-penetration, and also because we forget how little we conscire of its content. We may be compelled to revise our outlook by some of the remarkable data disclosed through psychical research. Of this I shall write later.

CAUSATION AND LAW

A man is driving a motor-car which skids and leads to slight injuries. When asked by his friend why he is lame, he describes the skid which he explains was due to the wetness of the road, the smoothness of his tyres, and to the fact that a child stepping off the pavement led him to swerve. These factors are accepted by all his friends as the "cause" of his accident, and they are certainly among the immediate contributory factors. But when we examine each of these (and others which might be named) we see that the wetness of the road leads us back through geography and meteorology to the solar system, and the car, the driver, and the child lead us back similarly to a remote past through a myriad inter-related events. Any given event can thus be regarded as the effect

[1] *Z.D.*, p. 451.

of innumerable causes (not necessarily all on the physical level), and it will in its turn be a contributory cause to other events which will follow it. The concept of causation arose as an attempt to account for change, and we take as a basis J. S. Mill's definition of "cause" as "the assemblage of phenomena, which occurring, some other phenomenon invariably commences or has its origin". It is clear that we have many problems to face. How extensive is this "assemblage"? Are mental factors to be included, and if so, what parts do freedom and chance play?

The contribution of Imaginism to these problems stresses first the fact of inter-penetration. Grass is "in" our brain and mind as well as in the field: indeed everywhere that its effects are present or its influence is felt, grass is present in a proper sense. Presumably this inter-penetration which is very limited and incomplete on the physical level of our world-system had its origin in the deep inter-penetration which characterised the original archetypal world. It still remains much more pronounced on higher levels than on the physical. What are described by physicists as forces of attraction and repulsion would be described by us as conditions favourable to, or inimical to psychical penetration. The invention of space facilitates development, but does not bring harmony. The play of attractions and repulsions with their constant change and unrest provide occasions for various imaginals to manifest, i.e. for qualitative novelty to occur. On the physico-chemical level we have abundant illustration of this in the syntheses which we call atoms, built out of electrons, protons, and neutrons, and then again in the syntheses we describe as molecules, built out of atoms. When an atom of sodium and an atom of chlorine form a molecule of common salt we observe the mysterious vanishing of certain qualities and the mysterious arising of completely new ones. The dominantly conservative features, such as the constancy of mass and preservation of atomic architecture, have always interested science, but the qualitative aspects which are even more important from a metaphysical standpoint have found no causal explanation: they have in fact been neglected. The Imaginal standpoint here offers a comprehensive viewpoint, on which we shall enlarge in Chapter 3.

Whether in the field of physics, biology, or psychology, or on any significant level of penetration into the nature of the world, we cannot get far in our explanations if we attempt to *derive* the higher from the lower. The lower may herald the higher, may indeed make awareness of the higher possible, but it never accounts for it. Nothing is derived solely from its antecedents.

"A fundamental revision of the concept of causation on the lines of imaginism is required. Every step of change includes a gift, a creatum which does not repeat any event in the past. It may include also the appearance of that which, up to this moment, has not been able to show in the world. . . . The lower supplies constituents needed for the making of the higher, or needed only to furnish the setting in which the higher appears."[1]

We cannot therefore account for common salt wholly in terms of our knowledge of sodium and chlorine, or of water in terms of hydrogen and oxygen. We cannot account wholly for the virus or gene in terms of protein molecules, or cell-function in terms of an assemblage of such molecules. We cannot wholly account for instincts in terms of nervous tissue or the wealth of the mind in terms of instincts or the capacities of the soul in terms wholly of the mind. Certainly there is no creative transformation if there is absence of material to be transformed, but what is constantly forgotten is that when the conditions are suitable, one or more imaginals can descend into the flux and give effect to novelty. "There results," says Fawcett, "an evolutionary movement which gathers strength at once from above and below." If therefore we accept J. S. Mill's definition of causation, we must be clear that the phrase "assemblage of phenomena" includes imaginal activity or gifts "from above".

The view of Imaginism is that in all events there is the conservative aspect and the additive aspect. Since the latter element involves either Divine consciring (through the manifestation of Imaginals), or the consciring of finite sentients:

(1) It follows that freedom may enter into events; for consciring is not rigidly determined but innovative. As we shall later see, freedom falls away into chance on low irreflective levels of consciring.

(2) It follows that the so-called inexorable "laws of Nature" have by no means the rigidity and inflexibility that we have so often supposed them to possess.

(3) We have a clue to the most commonplace of miracles: why events continue to happen—why chains of causation do not cease.

We shall deal with these in turn, but first we turn again to Mill's views of causation. There are some events in which conservation is dominant, and additive novelty is very small or very slow. All so-called mechanical and gravitational phenomena are of this type. Mill speaks of these events as illustrating the "composition of causes" for they can each be analysed into their contributory elements of the same quality. A simple example would be that two forces acting at an angle on a body displaces it in an intermediate direction with a certain resultant force. On the other hand there are events in which novelty is very marked and the conservative elements subsidiary. We may cite as typical most chemical and biological phenomena. Specific examples are the contraction of a

[1] Z.D., p. 261. G. N. M. Tyrrell in his book *Grades of Significance* (Rider & Co. Ltd.) has also very clearly and eloquently advanced this viewpoint.

muscle when a nerve fibre is subject to an electrical stimulus, and the production of water from hydrogen and oxygen. Mill would describe these as illustrating heteropathic causation. The qualitative uniformities which persist in all these cases are more properly to be regarded as habits of Nature than inflexible laws.

These two general types of causation (which are seldom distinct in practice) illustrate the conservative and the transformative methods of creating harmony in a situation of conflict. We certainly do not know enough to say *why* the reconciliation of inter-penetration by two atoms of hydrogen and one of oxygen gives rise to the particular qualities which characterise water. Imaginism stresses, however, that water with its qualities does not *emerge* from the synthesis, it is an imaginal solution habitually superposed upon the psychical penetration of hydrogen and oxygen when conditions of temperature, etc., are favourable. Of course, we can follow much more adequately the process of imaginal transformation of conflict in those cases where human consciring is the effective factor. Innumerable events in history might be cited as examples.

We shall briefly refer now to the existence of freedom and change as factors in causation, deferring a full discussion of these important topics to Chapter 11. According to the classical view, causation is irreconcilable with freedom, and from this opposition arose innumerable discussions about determinism and free-will. The attitude of Imaginism is that every event has in it *some* degree of novelty. The novelty derives from consciring, and this in its turn is free. Causation thus in principle includes freedom. It may of course be vanishingly small as for example if two persons each release an apple from the hand. Since between these two events there can be very little novelty entering, the results are likely to be similar. But if two persons each think of a number, these two events are of pure consciring based on the conservative elements of two private memories, and the results will probably differ. We can properly speak of "freedom" where the finite sentient has achieved reflective consciring, i.e. self-awareness. On lower levels, where irreflective consciring rules, "freedom" falls away into "chance". Of course, the boundary between these is difficult, if not impossible, to determine. In man himself a spearhead of reflective consciring co-exists with depths of irreflective consciring. On low levels chance reigns almost exclusively, as in the riot of gas molecules, the survival and growth of acorns, the fertilisation and survival of frogs' eggs. Because of this, these lower levels are under good central control (as we see from the reliability of statistical laws). At rather higher levels we have a measure of freedom, and therefore less complete central control. Unpleasant novelties may arise such as poison sacs in snakes and spiders. The limited consciring has introduced creative novelty where physical

conditions made it possible to do so, but this imaginal solution of conflict has had no consideration for the welfare of the whole but only for
that of a particular species. This clue leads us, if we pursue it further,
into the problem of evil in the world. We shall defer this, and remark
as we pass on that Freedom is only supreme on the heights—and these
are far above the level of man's present standing.

We shall comment briefly on the nature of Natural Law of which
we have heard so much. Scientists are themselves turning away from
rigid notions on this subject. Thus Eddington has remarked that "there
is no strict causal behaviour anywhere". Bertrand Russell has said,
"There is no conclusive reason for believing that all natural occurrences
happen in accordance with laws which suffice to determine them, given
a sufficient knowledge of their antecedents." The fact is that Law is a
concept, probably of social origin, and when we find sufficient uni-
formity of behaviour we group our observations together in this general
form. There are, of course, many cases where the conservative aspects
of consciring are dominant. But wherever a waiting imaginal can insert
itself, or finite centres of consciring are involved, some novelty is
possible and the supposed inflexibility of Law then vanishes. Habits,
of course, are formed when actions, once freely adopted, are repeated.
This is found not only in ourselves but increasingly in all lower sentients.
As Fawcett remarks:

"The value of the term 'habit' is that it enables us to dispense with that
convention, the rigid law, and to regard the conservative actions concerned
as merely *like* one another, yielding ever to the 'plastic stress' of innovation."

Finally, we may comment on the fact that events continue to happen
—that chains of causation do not all suddenly cease. It is popularly taken
for granted that something must always "go on"—that even if thermo-
nuclear weapons destroyed all life on the planet, waves would still lap
around the desolate shores of the world. Yet events are under no compulsion to continue: they do so because of the conservative aspect of
Divine Imagining. Progress—which is apparent when we take the long
view—would not occur but for the additive aspect of Divine Imagining,
which uses this method to impel the world slowly onward in the direction of its far-distant goal. This is the "plastic stress" or power

Which wields the world with never-wearied love
Sustains it from beneath and kindles it above.

We shall offer later a solution of the riddle of Evil. We shall also
postpone any suggestions as to the meaning of the cosmic process and
the goal to which it is all leading. We have already in our hands sufficient
of the viewpoint of Imaginism to make possible a new approach to the
data of science and psychical research, and this is our next step.

Chapter

3

THE SCIENTIFIC OUTLOOK ON THE WORLD

Scientific materialism . . . is an assumption which I shall challenge as being entirely unsuited to the scientific situation at which we have now arrived. It is not wrong, if properly construed. If we confine ourselves to certain types of facts, abstracted from the complete circumstances in which they occur, the materialistic assumption expresses these facts to perfection. But when we pass beyond the abstraction, either by more subtle employment of our senses, or by the requests for meanings and for coherence of thoughts, the scheme breaks down at once. The narrow efficiency of the scheme was the very cause of its supreme methodological success.

A. N. WHITEHEAD

Science as a discipline is magnificent, and indispensable; as a belief-system it is disastrous.

C. C. L. GREGORY AND A. KOHSEN

The avenue of intellectual enquiry is not a road to pure truth. Step by step these higher reaches of realisation may be won, but only by the development of the whole personality; not by training of the intellectual faculty alone. Do not let this be misinterpreted as an anti-rationalist argument. It does not mean that reason is to be abandoned in favour of pure intuition. Reason can, and must, be used on the higher grades of significance as on the lower. What is meant is that reason unassisted, when in possession of one grade, can never attain to the root-conceptions necessary to open a higher grade to its use. These root-conceptions must first be grasped by intuition, or, as I have preferred to call it, by the mystical faculty.

G. N. M. TYRRELL

MECHANISM AND ITS LIMITATIONS

TOWARDS the end of the Renaissance, science—such as it was—broke away from philosophy. It was a revolt against deductive reason unrelated to the facts of Nature, and there was a determination to make observation and experiment the new basis of science. The modern age with all its impressive evidences of applied science bears witness to the success of this method. What we may call in general terms "scientific thought" has been based upon patient experimental work, including accurate measurement, and it has been built up largely by inductive reasoning.

Whenever a theory or viewpoint has had notable success in a special field, there is a likelihood that it will be adopted in other special fields of enquiry, to which, indeed, it may not be without some relevance. Nevertheless there is a danger here, to which we shall refer later; it lies in supposing that the "higher" can be wholly understood in terms of the "lower". There is, however, a much greater danger than this, viz. that a viewpoint which has met with outstanding success in a special field may be adopted, in a popular sense, as a viewpoint on life. Such has been the case with scientific materialism, which in its crudest terms is the view that everything can be explained as mechanism in terms of matter and energy. It is a view long since abandoned by leading physicists, but it is still hindering the progress of biology and psychology, and —what is more important—it is still the most dominant factor in the popular outlook on life.

We do not propose to consider the history of scientific thought: this has been done by many competent persons.[1] It is, however, worth while glancing quickly backwards, in order to see how scientific materialism arose. We shall then consider how physicists themselves found it necessary in the end to discard these views and started to court philosophy again. The most characteristic feature of physics is that it was not content to classify things. It started to measure them. Names such as Kepler, Galileo, Descartes, Boyle, and Newton come immediately to our minds. Galileo is usually recalled as one who in 1633 fell foul of the Roman Inquisition through his support for the Copernican view of the solar system, but he was an inventor of no mean order and his researches dealt with many of the fundamental problems of moving bodies. It is interesting to note that in 1624 he was differentiating between the primary qualities of bodies such as shape, size, and position, and secondary qualities such as taste, smell, colour, and sound which depended on an observer. He regarded the primary qualities as having a higher degree of reality.

As everyone knows, it was the genius of Isaac Newton, whose famous *Principia* was published in 1687, which gave us the basic concepts of mass, force, acceleration, and the Law of Gravitation in a form in which they were to last unchanged for over two centuries. With these foundations to build on, accounting not merely for the motions of particles but also for the planets within the solar system, is it surprising that mechanics came to be regarded as the key to a basic understanding of the physical world? When the nature of light was being discussed it was two *mechanical* concepts—of particles and of waves respectively— which contended for acceptance. When, in the early years of this century, new experimental data were obtained which showed that the "billiard-ball" type of atom was impossible, the solar system became a model for atomic structure. We pictured negative electrons each in its own orbit going round a positively charged nucleus, much as planets go round the sun. With this mechanical model and certain new assumptions known as the quantum theory, Bohr was able in 1913 to account mathematically for the characteristic spectra of atoms.

[1] E.g. A. N. Whitehead, *Science and the Modern World* (C.U.P., 1926); or C. E. Raven, *Natural Religion and Christian Theology* (C.U.P., 1953).

It was a very great achievement, and in this amazing underworld of Nature it looked as though the reign of mechanism was as dominant as in the starry heavens. Matter in motion, acted on by forces which, though mysterious in origin, were law-abiding, seemed to nineteenth-century physicists to hold out promise of a complete understanding of the physical world. Although this optimistic view had to be abandoned, for reasons which we shall shortly mention, it is important to observe that the relevance of mechanics is only to the so-called primary qualities of bodies—mass, shape, size, and velocity. The so-called secondary qualities—taste, smell, colour, and sound—lie outside the mechanical world-picture and were usually attributed to the observing mind. The observing mind was supposed to create these qualities and project them on to the outside world. Writing satirically of this view, which Locke expounded, A. N. Whitehead says:

"Thus nature gets credit which should in truth be reserved for ourselves: the rose for its scent, the nightingale for its song, and the sun for his radiance. The poets are entirely mistaken. They should address their lyrics to themselves and should turn them into odes of self-congratulation on the excellence of the human mind. Nature is a dull affair, soundless, scentless, colourless; merely the hurrying of material, endlessly, meaninglessly."

Needless to say, we regard Whitehead's satire as richly deserved. How convenient to deposit in the human mind, as though once there they demanded no further explanation, those qualities of objects which do not lend themselves to measurement! It is precisely at this point that the mechanistic view shows its limitations. As a thought-system which builds into a coherent scheme selected data, viz. the measurable aspects of bodies, it is a great achievement. As a metaphysical outlook it is ridiculous, for it ignores all those aspects of the world which have *value* for us. The rich qualitative variety of Nature and its transformations are every bit as important as the world's metrical aspects in a complete metaphysical outlook.

Electrons may revolve and spin in a silent, colourless world. Planets may wheel in orbits which are the shortest paths in curved space-time. Quanta of energy may appear and disappear in an endless process of increasing entropy. But it is the colour of dawn over moorland, the scents of a woodland in spring, the lap of water on a lake shore, and the song of the skylark on a summer morning which disturb us with the sense of a Presence. The quality of the world must therefore find a leading place in our philosophy of life. I am disposed to agree with W. Macneile Dixon, who was once led to say:

"If I were offered the opportunity of living for ever in a paradise of surpassing loveliness I should not grumble if the last secret of the Universe were withheld from me."

I do not think the distinction between primary and secondary qualities is one which can be finally sustained, and from the standpoint of Imaginism it is unnecessary. All qualities observed by human beings, possibly with many others which *we* do not discern, but which a microbe or a god might discern, are aspects of objects of the external world, and in a psychical continuum they inter-penetrate all perceiving minds.

It cannot be over-emphasised that physics, like every other branch of science, selects and abstracts its data from a greater whole. Whitehead has described philosophy as the critic of abstractions and has drawn attention repeatedly to the errors which arise from mistaking abstractions for concrete realities, partial aspects for the whole.

PHYSICS AND IMAGINISM

The high hopes which were held in the late nineteenth century that it would be possible to explain the world of atomic phenomena by mechanical concepts were shattered by several happenings.

The first of these was linked with the name of Einstein. It began with the strange and unexpected result of an experiment made by two physicists who were measuring the velocity of light. Einstein showed that the only satisfactory way to account for their results was to revise fundamental ideas of mass, length, and time, which, he suggested, must depend on the observer's speed. This is now accepted.

The second, an even more radical shock, was linked with the name of Planck, and is called the Quantum Theory. It is not possible to give a satisfactory account of this without mathematics, and since we are writing for the non-specialist, it will be enough to give the conclusions to which it led. (1) Models of the atom and the microcosm in general are unsatisfactory and unnecessary. It is as though we drew mechanical designs in ink on blotting-paper. As the scale of our design diminishes, a point is reached where the design itself cannot be represented. (2) There is some inherent freedom which all the so-called fundamental particles possess. From the point of view of our attempts to measure and locate them, this leads to uncertainty.

It is a fair summing up to say that mechanism does not look at all promising as a clue to the structure of the microcosm, however convenient it may be as an aid to conceptual thought. With the elimination of a mechanoid basis for Nature, the way is at least clear for us to consider a psychoid basis, if there is evidence to support this possibility.

One of the contentions of Imaginism, startling to the physicist, is that sentience is in varying degrees embodied in entities below that arbitrary threshold which to the biologist divides the living from the non-living. Crystals, atoms, and sub-atomic particles are considered to be centres of irreflective consciring in varying degrees. Imaginism envisages that each more complicated structure, which embodies qualities not found in those below it, is accounted for by higher sub-imaginals "descending" into and using the products of lower sub-imaginals as their media or vehicles. Is there any good evidence in physics that these views are sound? I present below examples of physical phenomena which can best be understood from the imaginist standpoint.

(1) *Radio-activity*. It is common knowledge that radium slowly changes into another element because of instability in its nucleus, and that this process consists partly of the emission of α-particles. Experiment shows that if we start with 1 milligram of radium, half of it will remain after 1590 years. Of this $\frac{1}{2}$ mg. only $\frac{1}{4}$ mg. would remain after another 1590 years, and so on. From the point of view of an individual radium atom, the expulsion of its α-particle may take place the next minute, next year, or some thousands of years later. Each nucleus appears to have freedom in this respect. Do not let us overlook the fact that the nuclei are supposed to be all alike, and that 1 mg. contains about $3 \cdot 10^{18}$ atoms. Now, are we to suppose that each individual atom has knowledge of what all its neighbours have done or are doing, so that it might say to itself, "I must change now, and make my contribution to a half-life period of 1590 years"? Such a fantasy is of course absurd. Is there any alternative to something which we may call a radium sub-imaginal, of which all radium atoms are manifestations? This particular sub-imaginal has a limited life (as have some biological sub-imaginals) before it becomes extinct. Its process of ageing is reflected in the residual number of the species.

(2) *Interference*. This well-known phenomenon occurs with either electrons or protons, or with photons (light-corpuscles). If a suitable source of these is placed behind a narrow slit, we do not find a sharp shadow on this side of the slit, but the particles spray out and create what is called a diffraction pattern. The distribution of particles in this pattern is a characteristic one determined by their speed and the width of the slit. From the particle's viewpoint, does it know what contribution it is expected to make to the pattern and what its neighbours are doing? Of course not. The electron sub-imaginal or light-imaginal, as the case may be, has however certain properties which can be manifested when certain other conditions are satisfied. If a second narrow slit is placed parallel to the first one, the whole distribution pattern, now called an interference-pattern, is radically changed. The electrons or photons which contribute to the pattern must go through one slit or the other. Shall we suppose that in doing so they are aware of the presence of the second slit which leads them to choose a different direction from that which they would otherwise have taken? Of course not. The changed

conditions, however, make possible the appearance of a new property of the imaginal of which these particles are individual manifestations.

(3) *Reflection and Transmission.* A stream of photons falls on a transparent surface. A certain proportion is reflected and the rest is transmitted. The factors which determine this ratio are the angle of incidence and the refractive index of the glass. But the photons are all alike: are we then to suppose that individual photons make a choice, knowing what their neighbours are doing? The argument runs precisely as before.

(4) *Emission or Absorption by Atoms.* Let us consider the hydrogen atom, which consists of a single electron revolving around a proton. Normally this electron revolves in the innermost stable orbit which we will label No. 1. But if the atom is electrically excited, the electron may travel round a higher orbit No. 2 or in a still higher one No. 3, 4, 5, etc. Suppose some hydrogen gas is electrically excited and that millions of atoms have their electron raised to No. 3 orbit. These electrons can fall back to the normal one either by a single jump from 3 to 1, or in two jumps, namely from 3 to 2, and then from 2 to 1. In each of these jumps energy is emitted in the form of light and gives rise to three different spectral lines. Experiment shows that in given conditions these spectral lines have a certain intensity ratio. In other words, there is a fairly constant ratio between the number of jumps from 3 to 2 compared with those from 3 to 1. This is the crucial point: is the atom regarded as free to choose which jump it will make? Does an atom know what its neighbours are doing, so that it can conform to this ratio? The answer is of course not. The hydrogen-imaginal has a habit-pattern of behaviour which is manifested in the myriads of atoms which it creates and controls.

(5) *Crystal Structure.* From the plate of snow crystals, which may be of aesthetic as well as scientific interest to the reader, can be illustrated several of these principles. The crystal is a more complex structure than any we have so far considered. The snow crystal grows from the centre outwards, and a tiny nucleus such as a dust particle or a molecular aggregate often facilitates the first condensation of water-vapour which starts the crystal. The question I want to put to the reader is this: Has the crystal growing on any one of its six projecting arms any awareness of what pattern is being developed on its five neighbours? How is it that we do not find *different* symmetrical patterns on the six arms of the crystal once they have emerged from the common core? Indeed, we might go further with the same query and ask why there is symmetry on each of the arms. We may go further and ask why, if the forces are wholly physico-chemical, there are apparently no two crystals quite alike.

We have here an excellent example of a sub-imaginal field—of imagining at the irreflective level of crystals. We invoke the psychoid character of these humble entities, the inter-penetrating fields of the molecules, the "discovery" that hexagonal symmetry provides a harmonising of the conflict due to their inter-penetration, and the constructive power of the sub-imaginal field of the crystal which overrides those of the molecular sub-imaginals.

SOME REFLECTIONS

Do we get nearer to an understanding of objects by studying smaller and smaller parts? It must be obvious that the kind of knowledge we acquire by a process of progressive break-down or analysis may sometimes change radically. An artist's picture has to be studied as a whole if its significance is to be understood. Examination of it with a magnifying-glass may tell us more about the canvas and pigment—but nothing about the picture. Or again, the break-down products of chemical analysis will be wholly different in properties from the original compound. The study of parts or partial aspects may provide no indication of the nature and functions of the greater whole from which the part has been abstracted. Thus a study of liver or kidney function would provide no adequate data of the nature and functions of man himself. Indeed, the importance of environment, and relationship to a larger whole is being stressed today in all biological and physiological investigation.

These are illustrations of what we believe to be a general-principle, which J. C. Smuts has enunciated in his book *Holism and Evolution*.[1] He lays stress on three things among others:

(1) All objects of Nature animate and inanimate, and all ideas have their "fields"—inseparable from them. He says that "It is in these fields and these fields only that things really happen. It is the intermingling of fields which is creative or causal in nature as well as in life." He conceives such fields as conserving both their past and present, and in some degree including purposive or teleological elements.

(2) In the formation of greater "wholes" functions and properties arise which are new, and have not resided in any of the parts.

(3) There is a principle of "Holistic Selection" operative in organisms which through the medium of their fields places the resources of a greater whole behind any promising variation. This has particular relevance to Evolution.

[1] J. C. Smuts, *Holism and Evolution*, pp. 114-15. (Macmillan & Co. Ltd., 1926.)

Such views are wholly consonant with the general viewpoint of Imaginism. The first of these views is clearly the recognition that all things constitute a psychical continuum, and that from their inter-penetration arises conflict and change in the effort to find a new harmony. The second of these views is clearly accounted for by the fact that waiting Imaginals introduce themselves into situations when the development of the latter makes it possible. The third of these views describes in different terms the fact that individual organisms are created and sustained by higher sub-imaginal fields of which they are just a temporary expression. As we know, such fields are both conservative and additive of novelty.

We return to our starting-point. It is perhaps best to regard models as aids to thought, and this is permissible so long as we know it is "conceptual mythology" and not a portrayal of reality. Physics is full of conceptual myths. The concept of "matter", for example, neglects most qualities of objects and recognises only two—extension in space, and resistance to touch or motion. No one has ever seen matter, although we have all seen objects rich in qualities. When physicists wanted to measure *how much* resistance to motion bodies possessed relative to each other, the concept of "mass" was created. It is quite abstract, viz. the metrical aspect of resistance to motion.

Another concept is "energy". Mass and energy are today regarded as quantitatively equivalent, and are both governed by one conservation principle. When the former is transformed into the latter a number of wholly new qualities arise: where these come from is not explained by physics, which is interested only in the quantitative equivalence.

All we desire to draw attention to is the abstracted nature of the data of physics, and thus to emphasise that a metaphysical view is concerned with the greater whole which has qualitative aspects of not less importance than the quantitative aspects. We suggest that Energy is more fundamentally understood if it is regarded as Divine consciring on the lowest level (which is the physical level of our galaxy), that mass is a concentrated form of it involved in all psychoids or finite centres of consciring, and that the qualitative richness of the external world is a real part of its nature—not a creation of finite observing minds, but the manifesting of Imaginals and sub-Imaginals.

The philosophic views of A. N. Whitehead seem to me entirely consonant with these. It is well known that he regards electrons, protons, and atoms as organisms, physics being the study of smaller organisms and biology of the larger. He regards the classical view of the "simple location" of matter as an abstraction from reality. By "simple location" is meant that a bit of matter can be defined as being at a certain point of space for a certain duration of time without its relations to other parts of space and time being involved. In Imaginist terms he recognises the fact of inter-penetration in a psychical continuum. He says, "Each volume of space, or each lapse of time, includes in its essence aspects of all volumes of space or of all lapses of time." For certain practical purposes this consideration may not be significant—but for a metaphysical outlook it is very important; it is particularly relevant, as we shall see in the next chapter, to the data of physical research.

I venture to quote a passage from Whitehead [1] which summarises many of these ideas:

"The doctrine which I am maintaining is that the whole concept of materialism only applies to very abstract entities, the products of logical discernment. The concrete enduring entities are organisms so that the plan of the *whole* influences the very characters of the various subordinate organisms which enter into it. In the case of an animal, the mental states enter into the plan of the total organism and thus modify the plans of the successive subordinate organisms until the ultimate smallest organisms, such as electrons, are reached. Thus an electron within a living body is different from an electron outside it, by reason of the plan of the body . . . and this plan includes the mental state. But the principle of modification is perfectly general throughout nature, and represents no property peculiar to living bodies."

We shall turn now to some representative biological themes which have more direct relevance to our life as human beings.

THE NATURE OF LIVING THINGS

There are many features which make it convenient, for study purposes, to distinguish between living and non-living things. Self-sustained movement, as a whole, independent of externally applied physical forces, is one which impresses everyone. It is, however, possible to find primitive forms of life in which this feature is absent. Moreover, a biologist might say that, in principle, he can demonstrate experimentally that the energy intake and output of living things are equal, so that the feature of movement only indicates the presence of a piece of complex physico-chemical machinery. We should not say that a heat-engine or petrol engine was alive because it moved so long as we supplied the fuel!

A more distinctive characteristic of so-called living things is their ability to maintain themselves in the face of changes in their environment, provided these are not too extreme. If we live at high altitudes, the haemoglobin slowly increases to compensate for oxygen rarity. If we injure ourselves, many processes operate towards restoration. If we pick up an infection, the body has many lines of defence. Every organ of the body, and the organism as a whole, possesses a remarkable

[1] A. N. Whitehead, *Science and the Modern World*, pp. 98-9. (C.U.P., 1929.)

wealth of devices by which it can react to change and restore itself to a new harmony with its environment. It is of course conceivable that research will eventually establish that every one of these devices is *based upon* an ingenious physico-chemical reaction.

The most remarkable characteristic of what we call "living things" is their capacity for reproducing themselves. In some primitive cells, like yeast cells, this process is one of simple budding or subdivision. In most cells the process of subdivision of a cell into two daughter cells follows a complex and frequently observed ritual named mitosis, which give the impression of purpose, although "purpose" is not the correct word to describe the activities of such lowly centres of consciring. Molecules have not developed these habits so far as chemists are aware. It must, however, be recognised that while cells can be observed through an ordinary microscope, the largest molecules are only just coming within the range of photography through electron-microscopes, so that it cannot be claimed that their individual behaviour has been studied experimentally.

The view which we are presenting at the moment is that "life" is very difficult to define. The line between what we choose to call "living" and non-living may have no more existence than a line of latitude or longitude has on the earth's surface, although such lines may be convenient concepts.

It is common knowledge today that while bacteria are single-celled vegetable organisms which are always visible in a good microscope, there are much smaller particles called viruses which the optical microscope will not reveal and which pass through filters that can retain particles of size greater than one hundred thousandth of an inch. Pasteur suspected, but could not prove, that viruses existed in the cerebro-spinal fluid of dogs suffering from rabies. Viruses are now known to be responsible for many infectious diseases. Since they clearly multiply in living tissues and yet are much smaller than any known cells, their status as living or non-living entities is a particularly interesting one. In 1935 a virus was derived in a crystalline form from the sap of tobacco plants. For a considerable time it had been known to exist and to be responsible for mosaic blotches on tobacco leaves. The crystalline form was a guarantee of its purity, and its chemical structure was shown to be a protein molecule combined with nucleic acid. This is the same type of chemical structure as that of genes, of which we shall say more shortly. Both viruses and genes are very large and complex, but similar, molecules. The most important distinction between small bacteria and viruses, apart from size, is that the former can feed and multiply on non-living matter while the latter need living cells or tissues for their growth.

If reproduction is to be the criterion of a living thing, then at first sight viruses seem to be living, but as Darlington remarks[1]:

"Physiologically . . . we have to say that any particular crystalline virus is not living, because it is not capable of any living activity without the help of some other and more complex form of life—a chance which may or may not come its way."

We are on the interesting borderland where one of the greatest of the primary Imaginals—Life—begins to be able to manifest. The complex nucleo-protein molecule alone cannot sustain the note of Life (defined in terms of power to reproduce), but it is so near to this possibility that when it is placed in a living environment it resonates to the note and temporarily acquires the power. Rise a little higher in the scale. Let a series of different nucleo-proteins be arranged in rows to form chromosomes. Immerse the chromosomes in a suitably bounded medium (the nucleo-plasm), and surround this again by the cyto-plasmic medium containing a few other structures and a membrane, and we have, in principle, a cell capable of self-sustaining activity. The Life-Imaginal can find expression in and through it.

HEREDITY AND EVOLUTION

Although Robert Hooke first named "cells" in 1665, it was only with the development of microscopy in the first half of the nineteenth century that the cell was recognised in both plants and animals as the smallest unit of life. It is difficult to realise that it was in 1854, only a century ago, that a sperm was first seen making its way into the ovum of a frog, thus offering direct evidence of how a new individual began. Some six years earlier the microscope had shown that when a cell multiplies, its nucleus reveals the presence of a characteristic number of fine threads known as chromosomes. In the elaborate process of cell-division a longitudinal splitting of these takes place, so that the daughter cells each contain the same chromosomal material as the parent cell. This is an important feature because the chromosomes are the carriers of all inheritable characters.

Finally, the chromosomes were themselves found to consist of groups of "genes", much as beads might be threaded on a string. A single gene or sometimes a group of genes controls every inheritable characteristic of a plant or animal. The study of genes and the laws governing their behaviour constitutes a very active branch of biology known as genetics. The chromosomes of some creatures such as the fruit-fly *Drosophilia* have been the subject of detailed study, and maps

[1] *The Facts of Life*, p. 158. C. D. Darlington. (George Allen & Unwin Ltd., 1953.)

of the gene-positions in the chromosomes show what specific genes or groups of genes are responsible for different characteristics such as body-colour, wing-length, eye-colours, etc.

We have already mentioned that viruses and genes are very similar. Both are probably large single molecules consisting of a protein combined with a nucleic acid. Both breed true when they are in a suitable living environment. The gene is naturally in a suitable living environment, but the virus has to find its way into a living cell by infection. It is a kind of outcast which, freed from the habits of nuclear behaviour, appears easily to run amok. It is only fair to add, however, that there are well-behaved plasma-genes which normally reside in the cell cytoplasm and are self-propagating.

The rapid development in genetics, which is of great practical importance in the breeding and improving of plants and animals, has affected also views of the factors involved in Evolution. The views of Lamarck (1744-1829) are now generally out of favour. Expressed briefly, Lamarck's theory depended on the possibility of the transmission of *acquired* characters. The effective and constant use of organs leads to their strengthening and development, as we know in athletic training or in certain occupations. In contrast, the infrequent use of organs will tend towards their atrophy. Assuming that such acquired characteristics could be transmitted, we should have a very simple way in which animals could adapt themselves to change in the environment; but no evidence in support of this transmission has ever proved convincing. Lambs may have their tails docked for generations, but there is no increased tendency for them to be born without tails. About seventy generations of the fruit-fly *Drosophila* were bred in darkness, but the reactions of their progeny to light seemed quite unaffected.

Darwinism is the form of the theory of Evolution which is chiefly supported today. The views of Darwin (1809-82), were based on the observation that there is a range of variation among the individuals of any species. "Natural Selection" was the phrase he used to denote that some variations would doubtless confer an advantage on the creatures who possessed them, who would therefore be more likely to survive in the struggle for existence. These favourable variations would be transmitted to progeny, who themselves would have a better chance of survival. Changes in the environment would thus be responsible for "selecting" in the sense of favouring new and better-adapted forms of life. The types of variation which are possible material for Natural Selection are not acquired characters, but (1) the sudden unexpected mutations which occasionally took place in genes, and (2) the chromosome mutations which are constantly taking place in cell-division. The latter are by far the more important, and we know from the work of

Fisher, Haldane, and others that these changes are sufficient in number to provide the material from which the evolution of living things could take place. We are well aware today that many factors in the environment can affect both the chromosomes and their constituent genes. Among these are the exposure of tissues to X-rays, ultra-violet light, streams of neutrons or α-particles, and the ubiquitous cosmic-ray particles. Apart from such external agencies, the phenomenon of "crossing-over" in the process of cell-division is well-recognised. Here two chromosomes may interchange parts of themselves, so that a gene-sequence A B C D E in parent cells might become, for example, A D C B E in daughter cells. Because changes such as this take place in the germ-cells it is clear that sons and daughters of the same parents may be different in their inherited characteristics. This is not generally realised by the ordinary person, who seems surprised at hereditary variations in members of a family.

It might at first seem strange that there should be any difference, since the same genes are present in A B C D E, as in A D C B E. In fact, however, the effective influence of a gene depends on its genetic neighbours. The gene B might be dominant when its neighbours are A and C but recessive when they are C and E. This recognition of the importance of genetic environment or ordering suggests that there are factors operative over and above the chemical nature of the genes themselves. These may be expressed in terms of "fields" and "holistic selection" (see p. 68); or, in Imaginist terminology, we should stress the psychoid character of genes and the inter-penetration of their fields of influence, permitting new imaginals to manifest with the variation of these fields.

There can be no doubt of the importance of Darwin's viewpoint, which stresses Variation and Natural Selection as the twin foundations of our understanding of Evolution. They are also the foundations of our understanding of susceptibility and resistance to disease, and a few remarks about this may be appropriate. We know that bacterial infection sweeps through a community which meets a particular disease for the first time, and yet that as the years pass, the disease generally loses its virulence. The view now held is that susceptibility and resistance to disease are fundamentally genetic in character. When a disease is said to be very infectious it means that a considerable proportion of the population possesses gene-arrangements in their chromosomes which make persons susceptible to bacterial invasion. Genetic changes are constantly taking place, however, both in human beings and in bacteria. Natural selection is operative on both sides, so that human beings gradually acquire genetic arrangements which are increasingly resistant to disease. On the other hand, new genetic arrangements among the bacteria are necessary from their viewpoint if they are to multiply. C. D. Darlington expresses it thus[1]: "Infectious disease therefore works by a lock and key mechanism. It is a mechanism in which the lock and key are continually changing." An example of this is that in hospitals where penicillin has been in regular use for some years, many bacteria formerly susceptible to its action are now resistant. The biochemical fights against disease by the production of new specifics will need to continue so long as Variation and Natural Selection operate. In this constant battle, bacteria and viruses have the particular advantage of a life-cycle which is very short compared with that of human beings, so that their genetic change can be a much more rapid one.

EVOLUTION AND IMAGINISM

It is clear that the study of genetics throws considerable light on what might be called the mechanics[2] of Evolution. Genes appear to have a place in biology similar to that which atoms or sub-atomic particles have taken in physics. The issue which we discussed before is again relevant: how far does the study of smaller and smaller parts throw light on the whole? Here the living organism is the whole, and we find as our smallest significant unit a nucleo-protein molecule of great complexity. No one has ever supposed that an electron, a proton, a neutron, or a meson have colour or scent, taste or sound associated with them; but a greater whole—the atom—makes it possible for these waiting Imaginals to manifest. Nucleo-protein molecules contain thousands of atoms in a complicated type of structure which biochemists are slowly unravelling. This greater whole, the gene, has potentialities which are not present in any of the parts—it is made possible for certain transmissible qualities to appear, because other Imaginals or sub-Imaginals can now insert themselves into the phenomenal world. Nucleo-proteins are not themselves "living", but when they are synthesised in a greater whole,—the cell,—the new Imaginal of "Life" is able to manifest.

The *analytical* method of scientific study progressively eliminates the appearance of Imaginals, and thus leads us back to elementary entities which are the bases but not the adequate causes of these higher appearances. It is a common fallacy of the materialistic outlook to suppose that the higher can be "derived" from the lower, that physiological process is wholly a matter of energy transformations of a physico-chemical character, that instincts "derive from" neural patterns, that the human

[1] C. D. Darlington, *The Facts of Life*, p. 151. (George Allen and Unwin Ltd., 1953.)
[2] The term is used for convenience as referring to the chemical level of events, and is not to be taken as descriptive of the truth about even these elementary processes.

mind "derives from" instincts, that man "derives from" an anthropoid ape, and so on. (By "derives from" is meant "adequately explained by" or "causally accounted for".) It cannot be too strongly emphasised that the qualitative richness of the world has to be properly accounted for, and this cannot be done by the abstract concept of matter in motion.

In the evolutionary process we find imagining at work on every step of the ladder. As Fawcett[1] reminds us:

"For us there is no rich fancy in the absence of a rich pre-existing memory. For the macrocosm there is no rich creation in the absence of rich supporting conservation. The story of evolution pre-supposes divine creative fancy, but enduring or waiting elements, many all too easily overlooked by men of science and philosophers, concur with novelty during every stage of process. These elements insert themselves into the creative flux and are transformed then along with it. There results an evolutionary movement which gathers strength *at once from above and below*."

A nucleo-protein molecule is still a molecule—even if it is convenient in biology to call it a gene. It is incapable of accounting for blueness in eyes, redness in petals, or the length of a nose; nor if it is buffered by other neighbours, or if it drops an amino-acid from its tail, can it produce brown eyes, white petals, or a short nose. We do not dispute that certain molecular conditions and ordering of the genes are conditions (from "below") enabling such characters to manifest. But we claim that these qualitative features arise from "above", because Imaginals are able in these conditions to appear. The philosopher must continue to remind the biologist that "it is no good tapping a cask for wine which is not there".

When I survey the account which Darwinism and its derivatives gives of the Evolution of living things from the Protozoa to Homo Sapiens, I am bound to say that the two themes of Variation and Natural Selection, together with all the detailed knowledge which genetics is supplying, hold out great promise of accounting for the factors in Evolution which derive "from below". I am equally clear that regarded as the sole and sufficient basis of Evolution they are completely inadequate. At every step there is apparent the activity of imagining, of a purposive drive towards the interim goal of increasing awareness, and of experimenting to further that plan. Some of the experiments have obviously been failures: this is readily granted as we look back at the many extinct forms of life. But something was learned by these experiments, as we can see by the significant facts that failures were not repeated and that successful devices were fully exploited.

It may be asked: Who or what made these experiments and stored

[1] *Z.D.*, p. 382.

this wisdom? The answer leads us directly to consider the factors in evolution which come "from above". We must bear in mind firstly that all entities from the electron upwards are psychical in essence. They are foci of fields of influence inter-penetrating with either attraction or repulsion, harmony or conflict. Each is a centre of imagining or consciring, but as it participates in a greater whole it is modified, and to a considerable extent controlled by the over-ruling imaginative activity of that whole: the electron by the atom, the atom by the molecule, the molecule by the cell, the cell by the organ, the organ by the organism. Of course, the imagining only becomes reflective (i.e. self-conscious) at higher mammalian levels. Secondly, we must bear in mind the wealth of Imaginals and sub-Imaginals which are in some degree competing with each other and finding constant entry into the phenomenal world as and when conditions "from below" make it possible. Thirdly, I think we should bear in mind, at least as a reasonable hypothesis, that orders of intelligence higher than man have been and are interested in the evolution of living forms. It may sound a fantastic proposition to the scientist whose conceptions do not normally include more than the evidence of his senses can support. But I shall proceed to discuss in the next chapter evidence of the psychic inter-penetration of our familiar world which cannot be ignored, and may play an important part in our understanding of it. Man himself has now learned sufficient of genetics to direct naturally occurring processes in his own interests. He breeds flowers and maize and wheat, and domestic animals of all kinds to suit his economic or aesthetic interests. So far he has not synthesised the living from the non-living, nor can he control in a planned manner genetic changes. This will doubtless come, but at present he has to select from variations which Nature offers. The direction of Variation through psycho-kinesis may, however, be a form of scientific activity available to intelligent beings higher than man, and may have been a powerful directive factor in Evolution.

Of the two factors Variation and Natural Selection the former is by its nature the positive and active one. The latter does little more than provide that the field shall not be overcrowded with inferior types, so that improved types may have a fair opportunity. When one surveys the pageant of evolution there is abundant evidence of imaginative activity even on the level of lowly organisms, and there are at other points imaginal solutions of perplexing problems which, it seems inevitable, must have been directed and imposed by intelligent beings who have reached beyond man's attainment. Certainly chance variations would be completely valueless in the face of major developmental problems such as the construction of the eye or the ear. I shall illustrate these statements.

Consider the single-celled organism *paramecium* which is common in fresh-water ponds. It is one member of the class of *cilio-phora* who have all solved the problem of locomotion by co-ordinated motion of cilia. These are minute and very flexible hairs projecting from the body surface which are connected at their bases by something of the nature of a primitive nervous network. The wave-like periodic motion of the cilia propels the creature forward at considerable speed, rotating on its axis as it moves. Moreover, this movement combined with the creature's shape wafts a current of water containing possible food particles into the oral groove. The reaction of paramecium to an obstacle is a remarkable bit of imaginative activity on a very low level. Its ciliary movement is reversed for a short time and then it moves forward again in a slightly different direction.

At certain important stages of evolution, such as the invasion of dry land by the first amphibians or the conquest of the air by primitive birds, a whole group of complex adjustments had to be achieved approximately simultaneously. One or two alone could be of no value to the creature. These variations were presumably effected by co-ordinated genetic changes. The conquest of dry land meant a whole group of imaginative developments: internal lungs to oxygenate the blood, limbs with their muscles, nerves, and blood supply to lift the body off the ground, a satisfactory type of external covering to meet a wide range of seasonal changes, new methods of providing for progeny, etc. The conquest of the air by primitive birds after several brilliant failures involved enormous imaginative advances on the reptilian structure. The most remarkable of these was the invention of the feather, which is remarkably different in its properties from the reptilian scale. Yet feathers alone would have been valueless without fore-limb development and a very different musculature. And these could not have been used but for the much more efficient heart and vascular system. From the materialistic standpoint it is difficult to conceive of change providing either simultaneously or in rapid succession the whole series of variations which collectively are necessary to provide a working novelty that would confer an advantage on the creature which possessed it. That all the necessary variations should appear simultaneously appears extremely improbable. If it is postulated that they appear in succession we must ask how it comes about that the earlier ones are conserved in the midst of change until the last of the necessary genetic variations confers a working advantage. From the imaginist standpoint we find no difficulty, since both conservation and creative novelty are aspects of imagining, whether it occurs in the evolving individual organisms or in the psychic field of the whole species or in the minds of higher Intelligences.

It is of great interest that Professor A. C. Hardy has expressed the view "that there must be at least one element in the process of evolution that is not mechanical or material in the ordinary sense". Moreover, referring to telepathy, he has said, "The discovery that individual organisms are somehow in psychical connection with one another across space is, of course, one of the most revolutionary biological discoveries ever made."

In suggesting how this may have an important bearing on evolution Hardy revives the idea of "Organic Selection" (first put forward by Baldwin and by Lloyd Morgan). This supplements the Natural Selection of Darwin with an "internal" type of selection, viz. that derived from the habit-pattern of the animal. Organic Selection suggests that the habit-pattern, which of course may change with a changing environment, exercises a selective effect on those gene complexes which will give structural change better adapted to the new habit-pattern. (This is different from Lamarckism, which certainly starts with the same recognition that change of environment will give rise to a change in habit-pattern but goes on to suppose that it is the physical variation arising from greater or lesser use of particular organs which modifies the genes). Professor Hardy writes[1]:

"If there is to be expected, as has been suggested, something akin to telepathy, no doubt unconscious, acting between different members of a species and binding them together in a particular pattern of behaviour, then I think the fact that changes in behaviour can bring about the selection of different gene complexes would give evolutionary significance to such a group or species behaviour complex. That is, of course, provided that such a group behaviour complex gradually changed with the changing experience of the individuals making up the group. . . .

It may be argued that such a group behaviour plan linking the different members together might act against change of habit. This I think in part might well be so—we could expect it to be conservative; but also I think it possible to imagine this conservative plan being gradually altered by the influence of more enterprising individuals. Let us suppose a species of bird usually fed on insects off the surface of the bark of trees; then suppose that, in a time of shortage, a few individuals discovered that they could find a good supply of insects by probing with their beaks into and under the bark; they would be likely to be copied by other members of the species. The emergency of a food shortage in a particular area would compel a number to act against the conservative traditions of the racial behaviour plan; if this action proved beneficial a wave of change in the behaviour plan might spread—not simply by copying, but perhaps by a telepathic-like influence spreading from the individuals who had made the new discovery. An inclination to explore below the bark might be transmitted. Now by organic selection change of habit would bring about change of structure—those whose gene combinations

[1] *Jour. S.P.R.*, Vol. XXXV, pp. 237-8 (1950).

produced a slight change in shape of beak that was more useful in the probing of bark than the older type would tend to get more food and survive more easily."

In a later paper[1] Professor Hardy develops these views further. He shows the inadequacy of all current biological theory (genetic or otherwise) to explain the handing on in the evolutionary process of homologous structures. He refers to Samuel Butler's concept of a subconscious racial memory, and after a survey of related types of structure, says:

"I find it quite impossible to imagine how such a mathematical plan of growth could have been evolved entirely under the selective influence of the very heterogeneous environment. It seems to me to have all the appearance of a definite mental conception like that of an artist or designer—a pattern outside the physical world which in some way has served as a templet or gauge for selective action; it is suggested as before, that it is this plan in the group mind which indirectly *selects* those gene complexes presenting its best expression. It is a species plan mirrored in each individual: a plan which in evolution may be stretched or warped in various ways, but always as a *whole plan* is stretched and warped, and usually according to a relatively simple mathematical formula."

It is easy to interpret all this in Imaginist terms. The telepathic linkage is identical with the psychical inter-penetrating fields of the organisms. Imaginative activity, both conservative and novel, is operative in this field in response to environmental change.

The imaginal activity may be on what *we* call the chance level of chromosome mutation; it may be on the level of the individual organism (as in a bird searching under the bark of a tree for a better food supply); it may be on the level of the group-mind, where a new sub-imaginal is able to introduce its influence, or where intelligent beings higher than man exercise forms of artistic experiment with living things comparable to our own humbler experiments in artistic achievement with pigments, clay, and marble.

Bergson,[2] examining the data of evolution, pointed out that while the mechanist viewpoint would have to accept a series of accidents leading to an advantageous novelty—itself an improbable happening—it is quite improbable that the same novelty would arise on a completely different line of evolution by an entirely different series of accidents. He gives as a particular example the structure of the eye. Bergson compares the structure of the eye in vertebrates with that in a common mollusc such as the *Pecten*. Both have similar arrangements consisting

[1] A. C. Hardy, "Biology and Psychical Research", *Proc. S.P.R.*, Vol. L, p. 126 (1953).

[2] Henri Bergson, *Creative Evolution*. (Macmillan & Co. Ltd., 1913.)

of retina and nerve fibres, cornea, and a crystalline lens, and many subsidiary structures. Now the divergence of the vertebrate and invertebrate lines of evolution took place at a very early stage when any light-sensitive organ would have been little more than a pigment spot on the body surface. If we were mechanists, looking at this from Lamarck's standpoint, we should suppose that constant exposure to light of very different tissues would ultimately transform spots on both into an elaborate eye. The likelihood of this transformation is comparable to the expectation that a photographic negative, or a bit of light-sensitive selenium, if exposed long enough to light, will finally give rise to a camera! If we were mechanists, taking the Darwinist viewpoint we should have to fall back on accidental genetic change producing a more efficient eye in a very large number of stages. It must be pointed out that the retina of the vertebrate is an outgrowth of the embryonic brain, while in the mollusc it is a direct modification of the ectoderm. Is it really plausible that two different independent series of happy accidents are going to result in similar end-products?

The more we look at the phenomena of growth and development the more overwhelming is the evidence for over-ruling directive powers using the lower sentients for their expression, working towards ends, planning experiments to achieve these ends and conserving the fruits of experiment. Consciring has its twin aspects of conservation (memory) and creativity, which are present in all finite sentients from genes upwards. Certainly in the most primitive sentients the conservative elements far outweigh those creative of novelty, and moreover this measure of freedom on the lowest levels runs out into chance. We stress, however, that lower sub-imaginals are used by higher sub-imaginals in manifesting, and these again by still higher sub-imaginals, and so on, in a vast ascending hierarchy (sub-atomic particles, atoms, molecules, genes, cells, organs, organisms, etc.). As we ascend, the range and power of consciring increase, so that control and direction of those which are lower is to some extent possible. Central control is indeed substantial over the lowest sentients. The controlling powers may not only be imaginal in origin, but also derive from the experimental consciring of advanced Intelligences. What we describe in the next chapter as telepathy ($\psi\gamma$) and psycho-kinesis ($\psi\kappa$) may be the methods of doing this. We do not regard Variation as by any means a matter of chance alone.

4

A SURVEY AND ASSESSMENT OF PSYCHICAL RESEARCH

If you have had your attention directed to the novelties in thought in your own lifetime, you will have observed that almost all really new ideas have a certain aspect of foolishness when they are first produced.

A. N. WHITEHEAD

These queer facts are not at all trivial, and it is right to make the greatest possible fuss about them. Their very queerness is just what makes them so significant. We call them "queer" just because they will not fit in with orthodox scientific ideas about the universe and man's place in it. If they show, as I think they do, that the Materialist conception of human personality is untenable, and if they throw quite new light on the age-old conflict between the scientific and the religious outlooks, we shall have to conclude that Psychical Research is one of the most important branches of investigation which the human mind has ever undertaken.

H. H. PRICE

The supreme importance, as I see it, of the labours of Dr. Rhine and his fellow para-psychologists lies in this: that they are providing a slow, painful but sure demonstration by the methods of science of a truth that the religions of the world have grasped intuitively or that is seen only vaguely through the eyes of faith. I mean the truth that man is more than a physical organism responding to stimuli—that while living in this world he is yet in contact with an extra-sensory order of existence whose relations to time and space transcend those of the world of matter.

.... The world will not listen to the voice of religion nor to the clear voice of Wordsworth calling across a century defaced by the two most hideous wars in history, but it pays lip-service to the voice of science. Let us hope it will listen to what the science of para-psychology has to say before it is too late.

S. G. SOAL

THE aim of this chapter is not to present a systematic account of psychical research, still less to provide data on which judgments of the reliability of these strange phenomena may be based. Such data can be found and studied elsewhere. We propose here to survey the types of phenomena which have been studied, with a view to assessing their significance for a judgment of the kind of world we live in.

It is probably still true to say that the majority of thoughtful and educated people have paid no serious attention to the findings of psychical research. Its ideas have not yet confronted them as significant and revolutionary for their whole philosophy of life. We shall shortly tabulate a number of phenomena, and we may confidently affirm that if any one of them is true, the materialist outlook on life is quite undermined. The mind of man is shown to exist in its own right—not as a mere epi-phenomenon of brain—and behind the physical level other significant levels are shown to exist, in which man participates and to which he can make response.

Some people imagine that psychical research is synonymous with spiritualism. This is of course untrue, and such a view could only be held in ignorance of both. The former is a critical and scientific approach to all para-normal phenomena. The latter is a religious practice based upon the conviction of man's survival of death and the possibility of communication between the incarnate and discarnate. It is certainly true that *some* para-normal phenomena raise the question whether their origin is to be attributed to the action of discarnate personalities or to be attributed to the exercise, in an unusual degree, of powers latent in all living minds. It is quite possible for a student in the field of psychical research to hold that the spiritualist view is either right or wrong. The present writer has been driven to accept its central contention as true, both by a critical appraisal of the evidence and by certain personal experiences. Some students of psychical research would support him, while others would not accept this position, but we should all agree that there are well-established para-normal phenomena which have far-reaching implications in relation to the nature and status of the human mind.

The late G. N. M. Tyrrell,[1] a distinguished worker in this field, on many occasions drew attention to the strangely neglectful attitude of otherwise thoughtful and reasonable people towards the findings of psychical research. One would certainly have supposed that where issues of the greatest importance to scientific and philosophical thought were involved there would be widespread concern to investigate and assess them at their true value. Apart from a small minority of persons this is not so. The attitude is on the whole one of neglect, or of derision, or of explaining away as coincidental, happenings which, if accepted, would be beyond the possibility of explanation by our present scientific knowledge. It is clear that these commonplace attitudes must have a psychological cause, and Tyrrell suggests that in the course of man's evolution his mind as well as his body has been adapted to the physical environment. In other words, there is an unconscious factor in man's mind which acts so as to prevent his interest and belief from wandering too far from the familiar world which his senses present to him. It leads him to assume that the physical world ceases to exist at the point where his senses cease to register it. It also leads him to suppose that "common-sense" is a safe guide when faced with the question as to what is possible and what is not possible in this world.

[1] G. N. M. Tyrrell, *Homo Faber*. (Methuen & Co. Ltd., 1951.)

"The mind always reacts to an impulse which penetrates it through and through, forcing upon it the conviction that the sense-world is complete in itself. If we can rise above this conviction and see things more impartially, it becomes evident that there is no dividing boundary between the normal and the para-normal; and there is no reason (apart from our instinctive urge) to regard the para-normal as less probable than the normal. The apparent boundary consists in the limited boundary of our senses, reinforced by the instinct which convinces us that the boundary is objective and not subjective."[1]

I think there is a great deal of truth in Tyrrell's contention. Even when every allowance is made for scientific caution and the desire not to be deluded, unwillingness to examine evidence is not a scientific attitude. Moreover, again and again we notice that where this evidence is being examined, events are attributed to chance in a way which would not be entertained for a moment in other fields of enquiry.

I have summarised in tabular form some of the main para-normal phenomena. Those in which the observer by para-normal means *receives* knowledge or information have been grouped together. Those in which Mind *acts* para-normally in relation to its physical environment have also been grouped together. We have then gathered into a third group phenomena in which there is an interaction of Mind with the physical environment of a more involved or mixed type. It is sometimes said that we are grievously in need of a unifying principle or a theory to draw together these varied phenomena and help us to see them in a co-ordinated form. It may well appear so as we glance at this tabulation. We do know, however, that the key to understanding of them exists

Para-normal Cognition	*Para-normal Action*
1. Telepathy.	1. Psycho-kinesis (Rhine type).
2. Clairvoyance, Clair-audience, etc.	2. Movement of heavy objects.
3. Pre-cognition and Retro-cognition.	3. Levitation.
4. Unusual knowledge through Dream, Trance, or Motor Automatisms.	4. Poltergeist Effects (kinetic, acoustical, thermal).
5. Apparitions (Subjective).	

Various Types of Psycho-Physical Interaction

1. Object-reading or Psychometry.
2. Hauntings.
3. Creative/Destructive phenomena
   (Materialisations, Apports, Objective Apparitions).
4. Hatha Yoga: Fire-walking and other psycho-physiological phenomena.
5. Para-normal Healing.

[1] G. N. M. Tyrrell, *The Nature of Human Personality*, p. 96. (George Allen and Unwin Ltd., 1954.)

in the lower levels of human personality. The body: mind levels of ourselves and the many sub-levels which they comprise, hold all the clues if we could only unravel them. The careful analysis of all spontaneous para-normal experiences and the pursuit of experimental parapsychology will doubtless continue to take us farther on the way of understanding—but always it will remain understanding from the "outside". The administration of drugs such as mescalin and the discovery of other closely related compounds may perhaps soon allow us to induce and study psychic faculty both subjectively and objectively. If this could be done concurrently it would be a great advantage. One cannot look at some of the ancient Hindu treatises on yoga[1] without gaining the impression that some of these contemplatives of ancient India learned vastly more about the structure of human personality by their subjective methods than we in the West are ever likely to learn by our objective approach. In other words, if the human mind is ever to be understood in its profundity it will only be by the use of some still deeper intuitive part of the self. How far such knowledge can ever be formulated in words is problematical: such translations as we have of ancient experience are admittedly not very enlightening to the Western student. Sooner or later it will be necessary for trained scientific persons to undertake these ancient disciplines which, it is believed, may develop psychic faculty and bring it under the control of the will.

PARA-NORMAL COGNITION

(1) *Telepathy*. This term was coined by F. W. H. Myers and defined as being the communication of impressions from one mind to another without the use of any of the channels of sense. The evidence for it is overwhelming: indeed we may say that it is as reliably established as any basic fact of science. But when we ask ourselves what we know about it and how it works, our knowledge is still very small. We know that minds differ in their possibility of mutual rapport or affinity, so that a person A may have a relatively good telepathic rapport with B, a smaller degree with C, and none at all with D. We know that the "link-up" between the minds of A and B is not on the levels of consciousness but between what the psychologist calls sub-conscious levels. The *process* of communication is quite below the threshold of awareness of either party. In experimental work A, the initiator of thought, would be called the agent, and the receiver B would be called the percipient. It is important to

---

[1] E.g. J. H. Woods, *The Yoga-System of Patanjali* (Harvard Oriental Series, Vol. 17, 1927); or Arthur Avalon, *The Serpent Power*, 3rd Ed. (Ganesh & Co., Madras, 1931.)

appreciate, however, that if *B* is what we call a sensitive or medium, he often has the power in trance to draw memories from the sub-conscious level of *A*'s mind and re-present them to *A*. This process, popularly called "thought-reading", can be very impressive to *A* the sitter, and its possibility must be constantly kept in mind in evaluating material obtained at a sitting with a medium. We know also that telepathy is unaffected by distance between agent and percipient—at least up to distances of hundreds of miles, as experiment has shown. Dr. Soal remarks: "There is no sense in talking about the distance between two minds, and we must consider brains as focal points in space at which Mind produces *physical* manifestations in its interaction with Matter.[1] Soal has shown that change in the location of the agent, unknown to the percipient, does not adversely affect the latter's scoring. Soal also showed that when a percipient was experimenting with an agent, another agent, who unknown to the percipient was trying to influence the latter, failed to do so.

It seems very probable that telepathy, in the sense of an inter-linkage of minds, is common on the animal level. The concerted action of flocks of birds wheeling in flight, of shoals of minnows changing direction, of myriads of fireflies extinguishing their light, and the co-operative activity of ants, bees, termites, and other such insects, suggests the activity of a common group-mind to which individual members are intimately related. There is also some interesting evidence of the relation between man's mind and those of some domestic animals. The whole subject is a vast one, with enormous biological implications, as we have previously suggested. For our purpose we need not pursue this in any further detail, but we must consider the implications of telepathy. These are indeed far-reaching.

Professor H. H. Price has said: "Telepathy is something that ought not to happen at all if the Materialistic theory were true. But it does happen. So there must be something seriously wrong with the Materialistic theory." This theory supposes that events in the brain precisely determine all events in the associated mind. But we know that, through telepathy, events in the mind of a percipient can be determined by events in the mind of an agent. The materialist may point out that the percipient's mind is still associated with a brain. It is not this general correlation which is the essence of materialism, but the hypothesis that brain-events are necessarily causal and mind-events consequential, so that mind-functioning depends in detail on brain-functioning. Once the essentially independent functioning of mind is established, the whole philosophic outlook is changed.

(2) *Clairvoyance, etc.* By this is meant awareness of some approxi-

[1] F. Bateman and S. G. Soal, *Jour. S.P.R.*, Vol. XXXV, p. 257 (1950).

mately contemporary event or object in the *material* world without the use of the senses. An apparent vision of an event in a distant place, or knowledge of the order of cards in a shuffled pack, where this knowledge was not accessible from any living mind, would be clairvoyance. It should be said at once that the evidence for this is overwhelming and the phenomenon is completely established. At first sight it raises new problems, for here Mind apparently achieves a cognitive relationship to physical objects—a more difficult conception than that of mind-to-mind relationship as in telepathy. It is here that we must consider carefully what experiment reveals. "Clairvoyance" suggests clear-seeing, and it is easy to jump to the conclusion that it is a kind of "X-ray vision" of the physical object. In some cases this *might* be the case, but in many other instances it cannot possibly be so. The reading of a folded letter in an opaque envelope, which at first sight seems clairvoyance, might be precognition of the future mental experience of the reader, or telepathic rapport with the mind of the writer. Clairvoyant "perception" of the order of cards in a shuffled pack is difficult to picture as a focussing of "X-ray vision" on one card after another through a pack. So is the correct reading of line 17 on page 281 of a closed book. These also might be explained as precognition of future mental states of someone who verified the observation made.

But it would seem that there is such a thing as precognitive clairvoyance. Tyrrell did a long series of experiments with a percipient who raised the lid of one of five closed boxes in which a small lamp was lit. The arrangement was such that Tyrrell as operator did not know himself which lamp he lit, so that thought-reading on the part of the percipient was ruled out. During the course of these experiments Tyrrell built a relay which was set in operation by the opening of any box-lid. The lamp was pre-selected as before by a random method, but the lamp itself was only lit by the action of the relay when a lid was opened. Success with this demanded precognitive clairvoyance on the part of the percipient. Tyrrell found that scoring was unaffected by this device. It cannot be claimed that "X-ray vision" through the wooden box was here the explanation, for the lamp was not lit at the time the choice was made.

It must be admitted that clairvoyance in the proper sense does take place. Pre-cognitive telepathy as an alternative explanation was eliminated by an experiment in which twenty-five cards (five each of five different symbols) were sealed in separate opaque envelopes. The percipient was asked to post these correctly in five separate pillar-boxes, each pillar-box bearing one of the symbols. The cards fell out of order into the bottom of each box so that the subsequent investigator never knew in what order the cards had been guessed. In such a case we *might* interpret clairvoyance as X-ray vision, even though in other cases it could not be so. The only example of a psycho-physical interaction which is in one sense familiar to us is the relationship of mind to the brain and central nervous system. This throws no light on how clairvoyance operates, for we are not clairvoyantly aware of the structure and properties of our own brain.

I think it is becoming clear that the dichotomy of the world into a mental order and a physical order existing side by side, which is the heritage of Descartes, is no longer a helpful view. It is certainly *convenient* to distinguish between mental and physical events: my pain or sensation of colour are very different in character from the electrical stimulation of my cerebral cortex which appears to cause them. We often divide things arbitrarily for convenience of study, but what concerns us now is how these two orders of events are related. If the point of view previously advanced in this book is right, even electrons are psychoid in character, and organisms of increasing complexity manifest increasingly mind-like qualities. Minds on the one hand, and primitive finite sentients on the other, are manifestations—even though widely separated in development—of one psychic order. Nature, it has been said, is a vast society of societies, in which the greater wholes are formed from the lesser, using them, and to some extent able to control them. We must try to break away from the commonplace sense-centred view of physical objects as dead material things. There are no such physical objects. Even a playing-card or a dice is an aggregate of molecules each of which is a primitive sentient composed of and controlling lesser sentients. On this view it is not inconceivable that human minds may have both cognitive and motor relations with physical entities. Every physical object has its psychical field of influence comprising the memories and primitive imagining of its sentients.

These views may at first strike the reader as strange and improbable. Perhaps he will suspend judgment until the whole variety of paranormal phenomena has been reviewed and then ask himself if any other view is adequate. Telepathy and clairvoyance are not on this view essentially different things. Both are the relationship of a human mind either with another human mind or with "mindlets". In both cases it is knowledge which is acquired, but in one case it rises into consciousness in a verbal vehicle, in the other in a visual vehicle. In so-called clair-audience an auditory vehicle is used.

Such a phenomenon as dowsing is possibly a form of clairvoyance—or perhaps we may more accurately describe it as the use of a motor-automatism to acquire knowledge by para-normal means. The so-called sub-conscious levels of the dowser's mind use a simple mechanical device to indicate to the conscious levels information they wish to have.

Some experts, however, consider the phenomenon much more complex than this.[1]

(3) *Pre-cognition*. This is one of the most startling and puzzling of all para-normal phenomena. The mind has a faculty for acquiring knowledge of future events where all processes of rational inference are ruled out. This phenomenon, like telepathy and clairvoyance, has also been established beyond any shadow of doubt not only by collected records of thoroughly authenticated cases[2] but by experimental work such as that of Professor Rhine, Dr. Soal, G. N. M. Tyrrell, and others. J. W. Dunne[3] has presented certain theoretical views about pre-cognition which are not generally acceptable, but his collection of pre-cognitive dreams is nevertheless valuable and interesting. The distinguished physiologist Professor Charles Richet, who for thirty years studied para-normal phenomena, was prepared to say: "Pre-cognition is a demonstrated verity. It is a strange, paradoxical and seemingly absurd fact, but one that we are compelled to admit. . . . The explanation will come (or will not come) later. The facts are none the less authentic and undeniable." In the experimental work with cards, or Tyrrell's work with lighted lamps, the pre-cognition only preceded the event by two or three seconds at most, but in the spontaneous type of prediction the anticipation has been of the order of days, months, or many years. It appears that we must recognise pre-cognitive clairvoyance, and pre-cognitive telepathy as both established by experimental work. The latter may be autoscopic, i.e. pre-cognition of one's own future mental states, or non-autoscopic where another person's future mental states are known. Whether there are *long-term* pre-cognitions of the clairvoyant type is, I think, not clearly established. The pre-cognised distant future is generally stated in so far as it affects some person's life.

A particularly interesting example of this is given by Dunne, who described a vivid dream in which he saw a volcanic island about to blow up. He made considerable efforts in his dream to persuade the French authorities of the immanent danger, and to arrange for transshipment of the 4,000 inhabitants. This particular number was a clear recollection of the dream. Some time later, when newspapers arrived, the *Daily Telegraph* reported a volcano disaster at Martinique with the probable loss of over 40,000 lives. A particularly significant thing was that Dunne mis-read the newspaper report as 4,000 and did not realise he had made a mis-reading of it until fifteen years later when checking through papers. The actual loss of life was subsequently stated more accurately than this first estimate. We have here an example of an auto-

---

[1] E.g. *Jour S.P.R.*, Vol. XXXVI, p. 674.
[2] E.g. H. F. Saltmarsh, *Foreknowledge*. (G. Bell & Sons, Ltd. 1938.)
    J. W. Dunne, *An Experiment with Time*. (A. and C. Black Ltd., 1927.)

scopic pre-cognition in a dream of his mental state when he first read the newspaper account.

Readers of Dr. Eugene Osty's book[1] will find numerous examples of "sensitives" or "mediums" who appear to achieve a kind of telepathic rapport with what (we can only conclude) are very deep mental levels of the sitter. They are sometimes such that many future experiences of the sitter are apparently read as in an open book. Most sensitives commonly achieve rapport with more superficial mental levels of the sitter, and as a result it is often fears, desires, hopes, and accessible memories which are withdrawn and reported. This is of course a commonplace experience of séance rooms both public and private. But what are we to say of an experience such as Mrs. Bendit describes?

"The swarthy, black-eyed woman asked me in the usual way to cross her palm with silver, then she lightly touched my finger-tips for a moment, shut her eyes and poured out a torrent of speech. Her character-reading was astonishing; and she mentioned without hesitation a number of incidents in my past life. She was particularly clever in her analysis of my psychic abilities, seeing both their weakness and their strength.

"Eventually she began to foretell the future. It sounded incredible, not to say impossible. She sketched correctly the kind of professional life I was then living and said that it would change radically. 'You will marry a man who is either a doctor, or who is in a profession associated with sharp bright instruments,' she went on, adding various details about him. 'You will work together and write books together. You will travel together and neither of you will work alone in the future.' She then foretold a number of events which would lead up to this. Then, guessing my doubts, she said, 'You don't believe me, so I am going to tell you three unimportant things which will come true within the next seven days. When they do, you'll remember what the gypsy said, and you'll see that in the next few years the big things will happen too.'

"She then told me that I should very shortly receive a gift of stones; that I would also be given a ring; and that, on some very stony ground, I should find two sprays of white heather where no other white heather grew.

"I said nothing of all this to my hostess, but that evening while I was dressing for dinner she came into my room, bringing a box of unset cairngorm stones, beautifully cut. She said, 'I got these for you for last Christmas. But you will remember that I had 'flu and was too ill to send them off. So here they are.' Three days later, a registered parcel arrived from London. It contained an old ring and a note from a friend, who said, 'I meant to leave you this ring in my will, but I don't see why you should not have it now, so I am sending it at once.' Then, on the fifth day we were out for a picnic and on the way home, as we went through a very desolate pass in the hills, my hostess said, 'There's rather a fine cairn just at the top of this hill. Let's climb up and have a look at it.' I had nearly reached the top of the rough and

[1] Eugene Osty, *Supernormal Faculties in Man*. (Methuen & Co. Ltd., 1923.)

stony track when I saw, growing in solitary beauty, two sprays of white heather. There was not another scrap in sight.

"I confess that I was impressed, when these odd events came true exactly as had been foretold. I was still more struck when the larger issues developed, especially as they represented a turning-point in my life such as I had never even contemplated."[1]

It would appear that at some deep level of the human self there is available knowledge of certain future experiences which the superficial self will have to confront. This raises all kinds of questions, but we shall delay consideration of them for the present.

There was an interesting and I think signficant observation which Dr. Osty was able to make through his good fortune in being able to study several excellent sensitives. He noted that where an event was pre-cognised several times prior to its fulfilment, the sensitive appeared to have access to more detail as the event itself came nearer in time. It is as though the view of a distant place might be obscured by intervening mist, but as we travel towards the place the mist obscures less and less.

This may be important in relation to the status of events in Time.

When we start to ponder on this enormously complex problem we always become involved in three different but not unrelated issues:

(a) The nature of Time and the status of events in Time.
(b) The problem of freedom and determinism.
(c) The nature of Causation, and in particular, what causes the pre-cognition.

These are discussed further in Chapter 11, but at this stage we shall make our first survey of them.

I am going to describe three theories or viewpoints, with their advantages and disadvantages. I shall attach labels to them arbitrarily for convenience of discussion.

(a) The "Dunne" Viewpoint. This regards time as a sort of dimension in which all events, past, present, and future, co-exist. It is the idea sometimes called an "Eternal Now". The events of a person's life, for example, might be regarded as beads which exist on the string of time.

They are, however, experienced one at a time, as though we were only able to view one bead after another through a slit which moved steadily from one end of the string—from birth to death. In spite of all efforts to avoid or disguise the fact, this viewpoint is not compatible with human freedom. We are back at the old idea of an Absolute in which all things inhere, and the time-process is not creative in any sense; it is merely a disclosure of what is eternally present. We must emphatically reject this position for reasons we have given (page 44, f.).

[1] Payne and Bendit, *This World and That*, pp. 159-60. (Faber and Faber Ltd., 1950.)

(b) *The "Common-sense" Viewpoint.* The past is fixed and unalterable, while the future is blank and uncreated. The "specious present" is our creative opportunity and as this element moves along the time-dimension into the blank future it fills itself with content and leaves this as a deposit in the past. On this view, we certainly preserve human free-will, but the cause of pre-cognition is mysterious. If there is nothing in the future to be cognised, what is pre-cognition? On this view I can see only one answer, namely, that so-called pre-cognition is a very superior kind of inference or deduction from a knowledge of causal factors as they exist in the past and present. *If* this were feasible, it would not really be a *cognition* of the future. The inference would prove to be true only if all the causal factors remained unchanged and no new ones entered before fulfilment. Acts of free-will can of course frequently enter to change the inference made.

The chief difficulties of such a view are these. It would be necessary to ascribe to a deeper level of the mind powers bordering on omniscience. Take the following case:

"Mrs. C. dreamed that she was being persistently followed by a monkey, and this terrified her, as she particularly disliked monkeys. At breakfast, as she was unable to throw off the unpleasant memories, her husband suggested that she should go out for a walk with the children. She adopted this unusual course, and to her horror—in the streets of London—was followed by a monkey."

It is a trivial illustration, but it represents the solid core of pre-cognitions where the data on which inference could be made seem quite inaccessible.

I shall not multiply examples, but they would include not only the dramatic spontaneous type, of which that quoted from Payne and Bendit's book is an example, but a large amount of experimental work where packs of cards are placed in mechanical shufflers and afterwards "cut" by a chance method. It is inconceivable that anything of the nature of *inference* based upon a clairvoyant perception of thousands or tens of thousands of small events can be the explanation of this solid core of pre-cognitions. Moreover, only causal events not involving the free-will of agents *can* be known, and interventions of this type are always likely to vitiate inference as to what will happen. Yet if the future is quite blank and unformed, is there any alternative explanation of pre-cognitions?

(c) *The Imaginist Viewpoint.* The more we reflect on these two preceding viewpoints, the more clear it becomes that neither can be valid and that the truth must lie somewhere between the extreme views of a determined future and a blank future. Assuming that there is some kind of a future in existence, which can under favourable circumstances be pre-cognised, of what nature can it be? We suggest that it must be a plan, i.e. a mentally imaged pattern in the Divine mind. It is a Divinely conscired plan by which the world-system may find its way through the Metaphysical Fall back to the goal of a higher perfection. Perhaps one may use as a parable the canvas of a slowly moving tapestry on which the design of the tapestry-to-be is faintly outlined. A great army of workers are seeking to weave it. Their freedom to weave differently from the pattern, and indeed to make mistakes, is always present. An overseer named "Divinity of Measure" secures that too many serious departures cannot take place. The imaged pattern is thus properly described as a plastic future, not as a rigidly determined one. The slowly moving tapestry is only "fixed" when it is woven by the army of workers and has moved beyond them into the past. There it is sustained conservatively by Divine Imagining in the Great Memory. Pre-cognitions are glimpses of this Divinely imaged pattern. This admittedly does not often suggest a divine origin, and raises for our minds the problem of evil. It must however be remembered that we are not dealing with a static mental conception, but one which is being constantly adjusted to meet the mistakes and foolishness of many lesser sentients whose freedom to imagine often runs amok and impairs it. Except in a certain broad sense, and in relation to "key-points" through which the weaving threads are obliged to pass, it is not in any detail determined. We can appreciate the grounds for the observation which Dr. Osty made of the increasing reliability of detail available to the sensitive as the event draws nearer to the time of actualisation.

Saltmarsh has logically pointed out that we have no justification for assuming that *all* future events in a person's life can be pre-cognised because some events have been. I have referred above to key-points through which the weaving threads are obliged to pass, and I am of the opinion that these are such events and situations which are part of the life-pattern of a person in a particular incarnation. These will be unavoidable, part of the karmic pattern printed there because of our own past and the past of others with whom we have been linked (*vide* Chapter 9, p. 212, f.). Such critical experiences are doubtless pre-cognisable, but what is not pre-determined is the reaction of our own self to those events. Perhaps very crudely we may illustrate this viewpoint by a diagram of physical events. I do not believe that what I had for breakfast this morning was pre-determined from birth, although I should be disposed to believe that my marriage to a particular person was so determined.

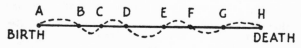

In automatic script through Miss G. Cummins, F. W. H. Myers makes a statement supporting the Imaginist viewpoint. He has referred to a certain subjective state into which it is possible to enter and says:

"So, while in this third subjective state, we turn again the pages of the Book of Life and read the future of our race. We gaze upon a drama which has not yet been enacted upon the earth, the vague echo of which is sometimes caught by prophets and soothsayers. We perceive the wanderings of those begotten by us, the fate of those who are of our blood, who bear upon their foreheads the seal of kinship with us. And, indeed, many of us sorrowfully close the Book of Life when we have thus gazed into a future that is not yet for men, sprung out of the Unknown, out of the boundless sea, which I must again remind you, is the creation of the all-pervading imagination of God."

So much for the status of the future. As for the means whereby pre-cognitions arise into awareness I think H. F. Saltmarsh's theory is essentially true. He suggested that the "specious present" which for our reflective consciring is but a fraction of a second, may be a progressively longer interval for deepening levels of our selves. Events which are all "present" to some deeper level may therefore belong to the past, present, or future of the waking self. Occasionally communication from such a deeper level to the waking self may therefore result in a pre-cognition. The deeper level to which I refer is probably found within the group-mind of the Group-soul to which the individual is related (see Chapter 13). It is the spirit which nourishes such a Group which mediates that part of the pattern of the great tapestry of the Divine Imagining which its souls are to weave finally to perfection.

I am well aware that the first reaction of most scientists and parapsychologists to the Imaginist view of pre-cognition may be one of dislike, if not disapproval. To introduce a Divinely conscired pattern to help us to understand pre-cognition is cutting the Gordian knot. The fact is that Time is a real and fundamental element in the world-structure having its source, as we have expressed already, in Divine Imagining. I have pondered on this problem of time and pre-cognition for some years, and venture to claim that it is along the Imaginist road that we shall have to travel.

Of retro-cognition we shall not say much. There are ostensibly some dramatic instances of the phenomenon,[1] such as the case of Miss Moberly and Miss Jourdain, who apparently "saw" gardens in Versailles in 1901 as they were in the mid-eighteenth century. A more recent case is that of two English ladies who on August 4th, 1951, while on holiday at Puys near Dieppe, apparently had a collective auditory hallucination

[1] Anne Moberley and Eleanor Jourdain, *An Adventure* (1911). See also "The Dieppe Raid Case", *Jour. S.P.R.*, Vol. XXXVI, p. 607 (1952).

of a raid which had taken place some nine years earlier on August 19th, 1942. There was a remarkable correspondence between the times of the various battle sounds and the actual times of various combined operations.

Miss Edith Olivier[1] has described an interesting experience near Avebury (Wilts) on a wet October evening in 1916. She apparently saw "a succession of huge grey megaliths which stood on either hand, looming like vast immovable shadows within a curtain of softly falling rain", but discovered some ten years later they had disappeared before 1800. A village fair, which from a little distance she saw in progress, she later found to have been an annual event, but to have ceased in 1850.

Experiences of this kind appear to differ in two respects from the general conditions of pre-cognitive experience. Firstly, they have not, as far as we know, been part of the past personal experience of the percipients, and secondly, they seem to be associated with localities. This latter feature in particular suggests a close connexion with a type of psychometry. The possibility of tapping the "memory of a place" seems the most obvious description of the phenomena, and suggests that we ought to consider seriously an extended view of "memory". So long as we are held in the paralysing grip of the matter-mind dichotomy of the world, we are shocked by the idea of the memory of a place or an object. With a psychoid conception of Nature our standpoint must be different. The past is, we believe, conserved by Divine Imagining (*vide* Chapter 2, p. 55).

It may be conserved in the imagining of the myriads of finite sentients which constitute a locality, or these may but serve to link the percipient's mind with the record of the past conscired by Divine Imagining. Still another possibility is that the retro-cognition may be in effect a communication of experience stored in the Group-soul. Such a hypothesis suggests (however strange it may seem) a possible explanation as to why this particular fragment out of the whole of past history is presented to a particular person. Such a one may in a former incarnation have experienced it as reality or may be in close rapport with another member of the Group-soul who did so. The reader will perhaps not dismiss this possibility pending the views expressed in later chapters.

Experimental work in retro-cognition is difficult because clairvoyance of existing records by which the retro-cognition could be verified is always a possible explanation. In any case the phenomenon probably adds nothing to the general metaphysical considerations which interest us. We shall conclude this section with the observation that

[1] Edith Olivier, *Without Knowing Mr. Walkley*, Chap. XVI. (Faber and Faber, 1939.)

non-inferential cognition of the future or past is quite outside any possibility of explanation on the basis of materialism.

(4) *Unusual Knowledge through Dreams, Trance, or Motor Automatisms*. The Mind's power of gathering knowledge other than through the senses or by rational inference has been reviewed briefly. Collectively we may speak of the mind's ψ-faculty, and in doing this we are regarding terms like telepathy, clairvoyance, and clairaudience as descriptive of the type of vehicle—verbal, visual, or auditory—which conveys the knowledge into our field of awareness. Pre-cognition and retro-cognition are also to be included under ψ-faculty, indicating as they do, that the exercise of this power may cover a wide range of time: past, present, and future. There are certain states of mind (differing from the normal waking state) in which ψ-faculty is sometimes exercised to a remarkable degree, and it is some of these which we shall now consider. The importance of these states is that they introduce us to knowledge which, while theoretically not beyond the power of ψ-faculty to account for, nevertheless obliges us to consider the hypothesis of the existence and intervention of discarnate minds as sometimes a simpler and more plausible explanation.

Let us consider dreams first. Take the following cases[1]:

Squires Case. The dreamer's friend, Davis, lost his watch. Both men were employed at that time on a farm. Squires was a sympathetic type and "could not keep his mind off the watch, and after two or three days thinking of it, went to bed one night still thinking of it." In a dream he saw the watch lying in long grass and noted its position and disposition in detail. The next day he went to the place and found it. Squires could not have seen the watch fall for he was working at the time some distance away.

Here we have no need to postulate more than the exercise of Squires' ψ-faculty (clairvoyance) stimulated by his prolonged concern.

Lamberton Case. Professor Lamberton tried to solve a problem by *algebraical* means. After a week or two he came to the conclusion he was "bogged" and dismissed it from his mind. In his bedroom there was a disused blackboard; and one morning a week later, when waking, he saw on this blackboard a diagram giving a *geometrical* solution. The diagram vanished at once, but he remembered it, and it proved correct.

Such a case is by no means characteristic of ψ-faculty. Here was an intellectual problem which baffled the resources of a trained mind. There is presented to him, not a clue towards an algebraical solution that he might follow up later, but a complete solution along another line.

[1] *Proc. S.P.R.*, Vol. XI, p. 397; *Proc. S.P.R.*, Vol. XII, p. 11; *Proc. S.P.R.*, Vol. XXXVI, p. 517.

This is the kind of dream which points to the existence of an "Intuitive Self"—a level of the hierarchy constituting the Self which lies beyond the highest reaches of the intellectual mind. It is the level from which creative inspirations and insights spring unbidden, whether the form of their expression is in colour, music, mathematics, or poetic imagery. We are approaching here perhaps to the secret of finite consciring, perhaps to the treasures of the Group-soul.

Chaffin Case. An eccentric farmer, J. L. Chaffin, made a will in 1905 leaving his farm to the third of his four sons. In 1919 he made a new will dividing the property equally between his sons, but no one except himself knew of the second will. He died in 1921, and the earlier will was proved. In 1925 the second son started to have vivid dreams of his father, in one of which the latter appeared wearing his old overcoat, and saying with a gesture, "You will find the will in my overcoat pocket." Action was taken, the overcoat was found, and in its lining was a paper referring to a particular passage in his old family bible. When this was found, the second will was discovered in the folded pages.

In this case, if an explanation is sought in terms of the exercise of ψ-faculty by the second son, we have to account for the dream-figure of the old farmer rather than the dream-image of the bible. We have also to account for a four years' delay in the exercise of his ψ-faculty and the absence of any obvious stimulus to its exercise at this stage. The more plausible explanation is, I think, the ostensible one of intervention by the surviving discarnate mind of the old farmer.

When we approach the subject of mediumistic trance we are dealing with a topic on which scores of books and papers have been written. We are faced with the task of presenting a fair assessment in a few pages, and we must ask the serious reader to study some of the many works written.[1] The ordinary person who thinks at all about states of consciousness probably recognises only those of waking, dreaming, and dreamless sleep. There are innumerable others, but all of them are perhaps most simply regarded as the withdrawal of the spearhead of consciring from exterior to more interior levels of the personality. Associated with this there is, in some cases, the flattening out of the "spearhead" from a state of focussed attention to one of diffuse inattention. Breadth is achieved at the expense of intensity. The "medium" or "sensitive" is a person who can do this and at the same time maintain a channel of communication with the outer levels through automatic or controlled writing or speaking. We must frankly admit that our ignorance of the structure of human personality is

[1] *Human Personality* (2 vols.). F. W. H. Myers. (Longmans, Green & Co. Ltd., 1903.) *This World and That.* Payne and Bendit. (Faber and Faber Ltd., 1950.) *Mind in Life and Death.* Geraldine Cummins. (Aquarian Press, 1956.)

abysmal: it will be one of the main tasks of the future to throw light on this supremely important field.

Sensitives differ enormously both in the nature and quality of the knowledge they disclose and the conditions under which they function. At the one extreme we have the rare type of sensitive who is apparently in a normal waking state of consciousness and who is in full control of all phenomena which can be switched on or off at will. The simplest assumption is that here ψ-faculty is to a remarkable degree under personal control. We have other sensitives whose state is somewhat detached or withdrawn, through many degrees of auto-hypnosis to the other extreme of the "dead-trance" medium who is in a deep sleep. In all these cases we find discarnate personalities purporting to communicate through the sensitive. In the fully conscious type of sensitive this is ostensibly by means of telepathic or clair-audient rapport, in the dead-trance type of medium the claim is often made that the brain and larynx of the medium are being directly manipulated and used. As to the nature of these communicating personalities there are, broadly speaking, three hypotheses about them: (*a*) that they are the veritable personalities which they claim to be, viz. discarnate human beings; (*b*) that they are temporarily dissociated fragments of the medium's own personality; (*c*) that they are dramatic impersonations by some level of the medium's own mind, as an actor might play successively many parts. In psychical research where we have to deal with phenomena of great complexity it is often short-sighted to contend that one hypothesis is right and others are wrong. They may all in different degrees contribute to the truth. Let us look very briefly at these hypotheses.

It is well-known that in certain stages of trance the medium can exercise ψ-faculty to a remarkable degree. Telepathic rapport with the minds of the sitters, and the exercise of clairvoyance by the medium where appropriate, can provide sensational evidence which the uncritical sitter may unwarrantably assume is coming from a discarnate friend. But when every allowance has been made for this, there is, in the case of some mediums, a wealth of evidence which it appears more plausible to attribute to discarnate minds.

A correspondent[1] who has had many years of experience with trance mediums has written to me as follows:

"Personality is a very real thing. . . . The case under review is not merely that of a psychic sensitive going into an abnormal condition and 'fishing up', so to speak, certain hitherto unknown pieces of information. Those who speak to us through the mouth of the medium or by other and even more striking means have all the qualities of complete, well-rounded unmistakable personalities. Each one is as distinct as those of our friends in normal life.

[1] I am indebted to Mr. H. Norman Hunt for these views.

They have mannerisms, accents, dialects, prejudices and favourite topics; some are mentally acute, some argumentative, some filled with gentle affection and a naïve simplicity. They vary as infinitely as do human beings on earth.

"I have held long conversations with, I suppose, hundreds of such persons of every type. I have been taught by many, laughed with some, argued with others, precisely as one does in ordinary life."

It is difficult to deny the strength of this kind of evidence, where mannerisms and temperament, accent and outlook, and innumerable subtle trains of personality are sustained without difficulty. In spite of all the nonsense found in some of Mrs. Piper's trance utterances, it was precisely this kind of subtle evidence of the personality of his deceased friend George Pelham, who communicated through Mrs. Piper's entranced organism over a period of many years, which convinced the sceptical Dr. Richard Hodgson of his friend's survival.

In Dr. Horace Westwood's remarkable book[1] he describes his intellectual pilgrimage from considerable scepticism about psychical phenomena to conviction both of the reality of these, and also of the reality of communication with discarnate personalities. The sensitive was a little girl called Anna, eleven years of age, and a member of his family circle. Dr. Westwood writes:

"The fact must be stressed that at all times she was in full possession of all her normal faculties. Never for one moment was there even the suggestion of a lapse of consciousness. While the alleged controls never 'broke through' or manifested in my absence, or without my expressed wish, when they did come through, Anna was always master of the situation. In almost every experiment, for example, she would at times throw off the control in order to make some personal comment or observation, thus showing that her own mind was watchful and fully alert. When she allowed the experiment to proceed without interruption, she never failed afterwards to indicate her complete awareness of all that had taken place."

Out of scores of remarkable phenomena carefully checked and described by Dr. Westwood, I quote two examples:

"We blindfolded Anna and sat her at the piano. Anna herself, of course, had taken a few music lessons, but was by no means an accomplished musician. However, what purported to be Kate began to play through her, and as long as I live I shall never forget that night. She began with a slow melody, the like of which I had never heard before, for it was solemn in its majesty and almost unearthly in its beauty. As I watched the child play, the bodily action and the finger technique were entirely different from Anna's own. Moreover, I had this strange reaction—a feeling that the instrument was incapable of

[1] Horace Westwood, D.D., *There is a Psychic World*. (Crown Publishers, N.Y 1949.)

expressing what the player wished to play. . . . The whole performance was on an elevated plane, indicating a mental range and musical understanding far beyond the child's normal power."

"One day . . . there came another entity, who refused to give any information about himself and who persisted in remaining nameless beyond the designation of 'X'. No sooner had he begun to write through Anna, than I realised we were in the presence of a decidedly superior intelligence. . . . With Anna at the typewriter (blindfolded) either in response to questions I would give orally, or else write, we discussed many things of a philosophical nature.

"Certainly the things we discussed were not within the range of a child's usual intellectual interest. Moreover, the answers given indicated a reflective capacity and maturity normally impossible to an eleven-year-old. Often the replies were totally foreign to those I would have given. Since this record is purely a narrative of events I shall not burden it with these philosophical reflections. However we discussed such problems as the existence of God, the nature of the universe, the character of being, the processes of the unfolding of the soul, the destiny beyond death, and so forth."

I cannot pretend to have any doubt about the survival by human beings of the change which we call death, nor have I any doubt that through some sensitives we have many genuine examples of communication between the incarnate and the discarnate. On the other hand, sensitives (such as Mrs. Piper) at certain times appear to have been the vehicle of veridical communications, and at other times were almost certainly producing dramatisations of subliminal material. There are other mediums in which *all* that purports to be "communication" may well have its origin in the strange underworld of the medium's own mind. Much automatic writing is doubtless of this type, and would be of considerable interest to psychiatrists. On the other hand, I have personally received automatic scripts from a sensitive which have given to me clear evidence that I have been in communication with a particular friend of mine "on the other side".

(5) *Apparitions* (*Subjective*). There are many excellent collections of cases of apparitions, for this phenomenon has been the subject of study by the Society for Psychical Research since its foundation over seventy years ago. The most important recent contribution, especially on the theoretical side, is that of G. N. M. Tyrrell.[1] In 1890 a census question was circulated widely to ascertain how widespread were experiences of this kind. "Have you ever, when believing yourself to be completely awake, had a vivid impression of seeing or being touched by a living being or inanimate object, or of hearing a voice; which impression, so far as you could discover, was not due to any external physical cause?" Of the 17,000 replies, almost 10 per cent. answered in the affirmative.

[1] G. N. M. Tyrrell, *Apparitions*. (Gerald Duckworth & Co. Ltd., 1953.)

Another census on a smaller scale in 1948 gave affirmative replies from about 14 per cent. of people. Analysis of the affirmative replies showed in the first census that 32 per cent. were phantasms of living persons, 14 per cent. of dead persons, and 33 per cent. of unidentified persons. The corresponding proportions in the later census were 40 per cent., 9 per cent., and 27 per cent. It is interesting to observe that, contrary to popular belief, phantasms of the living are much more frequent than those of the dead. Analysis of the senses affected showed: visual, 54·8 per cent.; visual combined with auditory or tactile, 11·6 per cent.; auditory, 25·6 per cent.; tactile, 7·1 per cent.; auditory and tactile, 0·9 per cent.

It is not, I think, generally known that apparitions have been created deliberately and experimentally. The well-attested cases of this are not numerous, but there are a number of records which show that concentrated efforts of the will-to-appear to another person have led to the latter perceiving an apparition of the agent. In such cases the group of actions carried out by the phantasm before its disappearance are not always those envisaged by the agent, and there seems no reason to doubt that the phantasm is a joint construction of certain levels of the subliminal mind of the agent co-operating with similar levels of the mind of the percipient. We know very little about the various levels of Mind. We are all familiar with the fact that in dreaming, one level throws up the motif or theme, another level dramatises it and still another level is an interested spectator. Such levels (or others) may co-operate to create phantasms. The study of experimentally produced apparitions might help considerably towards an understanding of the Mind and its powers.

Before theorising further, we must refer to the great majority of apparitions which are, of course, spontaneous. Most of them appear to be associated with some crisis in the life of the agent, such as the approach of death, an incident of grave danger, an accident, a shock or a serious illness. In addition to these there are the genuine post-mortem apparitions, where ostensibly a discarnate personality is the agent and in co-operation with mid-mind levels of the percipient creates a phantasm of himself. Here the motive is apparently to demonstrate the agent's survival of death, to convey some information of an important kind, or to carry out a compact made between the two parties when both were incarnate. There is a fourth class of apparition—the traditional ghost or haunting—which seems to differ from the others in being associated with a particular place or locality.

The importance of the study of apparitions from our metaphysical standpoint is for the light they may throw on the structure of the human mind. Questions immediately arise. Is there any difference in our perceiving a physical object such as a rock or tree or table, and our perceiving an apparition? What is its status: in particular, is it subjective or objective? Is it in any sense a vehicle of self-consciousness, i.e. is a human mind or soul "embodied" in the vehicle?

Broadly speaking, the theory most commonly held about apparitions is a telepathic one. Apparitions result from a transaction between certain levels of two (or more) minds in which one mind (the agent's) provides the initiative or dynamic, while the percipient's subliminal mind elaborates it and throws it up on to the screen of awareness in a visual dramatic form. If we ask in what way this process is different from clairvoyance initiated by a telepathic impulse, I think it is best to confess that we have not enough knowledge of the human mind to differentiate clearly between them. In the result, an apparition gives the impression that it is an intrusion into the physical world, and clairvoyant perception normally gives the impression that it is knowledge of the physical world. This is not really saying much unless we can be clear about the status of the physical world and the nature of perception—matter on which philosophers differ.

Tyrrell's viewpoint is that ostensibly there are two ways in which the whole apparatus of sense-perception can be put into operation. The first and commonplace way is by light impinging on the retinae, by sound-waves impinging on the eardrums, and so forth. The second way he considers to be "central" rather than "peripheral", viz. by a suitable mental stimulus, such as may arise from the co-operation of the mid-mind levels of the agent and percipient. Tyrrell then goes further and makes the rather startling suggestion that perhaps after all there is only *one* way in which the apparatus of perception is operated—and this is the central or mentally caused one. The function of the brain, stimulated by light, sounds, and pressures from without, would merely be to act as a stimulus and as a directive agent to the mind. The mid-mind levels would then create the sense-data, modelling them faithfully on the outer world. Tyrrell suggests that the efficiency with which this is done is "not due to causal efficacy but to biological necessity". In other words, upon the reliability of perception is based an animal's chance of survival. He suggests that when central excitation creates perception in the absence of directive brain signals there results a hallucination or apparition—usually a somewhat amateurish performance compared with ordinary perception.

We shall not discuss these views for the present. I think it would be correct to say that Tyrrell's answers to the questions we raised earlier would be that the act of perception is similar for physical objects and for apparitions, that an apparition is subjective, and that it is in no sense a vehicle of an independent centre of consciousness. My own view is that while there may well be apparitions of this type, there are also apparitions which do not differ in their existential status from physical objects, i.e. they could be photographed, recorded on a tape-recorder, and could depress a spring balance. In other words, there are also objective apparitions, and it is possible that there may well be a continuously graded series of apparitions of which one cannot say that they are wholly objective or wholly subjective. The terms objective and subjective, while convenient for certain purposes, are, as I have suggested elsewhere,[1] very arbitrary. Dream imagery which I regard as objective while dreaming is interpreted as subjective when I awake. These terms are therefore relative to the level of personality on which the spearhead of consciring temporarily rests. I shall say more of this later.

PARA-NORMAL ACTION

We turn now from the sensory or receptive aspects of mind, in which we are concerned with knowledge of the physical world or knowledge of the content of other minds, to consider unusual modes of action of mind in the world.

(1) *Psycho-kinesis (Rhine type)*. If I want to lift a weight, construct a table, paint a picture, or move from one place to another, it is commonly believed that I have only one way of doing so. This is to use the musculature of my body. But is this the only way? The mind has been shown to have extra-sensory ways of gathering knowledge; may it not also have extra-muscular means of performing actions?

In March 1943 Professor J. B. Rhine and his colleagues at Duke University, North Carolina, published the results of approximately ten years' work on psycho-kinesis (P.K.). The basic procedure was to attempt to influence the fall of a die by the mental attitude adopted. Given a perfectly unbiassed die, the chance is one in six that any chosen face will come uppermost. After making a very large number of throws, the application of statistics to any deviation from the expected chance score will show the odds against this deviation being due to chance. To eliminate any possible effect of slight bias in the die, if a certain number of throws have been made mentally favouring 6, then an equal number of throws should be made mentally favouring 1. Experiments of this type, duly witnessed, and varying all the conditions, have been made by the tens of thousands. Dice have been thrown singly and in quantity. They have been rolled down corrugated surfaces and discharged from rotating cages. They have been made of different sizes, materials, and shapes. In a critical survey of the American P.K. research, D. J. West[2]

---

[1] *The Imprisoned Splendour*, p. 239. (Hodder and Stoughton Ltd., 1953.)
[2] *Proc. S.P.R.*, Vol. XLVII, p. 281.

has said, "The case for P.K. does not seem to be challengeable; it is probably even more clear-cut and conclusive than the case for E.S.P. (extra-sensory perception) itself."

Some features of interest and significance disclosed by this research are as follows: The throwing of large numbers of dice simultaneously did not appear to reduce the above-chance scoring: if one were dealing with a physical force one would have anticipated a smaller effect when a larger mass had to be moved. The important factors were mental. Novelty and interest were stimulants, and when these diminished—as in prolonged experiments—marked decline effects set in precisely as in E.S.P. experiments. The action of drugs on the exercise of both P.K. and E.S.P. appears to be similar. Tests up to distances of twenty-five feet have shown no significant effect of distance between the experimenter and the dice. There is indeed much to suggest that these two aspects of the mind's function are closely related. They are probably twin aspects of the mind's ψ-faculty, and when the mind can be disengaged from the closeness of its linkage with the material brain, its extended knowledge and its extended powers may become available together. The notation[1] $\psi\gamma$ (for E.S.P.) and $\psi\kappa$ (for P.K.) are sometimes used as a reminder of this relationship. Rhine has suggested that the exercise of P.K. necessarily implies the exercise of E.S.P. also, for the dice movements are not followed by ordinary visual means. It may well be so, but I do not feel convinced by this argument, for it is to me inconceivable that the mind's activity is octopus-like, waiting to give a little favourable push to a die when it is balanced momentarily in unstable equilibrium. The action of a superposed magnetic field on individual magnets would be a better simile. But if we hope to gain understanding of some of these extraordinary phenomena it is not towards mechanism that we can look with any optimism.

The biological field offers a wide range of material for the study of psycho-kinesis. N. Richmond has recently reported interesting positive results of the P.K. effect on paramecia. This is a small single-celled organism found in fresh-water pools which propels itself by cilia that cover its body surface. His results incidentally provided further evidence that E.S.P. and P.K. were available together.

Valuable as they are in providing indubitable evidence of psycho-kinesis, the dice-experiments (like the card-experiments) are dealing only with the fringe of ψ-faculty. We now turn to the more sensational phenomena.

(2) *Movements of Heavy Objects*. In the presence of certain rare persons, usually called "physical mediums", and under circumstances where fraud has been completely ruled out, there sometimes take

[1] These Greek symbols may be pronounced Psi-gamma and Psi-kappa respectively.

place strange and impressive psycho-kinetic phenomena. The records of mediums such as Eusapia Palladino,[1] Rudi Schneider, Anna Rasmussen, D. D. Home, and others contain accounts of "violent movements of a pair of curtains which billowed and waved over the sitters' heads from time to time", the levitation of objects, the ringing of bells floating in mid-air and so forth. F. W. H. Myers, who edited and published reports[2] on the phenomena which occurred in the presence of W. Stainton Moses—of whose complete integrity there was no question—considered that there was no half-way house of reserved judgment possible. Either these things happened as recorded or several competent and critically minded witnesses were consistently deluded in the evidence of their senses over a period of years.

Sir William Crookes, O.M., P.R.S.,[3] a scientist of unquestionable integrity and distinction, witnessed many such phenomena in the presence of D. D. Home. In the presence of other witnesses and with complete control of the experiment, a weighing-machine carrying an 8-lb. weight on three successive trials increased its reading to 23 lb., 43 lb., and 27 lb. respectively. Crookes also built a simple recording apparatus so that variations in the force, which appeared to emanate from the hands of Home, could be recorded. In his own house, where trickery or fraud of any sort could be completely ruled out, Crookes witnessed such phenomena as an accordion playing in his own hand while he held it with the keys downwards, or playing while floating around the room. He mentions also five occasions on which he had seen a heavy dining-room table rise between a few inches and $1\frac{1}{2}$ feet from the floor under circumstances where trickery was impossible.

Dr. H. Westwood,[4] who at the time was a complete sceptic about such phenomena, describes how (under instructions) he, his wife, and a young woman "K" each placed the fingers of one hand lightly on a board.

"At once, as though charged with a powerful electric force, the board (a heavy piece of pine planking eighteen inches by twenty-four) began to race over the surface of the table with such rapidity that we could hardly keep our hands upon it. This proceeded for fully three minutes. The board then came to the edge of the table, and tipping itself vertically, with our hands lightly touching the surface (though not supporting it in any way), floated gently downwards to within about an inch from the floor. Reversing the process, it then floated upwards, till it came to the end of the table, and laying itself flat on the surface began to race over the top of the table as before."

Dr. Westwood describes his complete amazement, and also the chagrin

[1] *Jour. S.P.R.*, Vol. XXXVII, p. 387-9.   [2] *Proc. S.P.R.*, Vols. IX and XI.
[3] W. Crookes, *Researches in the Phenomena of Spiritualism.* (Psychic Book Club.)
[4] Horace Westwood, D.D., *There is a Psychic World.* (Crown Publishers, N.Y.)

which he felt at the fact that against his will he was compelled to admit the existence of a psychic force acting intelligently on the physical plane.

It is superfluous to multiply examples of this sort. They are naturally bewildering to the reader, although of course they are inherently no stranger than extra-sensory phenomena. So far as the physical world is concerned, we tend to think we know what can happen and what cannot happen in it. We have strong preconceptions based upon our everyday experience, and it is against the weight of these that psychical research has to contend. When we have satisfied ourselves that a sufficient number of responsible persons, in conditions where they were quite satisfied fraud was impossible, have confirmed for themselves that these things take place, it is our duty to overcome our preconceptions and seek a wider standpoint in which such phenomena can find an intelligible place.

(3) *Levitation*. This is probably to be regarded as a special form of the preceding phenomena where a person (the medium) is himself the object moved. Crookes[1] mentions that there were at least a hundred reports of the levitation of D. D. Home and that he had witnessed three of them. "On three separate occasions I have seen him raised completely from the floor of the room. Once sitting in an easy chair, once kneeling on his chair, and once standing up. On each occasion I had full opportunity of watching the occurrence as it was taking place."

An interesting case of levitation has been described by E. A. Smythies,[2] late Forest Adviser to the Government of Nepal. This occurred to his young orderly, aged about eighteen, who had failed to do the necessary sacrifice to the "Bhagwan" or spirit at his home village. The Nepali view is that such a lapse would be punished by the "Bhagwan", who possesses the delinquent and may cause him to shout, dance, and generally behave wildly. Mr. Smythies described the episode:

"His attitude was approximately as shown . . . cross-legged with his hands clasped between his legs. His head and body were shaking and quivering, his face appeared wet with sweat, and he was making the most extraordinary noises. He seemed to me obviously unconscious of what he was doing or that a circle of rather frightened servants—and myself—were looking at him through the open door at about eight or ten feet distance. This went on for about ten minutes or a quarter of an hour, when suddenly (with his legs crossed and his hands clasped) he rose about two feet in the air, and after about a second bumped down hard on the floor. This happened again twice, exactly the same except that his hands and his legs became separated."

Mr. Smythies was quite convinced there was no fake, that the episode was unpremeditated and that the young man was an unwilling victim.

---

[1] *Loc. cit.*

[2] *Jour. S.P.R.*, Vol. XXXVI, p. 415 (1951).

He was satisfied also that any question of *jumping* from this posture was quite ruled out.

There are a number of reports of saints and yogis having been observed by their followers as levitated during deep meditation, but we need not attempt to pass any judgment on these. The phenomenon, if genuine, is presumably a special type of psycho-kinesis.

(4) *Poltergeist Effects.* These are remarkably well attested, and there can, I think, be no doubt of their existence. I take them to be psycho-kinetic effects of a spontaneous and generally uncontrolled type. They all follow the same general pattern. There are acoustical effects such as unexplained noises in empty rooms, sound of hammer blows or taps on walls, ceilings and bedposts, sounds of breaking glass and of many other varieties, where there is no apparent physical cause. In addition, there may be sensational kinetic effects where objects fly about or move senselessly round a room. Household effects may be broken and beds overturned. Rather less frequently there are pronounced thermal effects. These involve the expenditure of a good deal of physical energy. Where does it come from? Is the law of Conservation of Energy valid in this field or not?

For the sake of brevity I shall not burden this chapter with unnecessary examples of poltergeist activity, but shall assume that the reader will examine some of the accounts. We shall consider below what seem to be significant observations. We shall then frame some hypothesis to try to account for these facts, and finally, most important of all, we shall have to ask how these things contribute to an understanding of the kind of world we live in, and the sorts of beings we are.

One feature which is fairly common in poltergeist phenomena is that a young person seems to be causally associated with them. In the great majority of these cases it is a girl. It would seem that, given a certain type of psycho-physical structure characteristic of physical mediumship, there is a close link between the physiological activity of sex and the strange uncontrolled release of energy which we call poltergeist.

Having said this, it must be admitted that there have been notable cases where a young person was certainly not involved. One of the most instructive cases is that of the famous Curé d'Ars[1] (1786-1859). He produced and maintained these phenomena for over thirty years. They were associated with marked extra-sensory powers, and he once remarked to a friend about raising money for charitable purposes, "One can get anything one wants if one fasts and watches enough." The Curé d'Ars was described by Gerald Heard as an "innocent powerful and unintellectual saint". He was a man of many ascetic practices. On the one hand, he treated his physical body ruthlessly with scourging and

[1] See Gerald Heard, *Preface to Prayer*, pp. 68-76. (Cassell & Co. Ltd., 1945.)

fasting and he allowed himself very little sleep. On the other hand, his emotional life was focussed on intense supplicatory prayer for his sinful "flock". He certainly appeared to be generating an enormous amount of energy on some level of his psyche, and this found a safety outlet in the form of kinetic energy. We have here a clear indication that our physical bodies are far from defining the limits of our activity in the world: they appear rather to be but physical foci which normally restrict and canalise our range of influence.

Another significant feature of poltergeist phenomena is that there seems to be some primitive kind of mind expressing itself through them. The phenomena are not accounted for, by any means, merely as an explosive and sporadic discharge of energy. In the Derrygonnelly case[1] Sir William Barrett recorded that the "poltergeist" would at his request respond by the correct number of raps to a number of which he thought. He says that four times with his hands buried in his overcoat pocket he asked for the number of fingers which he had extended, and this was correctly indicated by the raps. Apparently there was a telepathic rapport between the entity and himself. In this particular instance the phenomena appeared to be associated with the person of Maggie, the twenty-year-old daughter of the family. It is also noteworthy that the phenomena subsided and never returned during a short service of prayer which was conducted on his second visit.

HYPOTHESIS AND SPECULATION

It must be admitted that we have here as surprising and complex a group of phenomena as we are likely to meet. It seems a far cry from the mental field or attitude which orientates a die to that which lifts heavy dining-room tables, or in irresponsible fashion plagues a farmer's family for weeks with sounds, which at times were "like those made by a heavy carpenter's hammer driving nails into flooring". There is a value, however, in restrained speculation which may suggest new lines of observation and experiment. It will nevertheless be understood that we are groping in a field where we *know* very little, and therefore our hypothesis can only be held tentatively.

We begin from the assumption of the psychoid nature of the world. This psychical order on its lower level becomes the physical world which we perceive through our senses, and at its upper level becomes, or merges into the world of mind. I think it is convenient to postulate a psychic aether or aetheric world which acts as a bridge between physical and mental phenomena. In thus postulating three significant levels— physical, aetheric, and mental—it is understood to be only a conceptual

---

[1] *Proc. S.P.R.*, Vol. XXV, p. 390 (1911).

aid to thinking, and that the reality is rather one world of which there is a graded series of aspects and qualities. The hypothesis of a psychic aether allows us to think of a medium which is linked with "matter" on the one hand: indeed, it may even be bearer of the secondary qualities of Locke. It is causally prior to matter, and when organised by mind into form, it can be imagined as being the three-dimensional "blueprint" to which "matter" in its primary aspects of resistance-extension must conform. The physical world is then a duplicate of certain aspects of the aetheric world, although the latter may contain many elements which have no physical representatives. On the other hand, the psychic aether is linked with mind. It is the carrier of thought-forms or images charged with a type of energy which can be most simply described as emotion. Such images have a certain inherent quality which is as characteristic of the mind that gave them birth as a finger-print is of its creator. Professor H. H. Price[1] uses the term "telepathic affinity" to describe this quality, in virtue of which a particular image can be apprehended by some minds (to which it is attracted) and not by others. In terms of this hypothesis clairvoyance might perhaps be regarded as perception of the modified *form* of the associated psychic aether, and object-reading or psychometry (of which we shall write later) might be regarded as perception of the modified mento-emotional characteristics of the aether. The former faculty, so to speak, operates near the physical end of the aetheric bridge and the latter faculty near the mental end.

From such a viewpoint we should expect man himself to have an aetheric body or vehicle, for the organised psychic aether would be the mould or prototype of his physical body. There has long been a tradition or belief in such an aetheric body which some sensitives claim to "see" and have described in detail.[2] One of Dr. Osty's sensitives, M. de Fleurière,[3] has described some of his sensations as follows:

"When I am in proximity to an unknown person, and especially when a light touch places us in contact, I feel as though I were permeated by an indefinable fluid that radiates from his whole person. . . . Just as one cannot find two faces absolutely alike, I think that I have never found two fluids that have given me exactly the same impression; there are those that seem to me gentle, agreeable, sympathetic, and even pleasant like spring breezes, light and transparent like the blue sky; they seem endowed with calming and beneficent power. On the other hand, there are some that are keen, sharp, violent, and repellent, pricking like needle points, hard and piercing like winter winds; these carry what feel like an antipathetic and discomforting principle."

[1] *Proc. S.P.R.*, Vol. XLV, pp. 307-43 (1939).
[2] Payne and Bendit, *The Psychic Sense*. (Faber and Faber Ltd., 1943.)
[3] Eugene Osty, *Supernormal Faculties in Man*, p. 170. (Methuen & Co. Ltd., 1923.)

Sensitives have also described what they believe to be types of energy circulation in the aetheric body. These features have not yet received the attention of Western physiologists, but there is a strong *prima facie* case for investigation in the light of psychical research. Applying this hypothesis to psycho-kinesis and poltergeist phenomena, I shall make the assumption that each level—mental, aetheric, and physical—has its own type of energy. (Metaphysically, as I have said previously, there is only one world, and the only energy is that of consciring.) There is normally no pronounced transfer or transformation of energy from one level to another, or we should never have had a principle of conservation of energy in physics. I take it that no energy problem arises in the dice experiments. The effect is a very small one, only apparent statistically, and it is perhaps to be regarded as a slight mental control of the psychic aether associated with the dice. (It would be of interest to know whether dice previously handled by the experimenter or carried about on his person could be controlled more effectively.)

When we consider the controlled movement of heavy objects, such as the lifting of a dining-room table, we may have the actual transformation of energy of the mental or aetheric types into energy of the physical type, effected, I would suggest, through the aetheric body of the medium. It is interesting also to note that cold breezes have sometimes been reported in association with these phenomena, and this suggests that the mind has taken energy, in the form of heat from the air, and reversing the normal entropy change has transformed it into kinetic energy.

Turning to the poltergeist type of energy output, we have a complex group of facts to account for. The case of the Curé d'Ars is instructive. The intensely emotional state associated with his supplicatory prayer was, so to speak, affecting his aetheric body from the one side and his rigorous ascetic practices of fasting, scourging, and denial of sleep were battering it from the other. He appeared to be taking in from the aetheric continuum (or generating on this level) energy in excess of that which he could use, and its conversion into kinetic energy, in which objects were moved about, seems to have been a safety valve.

In the cases where a young person is involved, it is notable that the phenomena are usually temporary, and we may presume that they are associated with some instability or change occurring in the aetheric body concurrently with the physical change of puberty and adolescence. It is this instability which presumably permits poltergeist phenomena to take place—an instability which was induced and maintained in the case of the Curé's ascetic practices.

The concept of a psychic aether is helpful in reference to hauntings, or the strange psychical atmospheres of certain places, in which in extreme cases a ghost or apparition appears at intervals in a particular locality. I think it is plausible that the psychic aether in some places has been saturated by some strong emotional imagery, and there is in effect a kind of reservoir of energy at the place which cannot be dissipated except when it is visited by a person of the right telepathic affinity. One person in such a place may feel a vague unrest or aversion to it, another of the right quality may see a full-blown apparition to which he has probably contributed something, just as the reservoir has contributed something. It is most interesting to note that in one of the best-attested cases of haunting by a ghost, Miss Morton[1] described how, when she became sufficiently familiar with the phenomenon to observe it with detachment, she was conscious of a loss of energy to the apparition. On the other hand, the emotional energy reservoir gradually became expended and the phenomena became slowly weaker, ultimately fading out. The hypothetical energy reservoir really plays the same part in relation to the mid-mind levels of the percipient as the agent plays in the normal type of apparition which is not linked with a locality. Presumably if a person with the right telepathic affinity and a suitably unstable aetheric body came into the locality, the aetheric reservoir might be dissipated by poltergeist effects instead of visual or auditory ones.

The observation of the Curé d'Ars that extra-sensory perception accompanied his poltergeist effects, and the observation of Sir William Barrett that there appeared to be some telepathic rapport or thought-reading between the source of the poltergeist activity and himself, is not surprising. We have already remarked on the close association of para-normal cognition and psycho-kinesis which are probably twin aspects of ψ. In what we call the normal state of mind, practically all ψ-faculty of the receptive type is canalised through the senses: there is only a slight residuum capable of statistical demonstration. Likewise all ψ-faculty of the motor type is canalised through the motor-brain and musculature. This "canalising", as we have described it, is effected through the aetheric body, and where the latter is temporarily changed or disturbed we might expect para-normal phenomena of both types to arise.

As to the nature of the so-called "poltergeist", I do not think we have any good evidence to suggest that it is an entity distinct from the mind of the key-person. (I except the minority of cases where a reservoir of emotional energy is associated with a particular place.) It may well be no more than a type of schizophrenic manifestation, where a split-off group of ideas is functioning in a state of tension apart from the overall control of the mind. This indeed is suggested by the extraordinary case related by Dr. John Layard,[2] where a schizophrenic individual unravelled her source of conflict in a real but also a symbolic journey

[1] *Proc. S.P.R.*, Vol. VIII, pp. 311-32.
[2] *Proc. S.P.R.*, Vol. XLVII, p. 237 (1944).

round the streets of a city, and where the release of tension and re-knitting of the mind was apparently associated with a dramatic polter-geist manifestation.

We cannot close our minds to the possibility that there may be discarnate entities of a low grade who find it possible to create poltergeist effects. The Nepalis obviously entertained some such view of the levitation phenomenon described by Mr. Smythies. We are dealing with matters in which our ignorance far outweighs our knowledge, and it is premature to say what is not true.

VARIOUS TYPES OF PSYCHO-PHYSICAL INTERACTION

We shall now consider briefly some phenomena which are not purely cognitive or motor.

(1) *Object-reading or Psychometry.* Some sensitives have the faculty, after touching the object or establishing some kind of mental relationship with it, of making many accurate statements about the person or persons who have previously been in contact with the object. Although it has not been the subject of experimental work to anything like the extent of normal ψ-faculty, there is enough evidence in my opinion to establish it as probable. Expressed in terms of the psychic aether hypothesis, we can visualise the process as follows. The psychic aether of an object (we may call it, for brevity, the aetheric duplicate) is impressed with a unique mento-emotional quality when it is touched by a person. It holds thenceforward a unique characteristic of this person (such as M. de Fleurière described on p. 109). A sensitive can then subconsciously identify the mind of this person, establish some measure of telepathic rapport with him—and the rest is thought-reading. Once this has been done, the object can be destroyed as being no longer essential.

A number of observations have been made as follows. (*a*) Different objects belonging to the same person usually result in the same degree of rapport as measured by the success obtained. Just as we find in telepathic experiments that a sensitive can establish different degrees of rapport with different individuals, so we find the same in object-reading. (*b*) If several persons have touched an object, the identifying mento-emotional qualities remain separate and recognisable unless there are too many of them. In the latter case the effect can be compared with the superposition of a number of fingerprints—there is none outstanding. (*c*) The nature of the object itself is not significant. (*d*) The life of the subject, as it is, can be cognised, irrespective of the time-interval since the object was touched by its owner.

One of the significant observations made by Dr. Hettinger[1] was that

[1] J. Hettinger, *The Ultra-Perceptive Faculty.* (Rider & Co. Ltd., 1940.)

to establish rapport it was not necessary for the sensitive to *touch* the article: it was sufficient for him or her to orientate the mind in a certain way towards it. This is an interesting but not a surprising result, for we should expect the mind to be able to relate itself perceptively to the psychic aether of an object just as it relates itself to its own aetheric body. It would be an interesting piece of research to see if the mind by suitable concentration on an object could modify the aetheric duplicate in the same way as by physical touch. In the light of what has been said about hauntings and the "atmosphere" of places, this would seem to be very probable. We suggest that the phenomenon of object-reading— imperfect though our knowledge of it is—throws some light on beliefs hitherto viewed as superstition. It may be that images and sacred relics, places of worship or of pilgrimage, and places of sacrifice have been saturated by the emotions and mental attitudes of generations of people and thus are the foci of psychic fields. Any sensitive person coming into the field may achieve rapport and make a mental response. Likewise it may be true that certain jewels and objects are ill-omened for similar reasons, viz. that they have had associated with them aetheric fields of a particularly undesirable kind.

There is a well-known case of instantaneous healing according to St. Mark (chap. v, 25-34) where a person, by contact with the hem of a garment, achieved rapport with the powerful mind of its possessor and was healed.

(2) *Hauntings*. This subject has been already referred to and it is not necessary to say more. Here the object is a locality, and it has been suggested that an aetheric reservoir of strong emotional imagery has been created there. Its gradual discharge depends on persons of the right telepathic affinity coming into the locality, and they "see" or "hear" the ghost-phenomenon. It is of course conceivable that the reservoir is constantly replenished by the constantly renewed attention of the mind which first created it.

(3) *Creative: Destructive Phenomena*. I group under this heading some physical phenomena to which our immediate reaction is one of incredulity. We think we know how physical objects behave: that objects to which our senses respond in the normal way cannot appear in, or disappear from, locked rooms—fraud and illusion being eliminated. Our prepossessions are strongly against these things. We can only repeat that there is but one scientific attitude—to ascertain the facts by rigorous experiment and to adopt an outlook consistent with these facts. Good physical mediums in whose presence these phenomena take place are apparently rare, and few of us are likely to have the opportunity of first-hand investigation. But solar eclipses are comparatively rare, and few of us are likely to have the opportunity of verifying the effect

Einstein predicted of the deflection of light in a strong gravitational field. We do not hesitate to trust the observations and calculations of a handful of competent observers of this effect, and what is more, we incorporate the significant consequences in our physical outlook. Should we be less just to men like Dr. Schrenk-Notzing, Dr. Osty, Dr. Geley, Sir William Crookes, Professors Flammarion, Richet, and Driesch? These have all expressed their conviction of the validity of materialisation phenomena, and they were men not easily convinced. I shall give one example only, for the sake of brevity.[1] In deep trance there appears to emanate from the body of a physical medium a substance (of unknown structure) usually called ectoplasm. It is connected with the medium, and appears to be condensed and moulded into moving, living forms. Such was the case apparently with Franck Kluski, a non-professional Polish medium of good education, whom Richet and Geley investigated together. The idea was that even the visual sense of critical observers may sometimes be misled, but that irrefutable proof would be available if the "ectoplasmic limbs" dipped themselves into a bath of molten paraffin wax, created a wax glove and then de-materia-ised leaving the glove behind. This is an abbreviation of Richet's account:

"Geley and I took the precaution of introducing, unknown to any other person, a small quantity of cholesterol into the bath of melted paraffin wax placed before the medium during the séance. This substance is soluble in paraffin wax without discolouring it, but on adding sulphuric acid it takes a deep violet-red tint: so that we could be absolutely certain that any moulds obtained should be obtained from paraffin provided by ourselves. . . . During the séance the medium's hands were held firmly by Geley and myself on the right and on the left so that he could not liberate either hand. The first mould obtained was of a child's hand, then a second of both hands (right and left) and a third of a child's foot. The creases in the skin and the veins were visible on the plaster casts made from the moulds.

"By reason of the narrowness of the wrists, these moulds could not have been made from living hands; for the whole hand would have had to be withdrawn through the narrow opening at the wrist. Professional modellers secure their results by threads attached to the hand which are pulled through the plaster. In the moulds here considered there was nothing of the sort; they were produced by a materialisation followed by a de-materialisation."

A particularly interesting scientific observation was made by Dr. Osty in his own laboratory in Paris in 1932. He arranged that an infrared beam should fall on a photo-electric cell, the current from which affected a quick-period galvanometer whose beam was photographically recorded on a moving drum. He established that ectoplasmic extrusions

---

[1] Charles Richet, *Thirty Years of Physical Research*. (Wm. Collins Sons & Co. Ltd.)

from the medium Rudi Schneider in deep trance could interpose themselves in the beam, and having apparently appreciable infra-red absorption, could finally obscure the beam. The most interesting feature was that the obscuration took place in a rhythmic manner coinciding in its period with the respiratory rate of the medium. Flashlight photographs showed nothing *visibly* obscuring the beam, and experiment also showed that the obscuring ectoplasm disintegrated under the action of visible light. There appear to be several kinds of ectoplasm[1]: one tangible but not visible which is unstable in white light, another visible but not tangible which is stable in red light, and another visible and tangible which is stable in white light. The whole subject opens up a vast field of enquiry, and as yet we know very little.

Granted the validity of the experimental facts of but one case—such as that of Richet and Geley, which we have cited above—there is no point at which we can stop and say, "I will believe no more." F. W. H. Myers, when editing the Stainton Moses records, took precisely this view. We have then to face the well-attested full-scale solid materialisation of Katie King[2] investigated by Sir William Crookes, Sir Arthur Conan Doyle, and others. These things may not be so rare as the records suggest. A gentleman, a retired farmer, whose integrity I have no reason to doubt, and whom I should judge to be far from fanciful in his make-up, told me of his own extraordinary experiences week after week with a medium in London some years ago. Finally to convince himself beyond doubt he asked for, and was given, a private sitting in his own home near Cambridge with his wife and two daughters as the only other persons present. He assured me that no less than seventeen full-scale materialised figures appeared to them on that afternoon: men, women, and children. The adults all spoke to them—and there was no doubt about the grip of their hands!

We have also the extraordinary phenomenon of the "direct voice" associated with some physical mediums. Dr. H. Westwood, the records of whose experiences are impressive[3] and are obviously those of a careful and at first a sceptical observer, has expressed his conviction of the existence of this phenomenon. He affirms that the voices have nothing to do with the vocal chords of the medium, of which he made certain by placing his fingers lightly on the medium's throat. He also established the objectivity of the voices by dictaphone recordings. The explanation offered by communicators was that they "built up a psychic vocal mechanism through which the voices were produced". Dr. West-

---

[1] Phoebe Payne, *Man's Latent Powers*, p. 115. (Faber and Faber Ltd., 1938.)
[2] Wm. Crookes, *Researches in the Phenomena of Spiritualism*. (Psychic Book Club, 1953.)
[3] *Loc. cit.*, Chapters XII-XIV.

wood says that his hand encountered nothing tangible in the space from which the voices came. Mrs. L. J. Bendit[1] has made some interesting observations and considers that the necessary quality of ectoplasm to mould an "aetheric larynx" is drawn from the throat region of the medium and sitters.

Mention should also be made of the strange phenomenon of "apports", in which, according to accounts, a physical object disappears from one place and reappears in another which may be quite distant. The circumstances preclude any normal means of transport and are generally such as to require one material body to have passed through another. Dr. Westwood has given one example[2] of this from his own experience; it was proposed and carried out as a demonstration by one of the ablest communicators. A specially marked piece of paper disappeared from between two boards and reappeared on a mantelpiece some six feet away under circumstances apparently permitting of no normal explanation. An extraordinary incident is recorded by Gregory and Kohsen[3] in relation to the mother of the former. A letter which she had written, and was being blotted between a folded sheet, completely disappeared in the process, with her son and daughter looking on. It was never seen again in spite of the most careful search. These are strange events to which we do not wish to attach too much weight in the absence of serious scientific investigation in this field. It is, I think, premature to theorise about them until our data, under strict conditions of control, are more abundant.

(4) *Hatha Yoga: Fire-walking*, etc. Here we approach an extensive field of para-normal phenomena which have never been the subject of serious and critical scientific investigation, but which it would be foolish to brush aside as mere superstition. It seems quite possible, in the light of what we already know of the para-normal, that generations of contemplatives in certain Eastern countries have discovered and developed a science of human personality contrasting with Western science, which has concentrated on the world around us. Vivekananda,[4] a very able Indian swami with an intimate knowledge of Western life, said:

"There are no such realities as a physical world, a mental world, a spiritual world. Whatever is, is one. Let us say, it is a sort of tapering existence, the thickest part is here, it tapers and becomes finer and finer; the finest is what we call spirit; the grossest the body. And just as it is here in the microcosm, it is exactly the same in the macrocosm."

[1] Phoebe Payne, *Man's Latent Powers*, pp. 129-30. (Faber and Faber Ltd., 1938.)
[2] *Loc. cit.*, pp. 58-61.
[3] Gregory and Kohsen, *Physical and Psychical Research*. (Omega Press, 1955.)
[4] *Complete Works of the Swami Vivekananda*, Vol. 2: Mayavati Memorial Edition, pp. 10-23.

He spoke very little of hatha yoga—that branch of the science which deals with the control by the mind of all physical processes—for he was essentially interested in the development of the higher aspects of personality and the road to spiritual enlightenment. But on one occasion, in a remarkable address on *The Powers of the Mind*, he spoke of his own study and practice of the discipline of this yoga:

"It took me thirty years to learn it; thirty years of hard struggle. Sometimes I worked at it twenty hours during the twenty-four . . .; sometimes I lived in places where there was hardly a sound, hardly a breath; sometimes I had to live in caves. . . . I have barely touched the hem of the garment of this science. But I can understand that it is true and vast and wonderful."

These disciplines, as is well known, follow a certain general pattern and involve mental practices of concentration combined with unusual breathing rhythms. They are not without danger to those who undertake them without adequate knowledge and supervision, but it would appear that in the end they may awaken or liberate the mind's ψ-faculty and bring it under control of the will. In one special form of yoga they may also bring under fully conscious control all the physiological processes which are normally outside the scope of voluntary influence. It is said that the ageing of the tissues of the body can be arrested; that the processes of metabolism can be controlled so that internal heat can be produced to meet the coldest environment; that bleeding can be inhibited, and so on. One of the most remarkable of these controls is that exhibited in the Hindu fire-walking ceremony.

A recent description of this, as it occurs annually in Fiji, has been given by G. and H. Sandwith.[1] It is worthy of careful study as being one of the most detailed accounts of the ceremony and the preparations made for it by the participants. Of its remarkable para-normal character there can be no doubt, according to this account. Forty tons of logs were burned for about fourteen hours to produce a trench full of hot charcoal. The Sandwiths report that their faces had to be shielded to prevent scorching at 12 feet. The essential feature appears to have been that those who participated had to be fully charged with some unknown type of energy (presumably generated on the aetheric level), and ten days of ritual preparation were devoted to this. Numerous tests were made before the culminating event: their flesh was pierced by skewers without the feeling of pain or loss of blood, and they were lashed without pain being felt or weals appearing. The same energy appears to have remarkable therapeutic power and the case is described of the almost instantaneous healing of a Hindu girl whose legs had been

[1] George and Helen Sandwith, *Research in Fiji, Tonga and Samoa*. (Omega Press, 1954); also Colin Simpson, *Islands of Man*. (Angus & Robertson, 1955.)

paralysed from birth. Occasionally imperfect preparation for the fire-walking has led to tragedy. It looks as though we have evidence in this ceremony of the generation of psychical fields with unusual powers and properties.

One of the fire-walkers said to the Sandwiths after the 1952 ceremony, "This is something that really works: it is not just talk and promises." In a verbal account which Mr. and Mrs. Sandwith gave to me they spoke of the spiritual experience which it had been *for them* as spectators of the whole preparations and of the event. I am tempted to quote Robert Browning in an association which would, I think, have surprised him.

> Let us not always say,
> "Spite of this flesh to-day
> I strove, made head, gained ground upon the whole."
> As the bird wings and sings,
> Let us cry, "All good things
> Are ours, nor soul helps flesh more now than flesh helps soul."

(5) *Para-normal Healing*. We shall refer to this only briefly, for three reasons. Firstly, it is a vast field involving different levels of the personality—of which we know so little. Secondly, genuine powers exist side by side with much that is doubtful, and we do not wish here to make a long digression to sift them. Thirdly, the phenomena of healing illustrate but add nothing new to the things we have already discussed.

I suggest tentatively that there is a common factor underlying mesmerism (which was probably not *all* nonsense), the "odyle" of von Reichenbach, and the unnamed energy with which L. E. Eeman is at present experimenting,[1] and this factor may well be a common fundamental type of energy on the "aetheric" level. It is probably the operative factor in what is sometimes described as "magnetic healing" or healing by the "laying-on of hands". I do not doubt there are powers on other levels of personality which can be used constructively or destructively—but, as we have indicated, it is not proposed to discuss them here.

[1] L. E. Eeman, *Co-operative Healing*. (Frederick Muller Ltd., 1947.)

Chapter

5

WHAT SORT OF A WORLD DO WE LIVE IN?

To myself, I seem to have been only like a boy playing on the sea-shore and diverting myself in now and then finding a smoother pebble or a prettier shell than ordinary, whilst the great ocean of truth lay all undiscovered before me.

ISAAC NEWTON

I am whatever hath been, is, or ever will be; and my veil no man hath yet lifted.

Inscription over the portal of the Temple of Isis

I heard them in their sadness say,
"The earth rebukes the thought of God;
We are but embers wrapped in clay
A little nobler than the sod."

But I have touched the lips of clay,
Mother, thy rudest sod to me
Is thrilled with fire of hidden day,
And haunted by all mystery.

A. E.

THOSE readers who struggled through Chapter 3 and have felt bewildered by the data of Chapter 4 may welcome a pause at this stage to look at things in perspective. We took two branches of science, physics and biology, dealing respectively with the domains of the so-called non-living and the living. Physics studies the aspects of the world which can be measured. Using mechanical models derived from large-scale experience of the world, and with the aid of mathematics, nineteenth-century physicists believed that they would ultimately understand everything about the physical world in terms of certain fundamental particles and radiation. They built a remarkably consistent mechanical picture and up to a point achieved outstanding success—the success, in fact, upon which all the impressive technology of modern times is based. It was only when modern physicists probed into the ultimate nature of the atom and its particles that mechanical models showed their inadequacy in this region, and it was only when high speeds, comparable with that of light, were involved that the simple concepts of mass, length, and time showed unsuspected complexity.

But all this wonderful scientific system of thought achieved its prestige and impressiveness by ignoring other aspects of the world. Whitehead wrote rather caustically of this: "If only you ignore everything which refuses to come into line, your powers of explanation are unlimited." What are the things which physics ignores? The answer briefly is: the qualitative aspects of the world, and the subjective aspects of our experience. Colour, scent, and sound are conveniently ascribed to the observing mind and these are of course the basis of all aesthetic values. Position and speed and the "resistance-extension" qualities of the physical world were taken to be the basis of what the world is really like. We do not wish to be misunderstood. Any group of scientists is entitled to abstract from the whole and study a limited aspect of that whole for purposes of fuller understanding. But scientific success is heady wine, and we usually find, with misplaced enthusiasm, at first the insinuation, and finally the belief, that here we have the clues to the whole. There is no light or colour, no scent or sound in Nature—there is only matter in motion. This affects our eyes, our noses and ears, and our brains—but these are only matter in motion too. As for Mind—it must be a curious property or product of sufficiently complex matter in motion! This is the essence of materialism, and leads to the absurd conclusion that one curious property of matter in motion explains to its own satisfaction all the others!

Biology studies the "living" aspects of the world on the physical level. Having classified and ordered its large-scale phenomena, it has followed the tradition of the older sciences with their analytical approach, and this has resulted in the rapid rise of genetics. Genes seem destined to play a similar part in the study of living things to that which atoms have played in physics and chemistry. Indeed, the distant goal of genetics might appear to be that of a subdivision of chemistry. We shall risk reiteration and again point out that matter in motion, even though it be a very complex molecule called a gene, is one aspect only of a greater whole. The qualitative aspects are necessarily neglected, and the complex biological phenomena which genes make possible—e.g. redness in petals and blueness in eyes—are not accounted for. These are the conditions "from above"—imaginals and sub-imaginals in a vast hierarchy which manifest when the conditions "from below" make this possible.

The reader will also recall that the whole picture of evolution presents many inexplicable features so long as the conditions "from below" are regarded as a sole and sufficient basis, but that the recognition of psychical fields inter-relating individuals, conserving useful variations, and maintaining teleological pressure, gives promise of resolving these difficulties.

When we consider the phenomena being investigated by psychical research, we enter a field intimately linked with the observing minds which interpret sensory experience, a part of which science has studied. It should always have been obvious that we had no right to assume that the world ended where our senses ceased to disclose it. It should have been obvious that it was only an assumption that Mind as the instrument of knowledge was limited in its ingathering to the five sensory channels, and as an instrument of action limited in its operation to the neuromuscular channels. The experimental facts now make this abundantly clear, and it is not too much to claim that our whole outlook on the kind of world we live in must be radically affected by them.

THE IMPLICATIONS OF ψ-FACULTY

The Cartesian dualism of matter and mind was useful as a conceptual aid to thought, and unsatisfactory as a metaphysical picture. Its replacement by a trinity of matter, a psychic aether and mind is now more useful as a conceptual aid to thought—but we do not pretend that it is true in any ultimate sense. The evidence of psychical research suggests rather that the world we experience through our senses and our mind is psychical and that so-called "matter" and "mind" are lower and higher manifestations of a psychical unity. The inter-penetration of matter by matter and of matter by mind does not then present an aspect of incredibility as otherwise it is prone to do.

Telepathy and clairvoyance may be ascribed to one and the same activity. It is not merely that in the former the knowledge takes verbal form and in the latter visual form, but that in the former it is a relation between comparable minds, and in the latter between entities on very different levels of the psychical continuum. (Perhaps one is a human mind and the other the aggregate of elementary sentients constituting a playing-card.)

In the case of apparitions, we envisaged them as varying between the subjective Tyrrellian type and the objective type not different in status from physical objects. We can regard these as temporary constructions on different levels of one and the same psychical continuum by the interaction of two minds. If it is asked what distinguishes a full-scale solid materialised figure (to which all the relevant senses of a critical observer bear testimony) from an ordinary human being, I think the answer must be: on the sensory level there is nothing except its transience. There is, as we know, a slow process of growth in Nature sustained by Divine imaginative activity, and the physical forms thus created in Nature have considerable endurance. It may be that the rapid materialisation process of the seance room is an imaginative activity of a discarnate mind closely akin to the process of growth in Nature but subject to some law which links the degree of endurance in time with prolonged creative consciring.

Object-reading or psychometry introduces us in a direct manner to the psychical characteristics of physical objects. We can express the experimental facts by saying that a sensitive's mind so relates itself to the psychical field of the object that it cognises a quality imparted to it by the mind of a previous owner, and can thereupon achieve telepathic rapport with that owner's mind. What is the nature of this identifiable quality we do not know. It is not apparently a transient or disappearing quality, but it remains with the object. Moreover, different specific qualities derived from different persons do not interfere with each other but remain discrete and separate. These features, of course, are characteristic of diverse memories held within a mind. We must be prepared to extend our conception of memory. Bearing in mind the psychical character of physical objects, they too may conserve a memory-record of all the experiences to which they have been subjected. Object-reading has much in common with clairvoyance. In the former it is the higher-level characteristics and in the latter the lower-level characteristics of the psychical field of the object which are cognised.

Let us turn now to the action of mind in displacing physical objects. What happens when we displace an object in the normal way by the use of our muscles? An imaginative act initiates the process at a high psychic level. This modifies the psychical field of the motor-brain, and in turn this modifies the psychical field of the nerves and muscles. At the last stage it would be regarded as a repulsion between two swarms of electrons—those which constitute the hand and those which constitute the object in the region of "contact". But on the view we have developed, the electrons are themselves psychoid, and what the physicist would call electrical repulsion we should describe as a psychical repulsion. All action in the world is psychical, but in psycho-kinesis the high psychical levels (of mind) operate *directly* on the low psychical levels (of matter), using energy of consciring to do so. In normal action the high levels of mind act indirectly, using a descending hierarchy of subordinate sentients to give effect to their wishes—a process in which these elementary levels of consciring provide the dynamic.

The physical principle of conservation of energy which has been established for low levels of the psychical continuum (the physical order) is evidence of what the Greeks would have called the "Divinity of Measure", or the over-ruling Imaginal dynamic which maintains the balance between conflict and harmony, repulsion and attraction. I do not doubt that in the rarer type of direct "para-normal" activity of mind there may be a local and temporary violation of the conservation principle where consciring on high psychical levels pours energy into the lower ones. The mode of effecting this is obviously safeguarded and not easily realised, but the reports (which I am disposed to accept) of phenomena connected with hatha yoga and kundalini yoga, together with the lifting of heavy objects and poltergeist effects, suggest that it can be done.

Speculating in this field, of which we know so little, what can we suppose takes place in fire-walking? At the high temperature of the charcoal beds we expect certain chemical actions to take place very rapidly, destroying all human tissues by breakdown and oxidation. In psycho-kinesis of the sensational type, very considerable energy from higher psychic levels is directed to lower levels in the lifting of heavy physical objects *as a whole*. The prevention of chemical changes in tissues, under conditions where those changes would normally result, must I think be regarded as a special form of psycho-kinesis directed *inwardly* so as to oppose molecular disintegration. Expressed in psychical terms, it is the control through intense imaginative activity (i.e. con-sciring) by the whole human psyche of the behaviour of those myriad minor sentients, the molecules, which form a part of it. In a normal state this control is only a general directive one, and it occasionally breaks down, as when cancer develops. These minor sentients—atoms and molecules—have normally a very limited freedom which is so small as to conform in practice to habitual behaviour, and this we describe in terms of "laws" in chemistry and physics. In fire-walking their habitual behaviour is suspended by a complete and intimate overall control initiated by high mental levels of the psyche.

FURTHER REFLECTIONS ON INTER-PENETRATION

Many unusual phenomena which we are prone to dismiss with a shrug, begin to fit into a plausible pattern of thought when we think in terms of the inter-penetration of two psychical fields—of a lower one by the higher. With this kind of outlook we can recognise the possibility of dramatic forms of para-normal healing. Common processes of healing doubtless arise from the normal measure of directive control exercised by the mind on the inter-penetrated body. When this inter-penetration is intense and complete, as in the unusual state of fire-walking, we may expect unusual healing to be possible (of which one example was cited in the previous chapter). We should also anticipate that an experience in which psycho-kinesis is as remarkably effective as this might be associated with very remarkable—even ecstatic—extra-sensory percep-tion, for these twin aspects of ψ-faculty appear to be very closely related. G. and H. Sandwith mention one personal observation[1] of a girl who "approached the fire with arms outstretched and a smile on her face as if she were going to meet her lover; she danced across the fire in an ecstatic state".

[1] *Loc. cit.*, p. 9.

We have been discussing an unusual state in which the higher psychical levels (the mind of the organism) have *completely* penetrated and controlled the lower psychical levels (the body of the organism). There is, however, a normal degree of inter-penetration so that no tissue is exempt from the constant influence of the mind of the whole.

Take for example the following statement of Dr. Kenneth Walker[1]:

"As a surgeon, I am sometimes called upon to cut away the ureter (the narrow channel that connects the bladder with the kidney) and to implant it into another part of the bladder. When my work has been completed I am ashamed of its crudity. Compared with the job done by a plumber, my joint is a poor and botched concern. Yet when I examine it a year after I am scarcely able to tell which is Nature's joint and which is my own. Some intelligence in the patient's body has made good my failure, paring off redundant tissue here, adding new tissue there, until perfection has beeen attained. Does that intelligence exist only in the brain? No, for if I divided all the nerves that reached that spot from the brain, the work is performed just as well. If we conceded intelligence to the body, we must also concede to it some degree of consciousness."

A few years ago a report of the treatment by hypnotic suggestion of a case of congenital ichthyosis (crocodile skin) in a boy of sixteen created considerable interest[2] in the ranks of the medical profession. Instead of normal skin there occurred a black horny layer with numerous papillae projecting 2-6 mm. above the surface over most of his body except head, neck, and chest. Skin grafts had been attempted, but within a month they became indistinguishable from the affected parts. Finally, Dr. A. A. Mason used hypnotic suggestion, beginning with the left arm, and reported that "from a black and armour-like casing the skin became pink and soft within a few days". The arms, which before treatment were 80 per cent. covered, were after treatment 95 per cent. cleared, and so on in different degrees with other affected parts. Apparently in the first few weeks of treatment the clearance was rapid and dramatic, but subsequently it reached a point of no further change. The cleared parts, however, showed no relapse after a year.

The usual assumption has been that organic (and particularly *congenital*) disorders as distinct from functional disorders are beyond the reach of suggestion. It seems clear that no such assumption is justified. The practical question is *how* the resources of the mind can be brought to bear effectively on the physical structure. There is evidence of a considerable amount of empirical knowledge gathered over the centuries by some Eastern peoples, such as the Hindu fire-walkers and

[1] Kenneth Walker, *Diagnosis of Man*. (Jonathan Cape Ltd.)
[2] *British Medical Journal*, No. 4781, August 23rd, 1952, pp. 422-3; or a summary in *Jour. S.P.R.*, Vol. XXXVI, pp. 716-18.

hatha yogis, which, if it were studied sympathetically by the Western-trained mind, would add enormously to our fundamental understanding of the world.

I turn now to comment on certain views which Professor C. G. Jung[1] first put forward many years ago and called the Principle of Synchronicity. In a remarkable commentary on Richard Wilhelm's translation of an old Chinese classic the *I Ching*, Jung claims that the highest expressions of Chinese thought have not been based upon the causality principle which has ruled all our Western science. With our training and outlook on the world we view all events as linked together in complicated chains of cause and effect extended in time. To us this makes sense of the world. The *I Ching* considers that events may be correlated in quite a different way: they may be synchronous in time and correlated in space. The mere fact of simultaneous appearance in time of widely separated events in space involves, on this view, significant relations between these events. Jung writes of the "qualitas occulta of the time-moment", and cites examples such as the simultaneous appearance of similar thoughts and the simultaneous arising of comparable Chinese and European periods of style. He makes guarded reference to astrology as a possible "large-scale example of synchronism". Jung has returned to an exposition of the principle of synchronicity in a recent book.[2] In one case a woman patient at a critical stage of the analysis was recounting a dream about a golden scarabaeus when a similar beetle (its nearest analogue for that climate) hit the window-pane. Numerous other examples are given which, however, are all capable of interpretation in terms of ψ-faculty, telepathic, clairvoyant, and precognitive. It is suggested in this book that we shall have to make a choice between ψ-causality and non-causal synchronicity. I do not know why we should be faced with "either/or", but if we are so faced, most Western thinkers will be predisposed to a viewpoint which retains causality and makes research reasonable. When the creeks and estuaries of a far-stretching coast-line fill with salt water, we do not invoke the principle of synchronicity, we look for the cause and say: the tide must have come in. So long as we adopt a sense-centred outlook, the simultaneous occurrence of significantly related but widely separated events must always seem surprising. *But if the physical level of the universe in which we live is but the lowest level of an inter-penetrating psychical continuum which in its higher reaches merges into transcendent levels of increasing reality, are we not foolish to deny that tides of creative influence may at times and seasons flow from these higher regions of reality*

---

[1] Wilhelm and Jung, *The Secret of the Golden Flower.* (Kegan Paul, Trench, Trubner & Co. Ltd., 1942.)

[2] *Vide* review by Professor H. H. Price in *Jour. S.P.R.*, Vol. XXXVII, p. 26 (1953).

into the lower? If Man, as we know him, is the highest of evolved or created beings, and if he is snuffed out like a candle when his body wears out, we may well try in vain to pierce the mystery of existence. But if the Universe, of which with our senses and our telescope we can perceive so little, is the home of an infinite hierarchy of conscious beings, some as far beyond us as we are beyond the amoebae, is it not at least possible—even probable—that some have a compassionate interest in the doings of the inhabitants of Earth?

If the physical universe disclosed by our large telescopes is just "matter" scattered on a lavish scale, there is no point in asking what is its meaning or purpose. But in a psychical continuum no fact is isolated. For this reason I do not consider there are any *a priori* grounds on which astrology can either be derided or dismissed. On the contrary, I should expect to find a very far-reaching science, of which what calls itself astrology today is little more than a vestige or a hint. If the lower levels of our psychical continuum are inter-penetrated by higher levels, and these again may be penetrated by still higher levels, what is true of Earth should equally be true of the other members of the solar system and the stellar universe. These may be the homes of advanced beings even as our physical bodies are the homes of myriads of lesser sentients, and as the planet Earth gives hospitality to ourselves. From this point of view I have sometimes wondered what Professor A. N. Whitehead had in mind when he said[1]:

"We must also allow for the possibility that we can detect in ourselves direct aspects of the mentalities of higher organisms. . . . The fundamental principle is that whatever merges into actuality, implants its aspects in every individual event."

It suggests the extension of inter-penetration to cosmic levels and the possibility of influences such as we have referred to—shocking as this may appear to be to the scientific mind!

THE STATUS OF NATURAL LAW

The matters we have discussed naturally lead us to consider the question of the status of Natural Law. In an imaginal universe the two aspects of conservation and novelty occur together. Nothing repeats itself without some degree of novelty entering in. On the lowest levels of Nature, where there are countless myriads of minor sentients (atoms, molecules, etc.), freedom is in any case very restricted and habit-patterns have formed which have become very stable. It is because of the constancy of response that we have "laws" such as we know in

[1] A. N. Whitehead, *Science and the Modern World*, p. 187. (C.U.P., 1929.)

physics, chemistry, and mechanics. There is nothing inflexible about them except the constancy of habit, but individual departures will not be numerous enough to influence their practical reliability. Natural Laws are thus statements of habitual modes of response: there is no Divine fiat behind them. There is an important principle here, for habit is not inconsistent with the freedom of these very lowly centres of consciring, and there may be rare occasions when the habit-pattern is suspended to a considerable degree by the action of powerful higher centres of consciring, as for example in fire-walking or sudden healings. Moreover, habits can be slowly changed where there is pressure from a higher level, and it does not follow that in a thousand million years a "law" of today will still be valid. Indeed, the processes of stellar evolution suggest that such pressures are operative. Professor Royce has suggested that the concept of rigid law was of social origin and became transferred to the realm of Natural Science.

When we rise in the evolutionary scale, the area of freedom widens and we are less prone to think of "laws". There is certainly a strong background of conservation, but novel behaviour becomes more likely. The conservative aspect is of course apparent as "instinct", which might be regarded as the habit-pattern common to all the members of a lowly sub-Imaginal. At the level of man instinct plays a much smaller part and novelty a much larger one, so that generalisations about human habits can be made only with reservation.

To sum up, there are no absolutely rigid laws in Nature, but there are many uniformities of behaviour which we have described as habit-patterns. These are reliable for practical purposes in the case of the lower sentients which conscire irreflectively. Freed from the concept of inflexible Law, we see that *causation itself embodies freedom* and chance. In an imaginal world it could not do otherwise, for imagining on any level means freedom to imagine! The old antithesis of freedom and determinism is no longer an insoluble riddle. We shall look at this further in Chapter 11.

OUR PERCEPTION OF THE WORLD AROUND US

We cannot pretend to answer the question "What sort of a world do we live in?" without facing the issue of perception. How do our senses inform us about the world? What really happens when a man says, "I see a tree"? It is a vexed question among philosophers, and broadly speaking there are two schools of thought. There are those who consider that perception is based on direct acquaintance with the qualities of the surface of an outside object (and this is approximately the plain man's idea). There are others who consider that this is not so, but that our only acquaintance is with a mental image which we have formed. I do not propose to enter into the endless complications of this controversy, but to make a few simple comments on the process of seeing and to state the imaginist view of perception as I understand it.

We must constantly remind ourselves that the eye has a very limited range of response. We know that there are octaves of radiation extending on both sides of that single octave which we describe as visible and which stimulates in us the sensations of colour ranging from red to violet. Our eyes are limited also in their magnifying power to a certain range of practical utility, and we know that there is much more to be seen when we supplement our normal sight with a microscope or a telescope. If the function of the eye-and-brain instrument is merely to convey a stimulus-signal to the mind which thereupon *directly* acquaints itself with the surface-properties of an external object (presumably as in clairvoyance), the question arises why the mind does not learn all there is to know about the object. One might even ask why different senses are necessary. Since there is no difference in the nature of the stimuli arriving at different parts of the cerebral cortex, one might ask how it comes about that the sensations to which they give rise are of such incommensurable types? Thus, a man born blind, though able to hear, cannot know what colour is; and a man born deaf, though seeing, cannot know what music is. For these reasons, and also because the eye-and-brain instrument seems of quite unnecessary complexity if its function is only that of providing a stimulus-signal to the mind, I do not think a *direct* (clairvoyant) acquaintance of the mind with an external world is a satisfactory basis for perception.

An alternative theory might be that the eye-and-brain apparatus may (a) signal the mind to direct its attention outwards and also (b) restrict or canalise the mind's outgoing in such a way as to provide a limitation on how much can be seen. Just how this canalisation or restriction is imposed, we do not know. If it is possible, then we have, in the result, a restricted form of direct acquaintance with the surfaces of external objects. Normal seeing becomes a restricted form of clairvoyance, a viewpoint which Moncrieff has attempted to develop in a recent book.[1]

An alternative theory, to which I incline, is that the eye-and-brain apparatus (a) signals the mind to direct its attention to specific invading content and (b) assists the mind to conscire an image of this with sufficient intensity.

We must leave behind the ingrained common-sense view that

[1] M. M. Moncrieff, *The Clairvoyant Theory of Perception*. (Faber and Faber Ltd., 1951.)

physical objects are clear-cut insulated entities different in kind from our thoughts and memories. We must think rather of one psychical continuum of which the physical aspect of Nature constitutes the lower levels and the world of minds constitutes the upper levels. The eye-and-brain apparatus is a specialised structure in the lower levels to permit specific content of these levels to enter the self and then be conscired with the high intensity characteristic of "sight" or perception. The tree that I see and the tree that I recall as a memory are not different in substance; they exist on different levels of the same psychic continuum and are conscired with different intensity (for reasons we shall shortly consider). There is no iron-curtain or barrier between the percipient and what is perceived—a difficulty which always remains with the old Cartesian dualism of brain and mind. It is only on the Imaginist view, with its emphasis on the interpenetration of different levels and of different objects of one psychical continuum, that we can begin to understand not only such commonplaces as normal perception but the rarer and more sensational data of psychical research.

We return then to the nature of perception. A part of the external world invades our mind via the channel of eye-and-brain. In this channel something is lost and something gained. The myriad minor sentients which compose a blade of grass or a tree are never conscired by finite minds, but only a relatively few colours, sounds, and shapes which serve the practical purposes of living are conscired. The penetrative content from without is now selectively reinforced by imaginal content from within. The perceived images are largely constructed for us by our own inner consciring on the foundations of the invasive psychic content from the outer world. (Wordsworth refers to "all the mighty world of eye and ear" as being for observers "what they half-create and what perceive".) The selective process carves out of the presented continuum a tree, for example, to which we attend. As we do so, the background of grass and hills fades out in the intensity with which it is conscired. Moreover, there is infinitely more below the threshold of reflective consciring which we do not perceive at all. We do not, of course, conscire the physiological processes of the retina and brain with intensity sufficient to become aware of them. We are not gods: but we may surmise that greater beings than ourselves may conscire with great intensity over a wide field, and not be limited to a focal point of interest in a background which is partly faded out, nor to a few beggarly qualities out of the myriad riches of the world.

We do not pretend to have touched more than the fringe of a vast subject, but our view is that imagining, the fundamental power in ourselves, contributes to the act of perception. Whitehead observed that "the material world is largely a concept of the imagination which rests on a slender basis of direct sense-presentation". I should prefer to say the physical world is created and sustained by Divine Imagining, and we are able to perceive a small part of this which invades us through our senses, through the reinforcement and contribution of our own consciring.

HIGHER LEVELS OF THE WORLD

We are able, then, to go a long way with the plain man. We should disagree with some philosophers who doubt whether there is an external world. We believe that "the world of space-hung, time-strung events appears not merely within us but *to* us".[1] We further believe that this world which our senses reveal to us is but the lower level of a psychical continuum which in its higher levels includes our minds and all the thought-imagery of our subjective life. "The concept of matter is a mental substitute-fact for natural objects when thought of in respect of being touched. . . . There are no *merely* resisting-extended (spatial) objects, . . . these are one of the imaginal devices which subserve practical reasoning."[2] Physical objects are rich in qualities of the same kind as those found in our thought-imagery.

Let us in conclusion turn our attention to the aspects of the world which science neglects. We have seen how it abstracts from the Whole for purposes of detailed study. Even biology is not concerned with the distinctions which constitute individuality. It is obviously of significance for biology what the members of a given species have in common, and of little or no significance wherein its members differ. When we rise to the level of man it is obviously of the greatest significance wherein one individual differs from another. In other words, feelings, desires, thoughts, aspirations, ideals are not the concern of science, and only to a limited extent the concern of psychology. In so far as it is a science it is concerned with reactions shared by all men, and not with those higher distinguishing characteristics in virtue of which we cherish the friendship or admire the character of one person rather than another.

Psychical Research goes farther: it investigates a world whose limits are not determined by the senses. It is obliged to recognise profound individual differences—on a certain level. Consider the differing mental affinities of people by which good telepathic rapport is possible between some and not between others. We recall, for example, a sensitive's reaction to different personalities (p. 109). Psychical Research, however, in its turn neglects elements in personality which are higher in the scale of significance. Those elements which we describe as Values:

[1] *Z.D.*, p. 32.   [2] *Z.D.*, p. 35.

sensitivity to Beauty, the qualities of Compassion, of Kindness and of Self-sacrifice, the high attainment of Wisdom of which the expression is found in intuitive insights: these, which are the highest achievements of individuals, are not within its ken. These partake of still higher levels of the world which we may appropriately call spiritual or transcendental to distinguish them from those described as psychical. Human personality participates in these higher levels, as rocks and trees and animals do not.

Professor Gilbert Murray has said[1]:

"We cannot see like a hawk or track like a dog or hear like a hunted deer; but we can see a Rembrandt picture and feel the thrill of a Beethoven sonata or a great poem. And surely it is noteworthy that just here our sensitivity passes beyond the realm of mere observation into that of feeling; beyond the facts that you observe there is the sense of other things, not fully known, which have value and importance. . . . Bergson has reminded us that millions of men have lived for thousands of years in a world vibrating with electricity, without ever suspecting that there was such a thing. Are we not probably now in the presence and under the influence of unknown forces, forces concerned with deeper or more remote values or beauties or loyalties, which are beyond the range of our exact knowledge and power of definition, but by no means beyond the reach of an undefined but strong and even passionate feeling: 'This is what I value', 'This is what I love', 'This is what I must obey'."

It is therefore in these higher reaches of human personality that we must explore if we want the clues to all else. It is not without significance that the sages have always taught that man was an epitome of the macrocosm, and urged him to know himself.

Bergson's view[2] that the function of the brain and special senses is restrictive—eliminative and not productive—is commending itself increasingly to thoughtful men.[3] The brain, on this view, restricts us from using vaster reaches and powers of Mind. I am pointing now to restrictions at another level, imposed by the mind itself upon the Knower, for mind seems to me but another instrument of that essential Self whose native habitat comprises those higher levels of the world which we have connoted by the term spiritual. The critic has every right to ask on what authority we make this assumption. I suggest that hints of it are found penetrating the psychical levels in the phenomena of precognition. Those data suggest that higher levels of the self beyond the limits of the rational mind can conscire over a considerable time-

[1] *Proc. S.P.R.*, Vol. XLIX, p. 169 (1952).
[2] *Proc. S.P.R.*, Vol. XXVII, pp. 157-75.
[3] *Vide Proc. S.P.R.*, Vol. XLVI, pp. 271-7 (1941); *Jour. S.P.R.*, Vol. XXXVI, p. 702 (1952); etc.

span. I suggest that clear evidence of it is found in our capacity to appreciate beauty in all the Arts, to respond to the numinous, and to love unselfishly: these things are beyond the highest of our intellectual processes. I suggest that the ancient discipline of Yoga practised in the East for at least three millennia has not been undertaken to no purpose. As students of this discipline are aware, the first steps are a withdrawal from sensory distractions and undertaking of the long and difficult process of *stilling the ever-active mind*. It is when this has been accomplished that higher levels of the Self are given the opportunity to reveal themselves more fully. Finally, I suggest that the experiences of Mystics of all races and creeds all down the centuries bear witness to the realities transcending our minds, and convey to those who have experienced them an overwhelming sense of their touch with Reality. In later chapters we shall deal with these higher levels of the world.

6

IS RELIGION MEETING OUR NEEDS?

There cannot be imagined a deeper gulf between men than that which divides those who are convinced that in meeting the present crisis in human existence men have to rely solely and exclusively on resources within themselves from those who believe that there is a meaning in life which men do not create but find, that there is an end which they are meant to live for, a goodness to which they may respond in surrender and self-commitment and a love in which they may absolutely trust.

J. H. Oldham

The supreme error in religion is seeking finality either in renunciation of the actual or in contentment with it. . . . There are specially three finalities in which men have ever sought to find rest. They are Fixed Organisations, Fixed Ideals, and Fixed Theologies. . . . Perhaps the sad story of man's whole history is that he would rather have "bondage with ease than strenuous liberty" and that this is just what life is appointed to disturb.

John W. Oman

No generation can merely produce its ancestors. You may preserve the life in a flux of form or preserve the form amid an ebb of life. But you cannot permanently enclose the same life in the same mould.

A. N. Whitehead

It seems fitting, and indeed necessary, to consider the place of religion in human life, for religion claims to have its concern with these higher levels of the world and to be able to mediate some of their riches to man. When a man writes about religion, if he has any contribution to make to the thought of others, it will not be through trying to write with cold scientific detachment but through proffering with sincerity his own deepest thoughts and intuitions—in short, what his little experience of life has taught him. Others may not agree with his conclusions: this does not matter. But to his own fragment of experience he may apply Ruskin's words[1]:

"So far as he knows, no one else can say it. He is bound to say it, clearly and melodiously if he may; clearly, at all events. In the sum of his life he finds this to be the thing, or group of things, manifest to him—this, the piece of true knowledge or sight which his share of sunshine and earth has permitted him to seize. He would fain set it down for ever; engrave it on the rock if he could; saying, 'This is the best of me; for the rest, I ate and drank, and slept, loved and hated, like another; my life was as the vapour and is not; but this I saw and knew: this, if anything of mine, is worth your memory.'"

[1] *Sesame and Lilies.*

THE HUMAN SITUATION

In a very able and persuasive book[1] J. H. Oldham expresses the opinion that "the sphere of the sacred has been almost completely eliminated from the life of entire communities". He quotes others who support this view. Dietrich Bonhoeffer, a German theologian executed by the Nazis for his part in the resistance movement, wrote from prison, "We are moving into an age completely without religion." Sir Walter Moberly, in his book *The Crisis in the University*, says, "In modern universities, as in modern society, some think God exists, some think not, some think it is impossible to tell, and the impression grows that it does not matter."

I do not myself think that the situation in regard to vital religion (as distinct from conventional religion) varies much from one generation to another. This is necessarily an opinion, not a judgment, for data on such an issue would be difficult to obtain. The position would rather seem to be that we are living in an age of fantastic scientific achievement which has placed in the hands of man great powers which he may use for good or evil ends. So full of menace is this situation that we have become more conscious of the lack of man's moral and spiritual development which would have provided us with reassurance that these powers would not be abused. If university students represent a reasonable sample of the community, my experience of living and working among them for many years does not suggest that there is any drift to agnosticism. I think that a minority (perhaps ten to twenty per cent.) are really interested in religion; a much smaller minority may be antagonistic, but the overwhelming majority show no marked interest in it. It should not be assumed that the majority are irreligious, but merely that the significance of real religion has never been presented to them with sufficient persuasiveness to make them want to set aside time to investigate its claims. When I use the term "persuasiveness" I refer not merely to intellectual cogency but to an embodiment in personality that draws out affectionate respect and admiration, and conveys to others, as words can never do, that there is a quality of life of which the secret is worth pursuing. (Gandhi was such a one in modern India.) In the absence of this quality the claims of religion will always be viewed by the majority of people as no more than one of the many interests which compete for their consideration in the leisure time which they can devote to things of their own choosing. The student of medicine seldom studies art or philosophy or music; the student of art seldom studies the classics or science, not necessarily because he is indifferent to their value, but because with the competing

[1] J. H. Oldham, *Life is Commitment*, p. 43. (S.C.M. Press Ltd., 1953.)

claims of duty, social interests, and recreation, their intrinsic attractiveness to him is insufficient. Religion is, rightly or wrongly, viewed in this way by the majority. It will of course be urged that religion should be a spirit inter-penetrating, guiding, and lifting to higher levels of satisfaction every part of life. I agree: I am trying to understand a situation, not defending it. In practice, then, it is true of most students and also of the great majority in the community that religion means very little because it has never been viewed as other than one of many competing interests which make a claim upon time and attention, and because it has never been regarded as very relevant to everyday life. I am sure that a large number of people identify religion with a set of ideas about other-worldly interests which the Churches for traditional reasons regard it as their job to sustain.

So youth with its *joie de vivre* passes into the age of responsibility, earning a living, rearing a family, and making some contribution to the community's life and generally it is only when the foundations of personal life are shaken for a time that most people pause to reflect what it all means. Loneliness, suffering, misfortune, and death strike home *to us*, and then we stand shaken and rebellious, or sad and wistful. Is this life all? Is love immortal, or does the grave close over all our hopes? Is life largely a round of necessary trivialities with no meanings and values beyond the present hour? Are its most precious things all perishing and transient, or is there some Goodness which we can trust, some Love which cares for us amid all the shadows and mystery of our present lot?

> Something there must be that I know not here,
> Or know too dimly through the symbol dear;
>   Some touch, some beauty, only guessed by this—
> If He that made us loves, it shall replace,
> Beloved, even the vision of thy face
>   And deep communion of thine inmost kiss.

So wrote Henry Newbolt,[1] and religion is the quest for conviction about this.

In the crises of life many voices speak to us. Here is one voice:

> The years like great black oxen tread the world,
> And God the Herdsman goads them on behind
> And I am broken by their passing feet.[2]

Here is another voice:

"Are not five sparrows sold for two farthings? and not one of them is

[1] "When I remember": *Collected Poems of Henry Newbolt*. (Thomas Nelson & Sons Ltd.)
[2] W. B. Yeats, *The Countess Cathleen*. (*Collected Poems of Y. W. Yeats*.) (Messrs. Macmillan & Co. Ltd.)

forgotten in the sight of God. . . . Fear not: ye are of more value than many sparrows. . . . Take My yoke upon you, and learn of Me; for I am meek and lowly in heart: and ye shall find rest unto your souls. For My yoke is easy, and My burden is light."[1]

Which voice shall we trust? Is trust avoidable if we desire knowledge? We are not now dealing with scientific propositions between which, on grounds of an intellectual kind, a choice can be made. We are dealing with two attitudes to living of which I can only know which is valid by committing myself to the one or the other. J. H. Oldham[2] has expressed this clearly. He says there are

"experiences of life in which I do not stand outside of something and try to deal with it, but in which I am myself involved, so that I cannot detach myself from the situation and deal with it from outside. Life is full of situations to which I can respond not with part of myself but only with the commitment of my whole being."

He illustrates the difference between the scientific attitude (response with the intellect) and the attitude of total response or committal.

"No amount of research in the laboratory, no amount of solitary thinking, will teach you what love is—or for that matter hate. And when you meet her, if it is a she, you will not learn what love is by any measurements or tests that you may apply, or by psychological observation however acute, but only by surrender, by committing yourself, which is a totally different attitude from that of counting, measuring, weighing and calculating, all of which you can do without being caught yourself."

The question is: if I can only know of the validity of something by committal of myself to it, is it reasonable to make this venture? How incorrigibly we turn to seek the support of intellect in all our doings! I say unhesitatingly "Yes" to the quest for life's ultimate meanings through religion—where this is rightly understood. Indeed, I should say that sincere questing in this regard is the essence of the religious spirit. I say "Yes" for these reasons.

(1) The nature of man himself bears witness to the restricted character of his experience on the physical level. I consider the evidence quite convincing that man survives the death of his body, and that on the next level of his existence wider vistas of experience unfold for him. He has then dropped one veil which obscures the light of Reality—even though there are many more.

(2) Many ordinary people, neither very clever nor very wise, but facing the suffering and adversity which is the common lot, have all down the centuries borne witness to their belief that the heart of things

---

[1] Luke xii. 6, 7; Matt. xi. 29, 30.   [2] *Loc. cit.*, p. 24; p. 27.

was good and not bad, compassionate not indifferent to their needs, and worthy of their trust. It is true that many others have not, and that some have violently opposed this view. There is no guarantee of truth in numbers or fervour, whichever side they favour, but one cannot be indifferent to the contrasting quality of life which these opposed views seem to produce.

(3) Jesus spoke in terms of clarity and simplicity of things which in our times of darkness we most crave to know. He went into no detail; He gave His assurance. But could He, in the circumstances of His time, have done more?

(4) There are those today—they are not perhaps numerous, but they are not excessively rare—who have had moments of illumination or insight, when they have experienced the reality behind appearances with an overwhelming sense of conviction and certainty. Such experiences they could no more doubt than they could doubt their own existence. Compared with such moments all others have afterwards seemed dim and unreal. The testimony of mystical experience is unanimous that we are all a part of a friendly universe and that at the heart of things is Love, Beauty, Joy, and Goodness, beyond the power of man's imagination to conceive or express. Although I have had no such experience, I find this testimony remarkably persuasive and convincing. It is to me so clear a pointer to the Truth about the world that I do not hesitate to commit myself to this outlook and this quest.

In his essay on "Is Life worth living?" William James concluded with these challenging words:

"Be not afraid of life. Believe that life *is* worth living, and your belief will help create the fact. The 'scientific proof' that you are right may not be clear before the day of judgment (or some stage of being which that expression may serve to symbolise) is reached. But the faithful fighters of this hour, or the beings that then and there will represent them, may then turn to the faint-hearted, who here decline to go on, with words like those with which Henry IV greeted the tardy Crillon after a great victory had been gained 'Hang yourself, brave Crillon! We fought at Arques, and you were not there.' "

WHAT IS RELIGION?

I have not so far attempted to define religion. William James spoke of it as "The feelings, acts and experiences of individual men in their solitude, so far as they apprehend themselves to stand in relation to whatever they may consider the divine." G. Galloway defined it as "Man's faith in a power beyond himself whereby he seeks to satisfy emotional needs and gain stability of life, and which he expresses in acts of worship and service." A. N. Whitehead says "Religion is the reaction of human nature to its search for God." E. D. Fawcett speaks of it as "Devotion to the most perfect reality which shows in our experience." It would be easy to multiply such definitions, but they all point to certain things. The whole man is involved: it is a total commitment which affects all the significant levels of man's living. We are challenged by what we conceive to be the Divine, and to it we make a glad response, realising that our only happiness must be in our increasing awareness of Him. I have hesitated considerably before producing the accompanying

Significant Levels of Man	Corresponding Environment	Proper Response	Way of Evolution
Spiritual	God	Worship	(Grace)
Mental	Persons	Understanding	Gnana-Yoga
Emotional		Love	Bhakti-Yoga
Aetheric	Things	Action	Kundalini-Yoga
Physical			Karma-Yoga

table. The chief danger is one of over-simplification and precision, conveying the impression that the universe with all its wonder and mystery can be intellectually grasped and that this knowledge can be filed in a system of pigeon-holes.

Such a view would be shallow in the extreme. On the other hand, if the ordinary person has ever tried to read books on the philosophy of religion, he will probably have felt the opposite danger of grasping and retaining nothing through over-generalisation. With this apology I shall use the appended table as a basis for expounding the nature of the religious way of life.

The first column recognises (for convenience of discussion only) certain levels of man. On each of these levels man participates in a whole world of phenomena. His physical body is one entity among a myriad physical objects: his mind is an entity among a myriad other entities of the mental world, and so on. There are two basic facts in this sort of analysis of man, of which I have written at length elsewhere.[1] Firstly, as we proceed upwards in our table, we are moving in the direction of increasing reality—from the more dependent to the less dependent. G. N. M. Tyrrell expressed this profoundly and concisely when he said

[1] R. C. Johnson, *The Imprisoned Splendour*. (Hodder and Stoughton Ltd., 1953.)

"There is no more fundamental way in which reality inheres in anything finite than as an *aspect* of something which lies a step nearer to the absolutely real."

Secondly, in the relations of individuals to each other there is an increasing closeness of relationship as we proceed upwards. Thus, for example, there is a considerable degree of separateness and therefore there is minimum interpenetration on the physical level, while this becomes less marked on the higher levels. The leaves and twigs of trees are both separate and conjoined, but we appreciate the increasing unity of the life which flows through them as we travel inwards towards the trunk.

The second column of the table reminds us of the most characteristic relationship with which we are concerned on different levels of ourselves. Obviously this is not the *only* relationship, for we must remember that column 1 is an artificial separation of different levels of personality which are all interrelated and interpenetrating. Thus when I say that the most characteristic relation of mind is towards another *mind* in a response of understanding, I recognise the secondary orientations which are possible towards *things* (as in scientific and psychical research), and towards God as in theology. When I say that the most important and characteristic relation of my emotional being is towards another person in a response of love, I do not preclude love of Nature or attachment to things nor such a response to the Divine.[1] The last column may seem a little esoteric to the reader who is not familiar with Indian religious thought.[2] May I therefore explain briefly that there are various ways or paths of self-discipline by which the aspirant may find his way to God. They are described as separate, but overlap in practice. The path of karma-yoga is that of "works" or action in the external world. It consists, however, of work or action not for its own sake nor for the sake of results, nor for any advantage to the doer, but regardless of the world's opinion whether of praise or blame, solely in the spirit of an offering and sacrifice to God. "You are concerned with action but not with the fruits thereof," says the Gita.

Kundalini-yoga need not concern us: few Westerners will ever practise it. It is a technique involving the practice of certain breathing rhythms designed to awaken latent psychic faculties and expand aware-

[1] If it is said that in so far as I love my neighbour, I love the Divine in my neighbour, I shall not disagree. But I am here endeavouring to clarify thought by the imperfect process of analysis. "He that loveth not his brother whom he hath seen, how can he love God whom he hath not seen?" Both are true.

[2] I use the Indian terminology because it reminds us that there are many paths to the one goal. "Yoga" comes from a Sanskrit root, from which derives also the English word "yoke". It means union or joining together, i.e. the path by which the finite self is joined to the Divine Being.

ness on a level close to the physical. Bhakti-yoga is the way of complete devotion or love. God is seen as manifesting Himself in all things and He is loved there. St. Francis in the Christian tradition and Sri Ramakrishna in the Hindu tradition would be outstanding examples of this way. Gnana-yoga is the way of the searcher after Truth. It is not academic or scientific knowledge which is effective on this path, but the deeper knowledge of life which is best called Wisdom. Finally, I have placed "Grace" in parenthesis as a reminder that on the highest levels of ourselves in virtue of which we are properly called the "children of God" (however embryonic our present development) there is no *commanding* of spiritual achievement: it is given. The spiritual self is nourished by all growth in stature on the lower levels of personality just as the body is nourished by its intake of food, but these are the conditions of spiritual growth, not the explanation of it. I think the experience of the mystics is our only guide here. From their experience we know that those high moments when the human spirit is lifted into a conscious awareness of the Divine are acts of grace for which they cannot account and which they cannot control. The centre and core of the highest form of religious experience seems to me to be such mystical expanded awareness of the Divine, which I take to be a vastly greater and more intense level of consciring. At a much higher level of our spiritual evolution I believe that such awareness will be permanent—not transient or non-existent as with most of us now. All that we ourselves can do is to aspire on this high level of our consciousness towards Him. We may do it consciously at specific times as in High Prayer, but our orientation at a sub-conscious level may be continuous.

I turn now to the meaning of the religious life on levels of mind and feeling, and this involves our relationship to persons. Here we are dealing with issues of the greatest importance to the religious outlook. We can of course treat persons with the detachment with which we deal with things. They may be treated as units in a social structure, pawns in a political game, or just employees, workers, hands, students, and so on. This is a possible attitude but not one enriching to personality. On the other hand, persons can be recognised as rills of Divine consciring like ourselves, focussing-points of consciousness of the All-Soul where, however meagre the essential development, there is the potentiality of god-likeness, even as the giant oak of the forest is hidden in the acorn. It is on this essentially human level where we view others as kindred to ourselves in thought and feeling that our greatest tensions and our greatest opportunities lie. It is for this reason that every religion has an ethical code to be a guide to what the religious life should be in action.

In Christianity we have two finely wrought parables, those of the Prodigal Son and the Good Samaritan, which summarise the essential teaching. We have that great religious document, the Sermon on the Mount, which, as often as I read it, still deeply moves me by its sublimity and by the panorama of those dazzling peaks which are presented to man as within his power to conquer.

"Ye have heard that it was said, Thou shalt love thy neighbour and hate thine enemy: but I say unto you, Love your enemies and pray for them that persecute you; that ye may be sons of your Father which is in Heaven; for He maketh the sun to rise on the evil and the good, and sendeth rain on the just and the unjust. For if ye love them that love you what reward have ye? do not even the publicans the same? And if ye salute your brothers only, what do ye more than others? do not even the Gentiles the same? Ye therefore shall be perfect as your heavenly Father is perfect."

The supreme Law of Love runs through the whole teaching of Jesus.

"This is my commandment that ye love one another even as also I have loved you."

The theme is echoed by the writers of the Epistles. It is clear to the student of comparative religions that, more than any of the great ethnic faiths, Christianity stresses the importance of right personal relations as a large part of the religious duty of man. This is understandable, for Buddhism and Hinduism have always held a different view of incarnate existence from that of the West. Believing in the constant cycle of births and deaths as a consequence of re-incarnation, the physical order is regarded as something from which it is desirable to escape. For the Buddhist, attachment to the transient things of the world is the source of all sorrow; for the Hindu it is to be immersed in unreality and *maya*. Said Gautama, "Hurt none by word or deed, be consistent in well-doing; be moderate in food, dwell in solitude, and give yourselves to meditation—this is the advice of the Buddhas."[1]

The different outlook is apparent. Although compassion and tolerance were among the highly praised virtues, the strong tendency to a world-renouncing outlook in both these religions leads on the whole to an emphasis on the solitary quest for personal salvation. In the religious quest non-attachment to the *things* of the world is to a considerable degree extended to human relations also. As we see from our table (p. 138), desire may be detached from things and persons to become focussed in aspiration towards God in His unmanifested form. No one can say how great may be the gains. All we do suggest is that on this road something is also lost,—something is disregarded which God thought worthy of creation and into the experience of which Jesus Himself entered through incarnation at Bethlehem. The "flight to God from the works of God" must always seem a strange compliment to the Creator.

[1] *The Dhammapada*, verse 185.

A right understanding of God immanent would surely help us at this point. Lawrence Hyde has expressed this viewpoint clearly:

"It is undoubtedly a perilous enterprise to centre the mind too persistently and exclusively upon high metaphysical themes—an invitation in fact to spiritual egoism. For almost inevitably more external conditions begin to appear as limited, elementary, impure and merely phenomenal, and this is fatal, for it is evidently a fundamental law of true progress that every lesser condition can be transcended only by accepting and even blessing it. In fact something even deeper is involved, for the seeker after liberation has to understand that in a mystical sense he is one in substance with all those whose horizons are more bounded than his own. . . . Whether we meet it in the East or the West, striving after personal salvation appears as a self-defeating enterprise. Safety lies only in becoming so absorbed in service to others and in the study of the mighty universe around us that—although contemplation must always have an important place in our scheme—we gradually enter into a state of 'salvation' without giving more than a minimum attention to our progress at any stage in our growth."

I accept the wisdom of this view, although I should not myself have wished to state it exclusively. It was the greatness of Buddha—if we are to believe the records—that, having through solitary disciplines found Enlightenment and being entitled to enter the supremely blissful state of consciousness called in the East Nirvana, he declined to enter it and turned back to help mankind to attain it. There may be various orders in which spiritual things may be achieved on the road to perfection. But I am sure Hyde is right when he says[1]:

"For the fact is that we emancipate ourselves from illusion not only by contemplating metaphysical ultimates, but by relating ourselves strenuously to the Divine as it shines out to us through the form of Nature and our fellow-men. Our road towards the heights lies essentially, not away from but *through* the physical universe, from which we shall only become emancipated when (in addition to achieving communion with the Within) we have mastered its mighty processes and attuned ourselves to its life."

For this reason the great Law of Love is Christianity's supreme proclamation to man, and those like Dr. Schweitzer, Father Damien, and many another who have given themselves in unremitting service of love to their fellow-men must rank with the saints of every age and faith.

If I may quote again from Lawrence Hyde:

"For the unfolding of the deeper nature 'love of the neighbour' is obviously of paramount importance, far surpassing in significance any achievement in the sphere of wisdom, aspiration or moral fortitude. For in continually transcending the bounds of his own personality the individual is modelling himself in the closest possible fashion upon the Divine Pattern."

[1] Lawrence Hyde, *The Nameless Faith*, pp. 50, 60, 156. (Rider & Co Ltd., 1950.)

So far I have said little of the direction of the mind and emotions towards things. I described this earlier as a secondary activity in contrast to the primary and characteristic direction towards persons. The mind is directed towards things as a guide to action in the world and as an effort to understand the world (in scientific and psychical research). This is not a specifically religious activity although it may be accompanied by emotions such as wonder, appreciation and even gratitude. Apart from our intellectual interest in the world, our emotional nature may itself be directed towards *things*. This may be an attitude of attachment and acquisitiveness against which all religions warn us. There is a story told of the Buddha, that there came to him a man of great wealth and great generosity, seeking his advice. Should he part with his wealth, and don the yellow robe? Gautama, observing his sincerity and that he was not attached to his possessions, replied, "I say to thee, remain in thy station in life and apply thyself with diligence to thy enterprises. It is not life and wealth and power that enslave men, but their attachment to life and wealth and power."

There is, however, a different attitude to things which we cannot describe either as attachment or non-attachment. It is one which finds them sacramental. In this attitude objects are not valued because they are possessed, or de-valued and set aside because they might be the basis of temptation, they are accepted as revealing something in finite terms of the infinite Imagination. Thus Wordsworth could say:

> To me the meanest flower that blows can give
> Thoughts that do often lie too deep for tears.

The endless process of the Seasons, the beauty hidden in unlikely places, the ceaseless flow of Nature's pageantry, were for Wordsworth a "mighty sum of things for ever speaking". On every level of the cosmos the sensitive spirit can be aware of the interpenetrating divinity, but how much we find depends on the measure of our development. Even so, great Love may for a time open blind eyes and reveal the unsuspected sacramental quality of the world, as a poet sings[1]:

> What wind brings to the lagging sail
> Rain to the drooping flower,
> Sweet fire
> And the broken bread
> And song's peace
> To the lonely hour
> You bring,
> And blithely, to your kind
> You come and lo!

[1] Harry Lee, *To a Friend*, 1924.

143

The sail is spread,
The flower dances in the sun,
The heart leaps heavenward
Like flame—
And God is in the broken bread.

Notice how the enrichment of personality through love is the occasion of revelation. Notice also the sequence: things, persons, God, and the profundity of Martin Buber's insight,[1] "The primary word I-Thou can be spoken only with the whole being . . . All real living is meeting."

Finally, let us turn back to our analytical table, and there we see that as incarnate beings we live in an environment of things which compels us to respond to it by action. Whether we attach great value to works or none at all, it is obvious that to some extent we are compelled to act. We must eat to live, and we must work to eat. Beyond this minimum, by their philosophy of life, men divide themselves into two groups, the world-affirmers and the world-negators. By and large, the West has been world-affirming and the East world-denying, although so sweeping a generalisation as this must have many notable exceptions. It all depends on the value attached to incarnate existence and the ends which it is believed to serve whether works are judged to be important or not. I am not, however, suggesting that these considerations enter into the minds of the majority of mankind who preserve traditions they have never seriously questioned.

Apart from this unconsidered attitude, people may be world-affirming and enter fully into the life of action for several reasons. They may say, "This is the only world we are sure of: let us make the most of it." This "most" may lead to pleasure-seeking, to adventure, to the fight for power, fame, or wealth, according to the temper of the individual. Others with a keen sense of moral obligation may say, "This is a testing ground for character, the battleground of good and evil: I must try to help the world." Others with keen sensitivity and insight see Beauty breaking through from deeper levels and they make it their business to unveil it. These are the artists, poets, and mystics.

On the other hand, persons may be world-negating for various reasons. There are perhaps two chief groups (not mutually exclusive). Some say, "All existence is sorrow. All life is a flux of change and transience. If we attach ourselves by desire to things and persons and situations here, they will pass away and we shall only feel bereft. What does action lead to? For the most part it is a round of trivialities, but even its most striking achievements are all evanescent and the stream of time carries them into oblivion. Let us escape from it to the Within where alone true joys are to be found." Others are world-negating not

[1] Martin Buber, *I and Thou*, p. 11. (T. and T. Clark Ltd., 1937. Trs. R. G. Smith.)

because they find the physical world intolerable but because they regard it as illusory. It is a dream from which the wise man will try to awake. There are other significant levels of the world, more real and more satisfying, and the wise man will therefore sell all lesser pearls to buy a pearl of greater price. Such are hermits and fakirs, ascetics, yogis, and contemplatives.

Although Christianity is on the whole decidedly world-affirming, we must not overlook the phases of world-denial characteristic of the Desert Fathers in the third and fourth centuries, and of the development of Monasticism and Puritanism; and although Buddhism is on the whole decidedly world-denying we must bear in mind what Tagore[1] has said:

"The preaching of the Buddha in India was not followed by stagnation of life, as would surely have happened if humanity was without any positive goal and his teaching was without any permanent value in itself. On the contrary we find the arts and sciences springing up in its wake, institutions started for alleviating the misery of all creatures, human and non-human, and great centres of education founded. . . . And that power came into its full activity only by the individual being made conscious of his infinite worth."

I think we are slowly emerging from the attitude of mind which supposes one religious viewpoint wholly right and another largely wrong: from the innocence or intolerance which supposes that because you were born in London or Edinburgh you can rejoice in the truth, whereas if you had been born in Benares or Bangkok you would have suffered under error. There are many ways to God the All-compassionate, and He has many children. His saints are not confined to one country or one race. What is surely required of us all is that we follow the light we have with sincerity and devotion, always looking for more illumination.

With this basic acknowledgment made, I go on to express my own conviction that the value of works is largely in the spirit of the doer; that the life of action is primarily valuable in that it offers us a succession of spiritual opportunities; that the occasion of incarnate existence is given to us, not to be despised, but that we may enter as fully as possible into it and offer service of love to our fellows; that in spite of its tensions and conflicts and frustrations there is wonder and beauty and mystery everywhere for those who have eyes to see.

Perhaps I can best say what Christianity is by describing the Christian man. He is not sanctimonious, nor is the word "God" always on his lips: he prefers to treasure it in his heart. He does not have a solemn countenance: he creates wherever he is the happiness that he has in

[1] Rabindranath Tagore, *Creative Unity*, p. 73. (Macmillan & Co. Ltd.)

being and the goodwill which he feels towards all who are sharing with him the great adventure of life. He has a keen sense of humour which he uses to cheer the downhearted: it is never forced or unkind, but over-flows from a fount of joy within. He sees the spark of good in the least likely people: and they often leave his presence inwardly surprised that they have potentialities they had never recognised. He sees the evil also, but of this he does not speak. Where a fellow human being has need of help, he is the first to offer assistance: he can be counted upon, he need not be asked. He does not spare himself. He is kind without ostentation, loving without sentimentality, and charming without knowing it. He is the rock on which others lean their weariness, the strength to which others trust their weakness. No fear can daunt him: with equal serenity he will win through or go down fighting, knowing beyond any per-adventure that "All is well".

ORGANISED CHRISTIANITY: THE CHURCHES

We make a strange transition in passing from the nature of personal religion to the nature of organised religion. We seem to enter a different world. That fine fervour which lifted men's eyes to undreamed-of horizons and set men's pulses throbbing with the wonder of a new spring-time of Divine revelation, that conviction and enthusiasm which drove Saul of Tarsus round the Mediterranean world and sent the early Christians singing to their death, became the Church. Professor Emil Brunner said recently[1]:

"The *ecclesia* of the New Testament is precisely not what every Church, at least in some degree is—an institution. It is a fellowship of persons and nothing else."

The Institution grew: it became respectable and then powerful. It made and unmade kings; it ruled with temporal power for centuries. It acquired vast properties and wealth. It instigated wars: it was merciless in persecuting those who did not accept its orthodoxy. In spite of all this, it never failed to nourish its saints, as long as they did not think too freely, and it kept alive the flame of private charity, culture, and educa-tion through dark ages. It is perhaps as unprofitable as it is saddening to draw back the curtain of history very far; let all honest men ponder the thought that the brightest aspirations of mankind may always be corroded by the acids of power and worldliness.

It is, I think, a debatable issue whether Christianity has gained or lost more by its incorporation in vast organised Churches. When Paul wrote to Philemon, he referred to "the church in thy house". This group-fellowship must have offered to its members the enriching values

[1] *Vide* J. H. Oldham, *loc. cit.*, p. 92.

of inter-personal relationship, and must equally have been a focussing point of service and good works. With no priest to accept responsibility, its lay members had to shoulder this, or know that the group would fail and vanish; and with no canons of belief to subscribe to, its members were free to follow the guiding of the inner light. The Society of Friends probably comes closer to the primitive tradition at this point than any of the organised Churches.

It can of course be urged on the other hand that there would be precariousness of existence about small separate groups; that without organisation there could be no united voice of Christianity in the state. It will also be urged that historical traditions and teaching might not have been preserved, and that innumerable variations of essential belief might have arisen. All of these points have weight, and have sustained the Churches in being: but at a great price. Responsibility is not greatly shared by ordinary lay people: we have largely the ecclesiastical "welfare state". The organisation itself demands much time and money to preserve its very being, and this reduces the amount which is available to serve the *ends* which called it into being. Moreover, a large organisation is exposed to certain dangers arising from power, prestige, and influence which small groups can never be called upon to face.

I propose to examine these dangers in some detail, since the analysis should disclose why the Churches as we know them today do not have the support and confidence of the great majority of the community.

(1) The first danger I shall call the danger of professionalism. In the ranks of its priesthood or ministry every Church has some first-class minds, men of great ability and vision. Even more important, it has many men of great devotion who are idealistic, self-sacrificing, and often overworked. Some of these are my personal friends. Each priesthood or ministry has unfortunately not a few "camp-followers" who neither as men nor as clergymen measure up to the expectations of the ordinary person. Such men have generally settled down to maintain the traditions of ritual and practice into which they have entered. They are out of touch with real life. They see things only from the standpoint of how they will affect their Church: they have lost a wider vision. The many currents of thought and idealism which are moving and working to high ends—if outside the fold of the Church—are viewed with suspicion. Unfortunately, such men are in the public mind more often taken as typical of clergymen than their sincere, abler, and self-sacrificing brethren.

I have already referred to the other danger of professionalism, viz. that lay responsibility is greatly diminished within the Church. Outside the Church it gives rise to a tendency to discount the sincerity and disinterestedness of a clergyman's views with the knowledge that he is "expected" to say these things. It is only fair to say that the keenest minds within the Church are perhaps the most distressed by all this. Thus, writing of honesty in religion, Principal John Oman has said[1]:

"No other sphere is so liable to misuse. Religious professions provide the largest scope for hypocrisy; religious creeds for enslaving the mind to forms: religious duties for what may be fanciful or fanatical. This is no more proof that religion is either unreal or unprofitable than the growing of weeds disproves the existence or value of good soil."

(2) The second danger of a large organisation is conservatism. "An irrational conservation," says Fawcett, "is the bane of the institutional religions." I have prefaced this chapter with quotations from Professor A. N. Whitehead and the late Principal John Oman. The latter, one of the ablest theologians of our time, has spoken in unmistakable terms of this danger of settling in finalities. The Pauline phrase about "the truth once for all delivered to the saints" is one of the most unfortunate that great man ever uttered. If any religion is living, it means that the Spirit of God is still working through it and using it. The activity of Divine Imagining manifests the twin aspects of conservation and creative novelty. The Churches are far too prone to accept the former and reject the latter. This is in such notable contrast with Divine activity in all other fields of man's concern. Take science for example. There is a profound sense in which discovery on man's part is the complement of revelation on God's part. It is because imagining in men is a rill of the great Source.

There is a big element of conservation in scientific knowledge, but this is not why the thoughts and gaze of men are today turned in this direction. It is because every day new visions are coming to birth: creative novelty is being realised. It is not too much to say that organised religion is little esteemed because it is out of touch with the *Zeitgeist*. It seems to be a thing apart, unmoved by the tides of inspiration which are fascinating the man in the street as he looks at the story of scientific achievement and expectation. It need not be so if the Church had courage. But it will be a very radical courage that is necessary: perhaps even the courage to die in order that it may be re-born into new life. I shall not attempt here to outline what all this implies in the realm of thought and action, but will merely add that a wider and indeed universal outlook is crucial to the springing up of this new life. Some words of Lawrence Hyde[2] convey this concern:

"Let us here frankly recognise that every religious cult, large or small, constitutes a zone of psychological suggestion, a medium which at one and the same time envelops the faithful in a sphere of warmth and security and

---

[1] John Oman, *Honest Religion*, p. 32. (C.U.P., 1941.)   [2] *Loc. cit.*, pp. 104-5.

excludes them no less definitely from alien inspirations and satisfactions. . . .
The individual whose existence is passed within such a realm is to a far
greater degree than he usually suspects, conditioned in his responses. He
exists in the sphere of a selective tradition. He studies certain scriptures
which have been isolated for him by his mentors from out of the scriptures
of the world. He is made familiar with one restricted type of symbolism. . . .
He is instructed by teachers who draw their inspirations from a limited
literature. He soon comes to emphasise evidence of a particular type at the
expense of a wider range of data. . . . After a few years the universal man
within him becomes overlaid and stifled by the devotee, the adherent, the
follower, the dutiful believer, the crusader—and the seeds of separation are
fatally sown within his soul."

For my own part I should be prepared to say to the would-be
member of a Christian Church (in words which are a slight variation of
St. Augustine's), "Love Christ, and think what you will. Endeavour to
apply His spirit, as you apprehend it, to every part of your own life,
and build your belief out of your experience."

I would like to inscribe over every church and temple the words of
Lord Balfour:

> Our highest truths are but half-truths,
> Think not to settle down for ever in any truth.
> Make use of it as a tent in which to pass a Summer's night,
> But build no house of it, or it will be your tomb.
> When you first have an inkling of its insufficiency
> And begin to descry a dim counter-truth looming up beyond,
> Then weep not, but give thanks:
> It is the Lord's voice whispering,
> "Take up thy bed and walk."[1]

(3) The third great danger is Authoritarianism. Oman has pointed
out that there are two attitudes to life and history that are very relevant
to religious organisations.

On the one hand is the attitude that it is of supreme importance that
a system of beliefs and a code of conduct believed to be right by the
Church shall be generally accepted and carried out. A powerful Church
securing this is therefore an end in itself. The other contrasting attitude
is that belief is of no value unless it is freely adopted as a matter of
personal conviction, and good conduct has no merit that is not the free
expression of dedicated service. For such, the motive is all-important,
and the Church is a means to an end. For my own part I am whole-
heartedly associated with the latter group. Oman has expressed this
eloquently:[2]

[1] Lines of Arthur James Balfour, first Earl of Balfour.
[2] *Loc. cit.*, pp. 17-18.

"How we measure security depends on whether we think a truth is held when none dare gainsay it, or right [is] right when none dare do otherwise; or that truth is truth for us only as we see it to be true, and right only as we judge it to be right. In short is either truth or right ever truly or rightly possessed except in freedom? . . . .

"If however the sole perfect order is knowing God's truth of our own insight and doing God's will of our own discernment and joyful consecration, and that what distinguishes children of God from mere works of God is just search for truth however imperfect, and aspiration after righteousness however inadequate, we can have some understanding of the need for the painful and wandering way man has had to travel, with its errors and its sins, its divisions and its conflicts."

The fact is that Belief, like Love, cannot be compelled. Life declares its character to us through joy and suffering, through prosperity and adversity, through love and service, through quietness and meditation, and the only belief-system which is worth the having is that which we have made our own in these experiences. Creeds and confessions of faith such as all the Churches preserve are maps and charts to the serious thinker, and to the large majority who are incapable of creative thought they may be a necessary and useful anchorage. The true Church should not say, "These are our maps and charts; they represent a lot of enquiry and exploration by wiser people than you. We consider them to be well-nigh infallible: they are hundreds of years old. Study them at home in our safe anchorage." It should rather say, "There is the open sea of spiritual experience and questing. Take our maps and charts with you, they represent the experience of others before you, but help us to keep them up to date."

Unfortunately, history has shown that creeds and confessions of faith have seldom been regarded in this way. All too often they have been touchstones of orthodoxy, and the claim to freedom of thought has usually been followed by persecution for heresy. It might be thought rather cynical to suggest that the only certain lesson we learn from history is that the lessons of history are never learned.

I prefer to think that we are slowly (but Oh! how slowly) moving towards an outlook where men will be more concerned to discover truth than defend tradition. How can new truth ever be received by men whose pre-suppositions are that we have already attained finality? Or how today can we respect a spirit which turns away from the search for knowledge to protect an attitude of faith?

It is a situation so much at variance with the spirit of free enquiry and research in every other department of thought that it is perhaps the most important single factor alienating the support of many intellectuals from the Churches. It may be thought that I am exaggerating.

I shall therefore quote without comment from the Gifford Lectures[1] of the late Archbishop William Temple, who was widely and justly regarded as a most distinguished theologian and churchman:

"For these reasons it seems to me, so far as I can judge, positively undesirable that there should be experimental proof of man's survival of death. For this would bring the hope of immortality into the area of purely intellectual apprehension. It might or might not encourage the belief that God exists; it would certainly, as I think, make very much harder the essential business of faith, which is the transference of the centre of interest and concern from self to God. If such knowledge comes, it must be accepted, and we must try to use it for good and not for evil. And I could never urge the cessation of enquiry in any direction; I cannot ask that so-called Psychical Research should cease. But I confess I hope that such research will continue to issue in such dubious results as are all that I am able to trace to it."

I have pointed out these dangerous tendencies operative in the life of the Churches because I believe that only in so far as they are recognised and strenuously fought can the Churches be more effective instruments of Divine activity in this new and thrilling Age on which we are entering.

When all these things have been said and pondered, no fair-minded person can fail to appreciate the value of the work some of the Churches are doing in our society. They are proclaiming, however inadequately, that "good news of God" which, where it is accepted, lifts the horizon of life above the commonplace and trivial round to eternal things. Without the devoted and self-sacrificing labour of many of its ministers, vast areas of social and personal need would be untouched and unredeemed. If churches were to vanish completely tomorrow, standards would slowly fall, and within a couple of generations men would find themselves coming together again to start a new Church. I am not in agreement with some ecclesiastics who think that outside the Church there are no Christians. Far from it. I am confident, however, human nature being at the stage it is, that *for the majority* of people the alternatives are at present such religion as the Church can assist to foster, or very little religion at all.

May I conclude on this personal note. After twenty years abroad I recently revisited England, wandered through her little hamlets and sat down at times to feel the quietness of many an old village church. There on summer mornings, with no sound filtering through the deep-set glass windows except the occasional rustle of wind through the leaves, the church clock with its leisurely tick-tock reminded me of the tale of the centuries. To this place, while thrones had tottered and

[1] William Temple, *Nature, Man and God*, pp. 458-9. (Macmillan & Co. Ltd., 1935.)

dynasties fallen, country folk had trudged through winter snows and summer sunshine. Here had been brought the human burden, and here it had been lightened. The grey walls spoke the ancient tale of births and marriages and deaths through immemorial years. Even though in that hour a little sentiment may have coloured the mind, who would not pray for such a place—that its years may not fail and its comfort may not cease?

THE SIGNIFICANCE OF JESUS

It is not easy to speak of Jesus in measured terms, for since the days when He walked the hills of Galilee, the meditations of mystics, the reflections of saints and scholars, the efforts of creed-makers, and the worship of untold millions of people have lifted the picture of His person above the level where unfettered judgment is possible. I have no special qualifications, nor, as a student in other fields, have I any desire to enter into controversy on the sources of our knowledge of Him, or the nature of His person. Christianity, however, has now become so inseparably bound up with the *person* of its founder that the intelligent layman has to form an opinion about Jesus if he is to adopt an attitude to Christianity. He can only do so on the strength of the scriptures as translated, and the expositions he has heard or read over the years. What follows is therefore a personal reaction, the little bit of truth I can see at present.

It appears to be the opinion of a majority of competent scholars that there has been preserved for us a "nucleus of factual happenings of which we can be reasonably assured". While recognising this historic basis, scholars are apparently divided on the question, "Do we have in the Synoptic Gospels, in the main, an authentic portrait of the real Jesus, or have imported theological interpretations so distorted the picture that the real man has been lost under the dogmatic vestments?"[1]

To the plain man, as distinct from the scholar, I don't think this is a vital matter. There does emerge from the reading of the Gospels a portrait of a man in whom love and wisdom seemed to be perfectly blended, a man of great spiritual insight whose life illustrated the high quality of His teaching, one who loved His fellows and gave ceaseless help and guidance to them, so that looking at this portrait all down the centuries men have said, "This was a perfect man." The historic accuracy of the portrait is far less important to most of us than the fact that a truly "Enlightened" man did live on earth, and that the power of His influence is still profoundly felt in the experience of men today.

[1] W. R. Matthews, *The Problem of Christ in the Twentieth Century*, p. 10. (O.U.P., 1950.)

Because He had reached Enlightenment, what He has to tell us about God, not only in what He said but in what He was, is of great value and importance. This kind of knowledge is a function of being; it can only come to us through those rare souls whose spiritual nature is so highly developed that their consciousness of God is clear and continuous. Perhaps the most important thing He revealed to us is that God is love. It is a truth which many appearances in the world seem to obscure, if not deny. Mankind might have struggled along through countless millennia before discovering it otherwise. In its implications for mankind, and in the formulation of a philosophy of life, it is supremely important knowledge.

In Schleiermacher's phrase, Jesus was fully "God-conscious", and the quality of His life is so outstanding that, considering it, men have said, "This is a revelation of what God is like, so far as it can be shown within the limits of a human personality." To believe in Jesus Christ is to believe that the foundation-principle of the world is Love joined with Wisdom.

It is because it seems to me Jesus so adequately revealed the nature of God, *so far as it has practical relevance to man's situation*, that I reject as completely in error all interpretations of the crucifixion which contrast a just and righteous God demanding "propitiation" or "ransom" or "sacrifice" with Jesus who in His compassion for humanity was prepared to offer His own life. These are obviously misguided theories of devout Jews. The truth seems to me to be that Jesus, just as much in His death as in His life, was revealing to us the nature of God. His death was the inevitable end of the kind of life He had lived, constantly challenging the hypocrisy and legalism of the ecclesiastical power of His day. When a man lives for a truth, he must be prepared if necessary to die for it. No one can do more. The ironic tragedy of the death of Jesus lay in the fact that the best man the world has known was brought to His end by the wickedness of the religious leaders of His day. The significance of the event may be inexhaustible, but these things at least emerge:

(1) That in it Jesus entered the fellowship of all suffering humanity.

(2) That He revealed the nature of God by making a perfect reaction to this tragic situation.

(3) That by His resurrection He symbolically as well as literally proclaimed His invincibility and the ultimate triumph of Love.

I do not think there is any sense in which it is true to say that "He bore our sins" except in the familiar sense that when we are bound in ties of love with others, their successes and failures, their troubles and sorrows and sins are sympathetically shared by us. We feel them as our own. In this sense Jesus bore the sin of humanity, but certainly not in some magical sense which implies He bore them *instead* of us. To abstract sin from persons sinning inevitably leads to bad theology.[1] The obvious thing about sin is that it is not a burden that can be detached, it is a defective state of being in which my personality is cut off from access to the higher levels. In religious language, I am "alienated from God". The process of at-one-ment or redemption (as it may be called if it is looked at from the viewpoint of the higher levels) is the restoration of this channel of communication or relationship. It is certainly not a process of exemption from the consequences of sin. These consequences have to be met and faced inevitably, sometime, somewhere, but with the reinforcement and "grace" flowing from the high self, they can be faced and dealt with when they arise, courageously and for ever.

Let us return to consider the person of Jesus. Dr. Matthews says[2]:

"From the earliest time the person of Jesus was central in the religion of the Church, though the attribution of divinity to Him was not explicitly made at the beginning. Even St. Paul, I think, nowhere definitely equates Jesus Christ with God."

It is clear that by the time St. John's gospel was written this equation was approaching, and from then onwards the Church's theologians were concerned with two difficult tasks: (1) reconciling worship of the Divine Son with mono-theism—the legacy of Judaism; and (2) reconciling the two natures of Jesus: on the one hand His human nature as our brother, tempted as we are; on the other hand His divine nature in which He is an object of worship.

The doctrine of the Trinity was the Church's answer to the first of these problems, and the doctrine of the two natures or "hypostatic union" was the answer to the second. Both orthodox "solutions" are surrounded by a cloud of heresies from which they are carefully differentiated. It is the second of these issues which concerns us at the moment. Dr. Matthews says of the doctrine of two natures that "it leaves us with so many difficulties that we must regard it not as a final word, but as a starting-point for further reflection". He gives as an illustration of such difficulties the controversy whether there are two different wills in Jesus Christ or only one.

Is it unreasonable to suggest that the difficulties are so numerous and insoluble because the original assumption of two natures, human and divine, is itself at fault? Surely there is only one "ground-plan" or

[1] The essence of sinning I take to be the conscious choice of a lower way when a higher way is recognised.
[2] *Loc. cit.*, p. 22.

principle of construction which constitutes individuality and relates the Many to the One. Let me try to express this as simply as I can.

Human personality is a synthesis of many significant "levels" or principles. Those which we have touched upon already and for convenience labelled as physical, aetheric, and mento-emotional constitute in man what are sometimes called the "personality". These principles in modern man are all reasonably developed, although the last-named may differ considerably in its quality in different persons. There are, however, higher levels in man which constitute his permanent soul. These are his centre of consciring and his higher bodies. The latter are in most people ill-developed—even embryonic, in the sense that consciring in them is at a low irreflective level. It is in order to raise this level, so that in the end the highest body may become the perfect vehicle of the soul with full reflective consciring, that incarnations are normally undertaken. We shall discuss this in Chapters 8 and 9. From time to time our earth has known great souls to whom the words "Christ-like" have seemed the greatest tribute that we could pay. With such a conception of the nature of man, Jesus stands so far as we can see at the pinnacle of man's achievement. His permanent soul was so fully developed that His personality was its perfect instrument of expression on Earth. He was conscious of His sonship, i.e. of His Higher Self as being a member of the Divine Society and therefore one with God. "I and my Father are one". "My meat is to do the will of Him that sent me".

His incarnation, so far as we know, was unique in this, that it was not undertaken in the interests of His own development but out of compassion to aid ours.[1]

Wherever there is a human being, there is a germ of this God-consciousness, however rudimentary. This is evolving in all souls who are aspiring, and our destiny is in St. Paul's words to "attain unto a full-grown man, unto the measure of the stature of the fullness of Christ". In another inspired passage the same author writes, "The Spirit himself beareth witness with our spirit, that we are children of God: and if children then heirs; heirs of God and joint-heirs with Christ". When we examine ourselves, the goal may seem very far off and our attainment small, yet I cannot help but feel that it is better to keep looking hopefully forward than sadly backwards with faces appropriate to our status as "miserable sinners". In this I am sure we should have His encouragement and blessing.

Of the Father to whom Jesus felt so close related I shall venture with great respect to say something in Chapter 7.

[1] I am aware of course of the Bhoddisatva ideal of Buddhism and Oriental teaching of the existence of Nirmanakaya Buddhas.

CHRISTIANITY AND THE PLAIN MAN

Much that I have discussed in the three preceding sections may not interest the plain man, and he, after all, is the backbone of our society. I do not think anyone would claim today that religion is fully meeting his needs, or even that he is concerned with this fact. Previously I expressed my opinion that the general attitude to organised religion is largely one of indifference and seldom of antagonism. I do not think it is at all just to the majority of people to suggest that the ethical demands of religion are such that they are not prepared to try to meet them and that therefore they deliberately turn away. The major cause of indifference is rather that organised religion has never seemed to them very relevant to ordinary life, and further that many church-members do not practise what they profess to believe, or give evidence of the value of their religious affiliations in everyday life. Yet I am convinced that there is a widespread hunger for a satisfying "philosophy of life", for some reliable anchorage, whether it is thought of as "re-ligious" or not, which will help to make sense of life, which will show people how to live better and how to find inner peace while doing so.

A living and vital religion ought, broadly speaking, to do two things for the plain man. It should be related to his tasks in everyday life, to the workshop, office, or factory in which he earns his daily bread. It should also set his life in the context of a greater whole so that the crises which overtake him—accident, suffering, disease, loss, and finally death—can be faced with serenity and fortitude because they are believed to be part of a meaningful pattern.

I must be honest and say that on the whole I consider organised religion today is not adequately meeting either of these needs. To many within the Church it is doubtless helpful and satisfying. To the large majority of the population it makes no contribution. I have only one conviction in relation to all these matters, and it is that the things which Jesus Christ taught are still most relevant to our day, and that the quality of life which He exemplified is still our deepest need. This being so, what can be done to bring the Christian Church, which is the historic vehicle of Christianity, into living touch with the majority of ordinary men and women? I do not think special missions and campaigns will make any substantial difference to the existing situation, but that only a long-term policy of a fundamental character holds the possibility of success. I should not expect everyone to agree with the suggestions below, but I am encouraged by words of Dr. John Oman[1]:

"As the Church should never be the end, but is only the very imperfect means for realising on Earth the Fellowship of the Spirit, we should not even

[1] John Oman, *Honest Religion*, p. 173. (C.U.P., 1941.)

try to persuade ourselves that its limitations and failures are other than limitations and failures, even if they may seem to be ecclesiastical excellencies."

(1) The Church of the future should interpret *in modern terms* the significance of the teaching of Jesus Christ for our day. The canon of the New Testament will always be a priceless book of reference both in relation to the historical background and the experience and development of thought in the early Church, and it will not cease to be an inspiration for questing man today. But the climate of thought in which its writings came into being is vastly different from our own; the symbolism and antique modes of expression are quite alien to the modern outlook. Saints though they were, the writers of these books were fallible men, and a theology which satisfied their minds in the early centuries cannot be expected to meet modern needs, nor need it be the basis of modern preaching. "He that hath an ear, let him hear what the Spirit saith to the Churches" *today*.

(2) The Church of the Future should revise its creeds, and all narrow canons of orthodoxy should go. The Dean of St. Paul's said recently[1]:

"The original creed of the Church, it seems, was the simple formula 'Jesus is Lord'. With this watchword the Church achieved the first and decisive expansion of Christianity into the pagan world. In my opinion that earliest creed should have remained the sole doctrinal test for membership, and the greatest misfortune which followed from the Christological disputes was the substitution of the criterion of acceptance of a set of theological propositions by which to judge a genuine Christian, for that which Jesus Himself laid down for His disciples 'by their fruits ye shall know them'."

When I look at the creeds of Nicaea and Athanasius, the Roman decrees of Trent, the Thirty-Nine Articles of the Church of England, or the Westminster Confession, I enthusiastically agree with the words of Dr. Matthews. It must always seem strange to the ordinary man that formulae of exclusion should operate to keep persons who could sincerely say, "Jesus for me is Lord", out of the Church which claims to be His body.

I believe also that the Church of the Future will cease to claim that there is only one way to God. The saints and mystics of all the great religious faiths have everything in common in their attainment although the ways they have travelled to it are different. The ecumenical move-

[1] W. R. Matthews, *The Problem of Christ in the Twentieth Century*, p. 24. (O.U.P. 1950.)

ment which is today bringing together in growing goodwill the many branches of the Christian Church should extend the same hand of understanding and fellowship to all those who devote themselves to the service of the one God according to the light they have.[1]

(3) The two preceding suggestions concern reform of outlook; this concerns re-vitalisation from within. Where are the Mystics in the Church today: men who can speak to us with the only real authority which springs from a conscious awareness of the Divine within? They have never been numerous, but today they seem very few and far between. The Roman Church through its contemplative orders nourishes a few: in the Protestant Churches I fear that they are rare. The Church of the Future will be re-vitalised not only by its Mystics but by a much greater proportion of its members finding a real touch with at least the fringe of such living experience and becoming less dependent on sermons and meetings.

It will also be re-vitalised by the recovery of lost knowledge, so that low-prayer will be scientifically practised, and healing through non-material means undertaken with knowledge. The "communion of saints" will not exclude the communication of saints in which persons here may from time to time be in touch with those on higher levels of being.

(4) The Church of the Future will not, I think, recognise one vocation as sacred and another as secular. It will have its ordained men and women in factory and workshop, business and trades-unions, sometimes as "workers", sometimes as executives, indistinguishable in their outward appearance from others, but distinguished by the quality of their living and each therefore a radiant focus of the good life. Cells or groups, having the bond of similar daily work, will grow round such persons, gathering together in spiritual questing at other times. As groups they will both study and worship together and make their impact within their daily environment. Individual churches in the big centres of population will be fewer and a man who is ordained to this responsibility will be chosen alone for his spiritual development and wisdom. He will be the spiritual guide and consultant of all who seek his help. He will call on the specialised and technical knowledge of his colleagues in all walks of life where this will help him. The small churches which serve country areas will be wholly run by groups of devoted laymen and women.

I shall not attempt, nor have I the qualifications, to work out the pattern of things to come: I am content to suggest that the Church needs to plan along new lines if it is to make an impact on the common man, which at present it is not doing.

[1] Cf. *Eastern Religions and Western Thought:* Radhakrishnan, pp. 296-7. (O.U.P.)

There is no easy way to this end, and certainly no quick way. Each of us meanwhile must, in J. H. Oldham's words,

"do what he can to transform that sector of reality, small or large, which lies within the reach of his influence in accordance with what seems to him truth and right, and trust the incalculable future to a wisdom and love infinitely greater than his own."

Chapter

7

THE NATURE OF GOD

O Lord, pardon me three sins.
I have in contemplation clothed in form Thee who art formless.
I have described Thee Who art ineffable.
And in visiting temples I have ignored Thy omnipresence.

SAMKARA (A.D. 788-820)

Still creating, still inspiring,
Never of thy creatures tiring;
Artist of thy solar spaces;
And thy humble human faces;
Mighty glooms and splendours voicing;
In thy plastic work rejoicing;
Through benignant law connecting
Best with best—and all perfecting,
Though all human races claim thee,
Thought and language fail to name thee,
Mortal lips be dumb before thee
Silence only may adore thee!

CHRISTOPHER PEARSE CRANCH (1813-1892)

ANYONE attempting to write about the nature of God must be acutely aware of the presumption of his undertaking. A microbe seeking to understand man might have a less difficult task than man seeking to understand God. And yet we have a little fragment of mind which we believe to be in some sense akin to the Mind which created and sustains the world around us, else how could we perceive and appreciate it at all? Even more important is the belief that we ourselves, the knowers, the lovers, the worshippers, the aspirers, are in our inmost selves akin to the Divine. Perhaps, therefore, there may be some sense in which "the drop may declare the ocean" or try to do so.

The historic attempts show how difficult, if not impossible, it is for man to rise above anthropomorphic concepts. Man found himself on Earth in the midst of conflict between good and evil, light and darkness, truth and error, and by a process of universalising he created dualism in its many forms. The Chinese had their two contending principles Yang and Yin, the Persians had Ahura Mazda and Ahriman, and philosophers have had their own dualities.

The mysterious powers of Nature, being beyond man's understanding or control, were regarded as controlled by superior beings, and thus arose polytheism. This has ranged in its forms from the crudity of primitive animism to the artistically elaborate pantheons of Slav, Celt,

Teuton, Indian, and Greek. It is abundantly clear that here man has conceived of gods in his own image.

Pantheism is, strictly speaking, a conception ranging between polytheism and monotheism. In its lower form the conception of a hierarchy of gods is introduced with one supreme god at the apex. There is a transition from this towards monotheism where there is only one God, and the so-called divine beings are personified *aspects* of the One. There is also a higher mystical pantheism of which the formula is that God is all, and this inevitably leads to the conception of degrees of reality in the universe, or to some distinction between appearance and reality, in order to account for evil.

We have finally the monotheistic concepts. In the form of Deism, God was creator of Man and Nature, but He is transcendent and not involved in their affairs. In the form of Christian Theism God is both transcendent and immanent. Man and Nature depend on God but are not to be identified with Him. There are many other variants of man's views about God, and it is probably unwise to have tried to compress into a few inadequate sentences views on which many learned books have been written. These sentences are not intended to do more than remind the general reader that for many centuries men's minds have wrestled with the ultimate mystery—the world ground from which everything springs.

I shall endeavour now to present a brief summary of the Christian view of God, and then to express some difficulties which current conceptions hold for me. Finally—and this is the essential contribution of the chapter—I shall endeavour to present a view of God as Divine Imagining, together with some deductions from this viewpoint which remove my difficulties.

THE CHRISTIAN VIEW OF GOD

The Christian view of God is potentially a growing one because it is capable of enrichment by the developing experience of men. It is based fundamentally upon the teaching of Jesus about God, both as to what He said and what He was. Jesus Himself had as the background of His teaching the conceptions of the Old Testament prophets who through many stages had arrived at a high ethical monotheism. To them God embodied perfect holiness, righteousness, love, and constancy. He made known His purposes in history, being active in the events of men, where He was just, yet full of loving-kindness. Jesus built upon this foundation.

The teaching of Jesus was essentially practical rather than philosophical in its character. It offered men sufficient knowledge for the essential business of living. The most distinctive element in the Christian view of God was, however, added by the reflection and meditation of the early Church, and it is found in the New Testament writers: God is like Jesus. Within the limits of human personality Jesus presented qualities which accurately reflect the nature of God. In addition Greek thought has certainly contributed to the Christian view of God as it is held today, and we must add the following affirmations.

(1) God is the creator of the Universe, and Omnipotent. He both created it and sustains it, and it is therefore dependent on Him. He is sovereign and over-rules its evolution. It is not orthodox to regard the Universe as created from the substance of God Himself: this is pantheism, viz. "God is all". It is orthodox to say that God created the Universe by an act of Will out of nothing.

(2) God is Spirit, Omnipresent and Omniscient. To say that God is omnipresent is not the same as pantheism, which asserts that God is everything. There is a difference between saying "God is in me" and "God is me". (The grammar may be pardoned for the sake of emphasis.)

(3) The moral attributes of God at which Hebrew thought had arrived are also a part of Christian belief. God is perfect in Holiness, in Wisdom, and in Love. By holiness is not only meant transcendence and unapproachability, but even more, supreme goodness. By wisdom is meant perfection of knowledge and the over-ruling of all events for the highest ends. Love includes compassion and a redeeming activity.

> Only Thou art Holy; there is none beside Thee
> Perfect in power, in love, and purity.

(4) The hymn of Heber's from which I have just quoted has another line:

> God in Three Persons, blessèd Trinity.

This expresses in its Augustinian form the orthodox belief held by the Church since the fifth century about the being of God. Once the deity of Jesus Christ was accepted by the Church, the preservation of monotheism required a very careful statement. The Athanasian creed says, "We worship one God in Trinity, and Trinity in Unity." As to the interpretation of this, there is no unanimity of opinion. Dr. William Temple wrote of "Three centres of one consciousness". Dr. Rashdall suggested that it is a "Trinity of Power, Wisdom, and Love". St. Augustine wrote of "Him that loves, that which is loved, and love". In all these cases what has become of the ideas of three *Persons*? With apparently insuperable difficulties to face, many Christian thinkers probably regard the doctrine as an inadequate attempt to formulate that which is above reason.

(5) In addition to all those affirmations which are appropriate to the transcendence of God, the immanence of God is also a part of Christian orthodoxy. The latter follows from a right understanding of omnipresence to which I have referred. The two aspects are placed together in the concept of a transcendent personality—the Heavenly Father. In virtue of being personal—or as some theologians would prefer to say, supra-personal—He can and does retain relations with mankind. This is of course the golden thread running through all the teaching of Jesus about God: that He loves men, cares for them, and seeks for their love. It was proclaimed in the greatest parables of Jesus and also in His life. "The Son can do nothing of Himself, but what He seeth the Father doing."[1]

In an extremely condensed form this may perhaps be considered the essence of Christian belief about God, although particular schools will be critical of some statements.

SOME DIFFICULTIES

It might be thought a presumption to interpolate personal difficulties into this chapter. It is, I think, justifiable to do so in so far as there is reason to believe that they are difficulties shared by others, and even more so where it is hoped afterwards to expound a viewpoint from which they seem to be resolved.

(1) *The Astronomical Difficulty.* In an earlier chapter I pointed out to fellow-physicists, whose science is based upon the measurable aspects of the world, that the qualitative aspects were of at least equal importance for any complete metaphysical outlook. I now venture to suggest to theological colleagues the complementary truth, that while supra-temporal values are their primary concern, and the qualitative aspects of the world to some extent reveal these, the quantitative aspects of the world cannot be ignored.

The Christian view of God was to a very large extent formulated at a time when the Earth was believed to be the centre of the Universe. It was round this centre that the cosmic drama revolved. Man was therefore believed to be the special object of God's concern, almost the unique object. The Psalmist was apparently moved by the spectacle of the night sky to a sense of the littleness of man in the presence of the total Creation.

When I consider Thy heavens, the work of Thy fingers,
The moon and the stars, which Thou hast ordained;

[1] St. John, v. 19, 30; viii. 28.

What is man, that Thou art mindful of him?
And the son of man, that Thou visitest him?
For Thou hast made him but little less than Divine
And crownest him with glory and honour.

He had, however, no mean sense of man's importance in the drama, and if there was an angelic hierarchy it was between *man* and God. This was inevitable at the time, but the outlook which modern astronomy discloses is so incomparably different that it is reasonable to ask if it has not profound implications for our view of God and His purposes. If the reader will glance at Plate XXV in Hoyle's recent book,[1] he will see a photograph of a small section of the Milky Way, where each point of light is a sun. Better still, if he will look at the sky on a clear moonless night, he will see at most five thousand stars with the naked eye. He must then recall that our own galaxy contains approximately twenty million stars for each one that he sees. Furthermore, far outside the remotest star of our galaxy are known to be hundreds of millions of galaxies in evolution. This is all *we* can observe with our telescopes. There may well be galaxies or even super-galaxies without end. I am not so naïve as to suppose that the Supreme Being finds particular satisfaction in the well-nigh infinite production and dispersal of merely physical objects in space. The physical aspect of the Universe seems likely to be its least important part, and lying within and behind this may be aspects of mind and spirit beyond our conceiving. It is quite reasonable to suppose that wherever the physical levels exist they are the outer vehicles or garments of a myriad experiments and adventures in creative consciousness, even though we know little about them. Every star may be an environment in which countless conscious beings are experiencing the joy of existence, and if so, they are as significant and important in their relation to God as we ourselves. It was, I think, an eminent astronomer who suggested that if God sent forth an angel to find the Earth, his task would be like looking for a particular grain of sand on all the sea-shores of the world. I can understand Professor Broad's feelings when he said:[2]

"Naturally I am not so silly as to suppose that this constitutes a *refutation* of Christianity. All I can do is to record the fact that for me personally the Christian story and the Christian theology in a Copernican universe wither like a plant taken from a hothouse and bedded out in the Siberian desert."

The geocentric outlook gave rise vèry naturally to a system of religious thought in which God was primarily concerned with *man*, and sent to

[1] Fred Hoyle, *Frontiers of Astronomy*. (W. Heinemann Ltd., 1955.)
[2] *Religion, Philosophy and Psychical Research*, p. 238. (Routledge and Kegan Paul Ltd., 1953.)

Earth His *only-begotten* Son. This outlook, moreover, naturally gave rise to the highest conceivable status being ascribed to Jesus, for He gave to us our highest conception of God. It is understandable in the light of this outlook that Jesus should be regarded as co-equal with God, and that a concept such as that of the Trinity should have arisen in the meditations of men upon this historic revelation. But in the light of the Universe disclosed by modern astronomy is such an outlook plausible? On countless trillions of worlds conscious beings, also His offspring, may have needed and may have had *their* supreme revelation of God. If we are earnestly seeking metaphysical truth—the truth about the whole—we cannot be content not to ask such questions.

I think Dean Inge once said, "God's Word for this world was Christ, but He may have had other Words for other worlds." It is clear that similar thoughts were passing through Alice Meynell's mind when she wrote her poem *Christ in the Universe.*

> Nor, in our little day,
> May His devices with the heavens be guessed,
> His pilgrimage to thread the Milky Way,
> Or His bestowals there be manifest.

> But, in the eternities,
> Doubtless we shall compare together, hear
> A million alien Gospels, in what guise
> He trod the Pleiades, the Lyre, the Bear.

> Oh, be prepared, my soul!
> To read the inconceivable, to scan
> The million forms of God those stars unroll
> When, in our turn, we show to them a Man.

I do not think these issues can be lightly brushed aside. Perhaps they are not very important for religion, but they are important for our metaphysical outlook. The reply to this issue is usually made from the standpoint of religion somewhat as follows. Moral truths are not related to spatial considerations. Values which we recognise by our own spiritual and intuitive response are valid everywhere and for all time: they are supra-temporal and supra-spatial. Hence, what we have learned of the nature of God in *our* experience is eternally true. All this I do not dispute, but these replies do not meet the metaphysical issues. *Our* experience is now seen to be so infinitesimal a part of the possible total conscious experience of the Universe, that I think we should be far more modest in our claims. I should unhesitatingly subscribe to the description of Jesus as *a* Son of God. Jesus never claimed for Himself that He was the *only-begotten* Son of God, and if the author of St. John's gospel had been writing today instead of in the second century under the influence of Greek philosophical ideas, he would probably have refrained from this assertion which is in any case far beyond any man's knowledge.

(2) *The Greek and Hebrew conceptions of God.* It is well known that the Christian conception of God embraces ideas from Hebrew and early Christian sources on the one hand, and from Greek thought on the other. The very brief synopsis already presented embodies attributes which are difficult to reconcile with each other. Writing of this Dr. W. R. Matthews said[1]:

"For my own part, I think that the two concepts of deity remain irreconcilable; however deeply our sight may penetrate and in spite of all the wonderful subtleties of theologians, the Greek and Hebrew and primitive Christian ideas have never been harmonised."

Greek thought as it was found in Plato and Aristotle and developed later in Plotinus, regarded God as the Infinite Nameless One, beyond knowledge. He was perfect, self-sufficient and beyond change: these are the attributes of an Absolute. In contrast with this the God of Hebrew thought was Creator of all things. He was the holy and righteous Judge whose verdicts were visible in history. He was deeply concerned with men and moral values. In Christ's teaching God was the Heavenly Father, loving men, seeking their love and loyalty to His rule, and caring for them beyond human measure or conceiving. In Greek thought, on the other hand, God was the transcendent One from whom, as Plotinus thought, the created universe came forth as an emanation. God is beyond good and evil, beyond suffering and desire. In the Hebrew and early Christian view, God is intimately concerned with mankind and even remembers the "two sparrows which are sold for a farthing". There are here two currents of thought in such marked contrast that they do not blend.

The antithesis can be expressed in many different terms: transcendence and immanence, the One and the Many, the Omnipresent and the Personal, but it is the same clash of conceptions. Here are two voices of the same hymn-writer:[2]

> Who can behold the blazing light?
> Who can approach consuming flame?
> None but Thy Wisdom knows Thy might,
> None but Thy Word can speak Thy name.

---

[1] *The Problem of Christ in the Twentieth Century*, p. 27. (O.U.P., 1950); see also Chapter V of *God in Christian Thought and Experience*.
[2] Isaac Watts (1674-1748).

But saints are lovely in His sight,
He views His children with delight;
He sees their hope, He knows their fear,
And looks and loves His image there.

In the one case He is beyond relations, in the other case His relations are real and near. In the one case He is not an object of knowledge, in the other case He is a possible object of knowledge, although not of course in His completeness. In the minds of the early Church Fathers Clement and Origen, in the powerful and brilliant mind of Augustine, in the tremendous theological achievement of Thomas Aquinas, and in the thinking of the ablest modern theologians, it cannot be said that the God of Greek philosophical thought and the Father of our Lord Jesus Christ are identical or even reconcilable. Yet it has been, and still is, the Christian view that we must hold both to be true: that God is both transcendent and immanent, that while He is infinite and omnipresent on the one hand, He is also personal on the other.

Faced with this type of situation our tendency is, very naturally, to analyse the content of each of the opposing terms in order to find, if possible, a new interpretation by which they will approximate to each other and finally meet. Thus, for example, "infinite" might be interpreted in terms of potency rather than actuality, as the *power* to manifest everywhere. "Omnipresence" might similarly be interpreted as infinite availability, or the power to be apprehended in every place. While "personal" conveys to us through our senses the idea of spatial limitation and of sharp differentiation from other persons and things, the new knowledge of Mind which we are gathering today points to the fact of human minds being in relationship in a way which is not dependent on space. It may be possible, as knowledge increases, in this way to bridge the gulf between these antitheses, but for my own part I do not feel confident that this is the right direction in which to look for a solution of the riddle. I shall postpone further discussion until the main thesis of this chapter is presented.

GOD AS DIVINE IMAGINING

In introducing this subject we shall briefly recapitulate the substance of the first five sections of Chapter 2.

In discussing the nature of God we can only extrapolate upwards from the highest we know in ourselves. In human nature at its best we may hope to find clues or pointers to the ultimate power, assuming that it must have some kinship with ourselves.

Imagining (or imagination, as it is commonly called) is usually thought of as one among many faculties of the mind, such as memory, anticipation, wit, perception, and reasoning. Some philosophers, in particular Hume and Kant, looking for a fundamental power in the human psyche, have suspected that imagining might play this part. Thus, in memory and anticipation this power is at work to create images and scenes out of past experience. Even in perception of the outer world, Whitehead suggests that it is "largely a concept of the imagination which rests on a slender basis of sense-presentation". We consider the outer world to be of psychical content akin to our own inner experience and entering us through the devices of the special senses. We note, however, that in the act of perception an amazing modification of this content takes place, so that millions of molecular and cellular processes simply appear to us, for example, as a patch of green grass.

Most surprising, perhaps, is the suggestion that Reason is the fruit of imagining. Certainly here the fundamental power is much overlaid and obscured by its logical products. But how did these products originally arise? By acts of imagining which were then tested by the facts. The practical demands of life gave rise to reason, for when faced with difficulties it was necessary to draw rapid conclusions and make decisions. Reason is really a system of tested and well-tried imagining. It will be noted, however, that all creative work in art and science still involves the primeval power: it bodies forth something new—a gift of creative fancy. "All the laws of science," as Karl Pearson has reminded us, "are products of the creative imagination." It is of course obvious that we may imagine many things which are not true, i.e. which do not correspond to reality, which is Divine imagination. Reason's function is then to act as a sieve for our imagining, rejecting some things and adding others to our body of knowledge.

This imaginal power which Kant thought might be at work in the depths of the human soul, and which Hume called "a kind of magical faculty in the soul . . . always most perfect in the greatest geniuses", is surmised to be the fundamental power in the Universe itself—the fontal reality from which everything springs. Imagining fulfils the conditions which such an ultimate principle must satisfy. There is nothing which we or any other beings can imagine that could not exist in Divine Imagining. It is all-embracing. When God imagines, *ipso facto*, He creates. It is however convenient to distinguish between the creating activity and the objects which are created. We therefore use the terms consciring and conscita for these two aspects of Divine Imagining. It is quite artificial to consider them as separate. They are inevitably linked together, for conscita only exist for the activity of consciring. All conscita are sustained in being by the consciring: if the latter ceased, they would vanish. We must keep in mind that Divine consciring always has a two-fold activity, one is conservative and preserves all things in being, the other is additive of creative novelty.

We have said that when God imagines He creates, and what He creates is real. Our imagining is on very much lower levels. On rare occasions it may create an immortal poem or piece of music or sculpture, more often its activity is small and perhaps transient. Indeed, the conscita may have no existence except for ourselves.

Just as Divine Imagining is consciring and conscita linked together, the latter dependent on the former, so also it is the One and the Many, the Transcendent and the Immanent, in each case linked together, the latter dependent on the former. Divine Imagining is not the Absolute of Greek and Indian thought which is complete, perfect, and above change. The only sense in which Divine Imagining is above change is that its nature remains the same. But because it is Divine *Imagining* it creates additively, it produces novelty. This implies change. Time-succession is therefore real, for it is rooted in the Divine nature itself. Believers in an Absolute have always on their hands the puzzle as to why the Reality beyond time should extrude a time-process. To describe the latter as an illusion still leaves unanswered the purpose of this illusion in which so many finite sentients are immersed. We have no such problem with Divine Imagining.

The other great difficulty of the Absolutists is with Evil. Evil must either be present in the Absolute, in which case all that the time-process does is to reveal it, or Evil is unreal and an illusion. In the latter case we are faced with the source of, and the reason for, the illusion. We shall discuss the problem of Evil from the imaginist standpoint in Chapter 10. Meanwhile we shall note that Evil need not permanently soil the world-memory. If anything in the past ceases to be sustained by the conservative aspect of Divine consciring it must perish as though it had never been at all. What cannot be redeemed may therefore be allowed to vanish when a world-system draws near to perfection.

We believe that Divine Imagining is the best description we can have of the Ultimate Power. It is very different from Divine Thinking. Thinking is *about* reality whereas Imagining is the reality itself. As we ourselves know, thought becomes more and more abstract as it becomes advanced in character. It is a useful aid to man, but it is not something which it is a compliment to ascribe to God. God does not think *about* anything. He conscires: and all His conscita, whether galaxies or human faces or blades of grass, are intuited through and through. He never chooses between alternatives which would involve thought. He conscires in the best way *imaginable*.

Consciring is the conscious energy of the Universe, the fundamental activity of Spirit which sustains all things in being, and is projected into beings like ourselves so that we too are "jets of conscious activity". What we call our consciousness is a rill of this Divine consciring which is our inmost self and functions with some sort of independence of its source. The "sort" of independence envisaged is perhaps that of an acorn from the oak tree which produced it. We know that this separateness is only marked on the outer physical level, and that on inner levels each acorn is only the latest manifestation of an inner principle of oakness. Given time and the endless processes of the seasons, this continuing principle will one day manifest in its full maturity from a new centre.

We shall endeavour to avoid using the term consciousness in relation to ourselves, for it suggests only a faculty of passive awareness. The jet of consciring which is our inmost self is much more than this. Our centre of being is not only actively aware but makes and grasps experience into a whole so that it becomes *my* experience, *my* conscita which I conscire. We shall speak of "reflective" consciring where in psychological parlance the activity of the conscious mind is referred to, and "irreflective" consciring where the activity of the so-called unconscious mind is involved. We conscire irreflectively when asleep; we attain the more intense reflective level when we awake. This is because the irreflective consciring of the numerous minor sentients in the brain is added to the soul's consciring and together these are sufficient to raise it above the threshold. A little fatigue or damage to the cortex will drop the level of consciring back below the threshold. Our reflective consciring is only the spearhead of our total consciring, most of which is irreflective, being in this respect like that of the greater part of Nature. When we desire to be creative, we have to *attend* to the task, which means focussing our consciring. At this bright point we are most aware, most creative, and most alive, but we know how much we have to exclude from reflective consciring to achieve this. As we commonly say, we cannot attend to two things at once. In addition, our creativity is seldom of the essentially new; much more often it is a rearrangement of given data.

In contrast with this, Divine Consciring attends to an unlimited field with undiminished awareness, and it is fundamental in its creativity. If the human parallel is any guide, we must infer that Divine Consciring is not a spearhead only, but fully reflective, attaining an intensity and radiance far beyond our experience. This is the answer to Schopenhauer, von Hartmann, and those philosophers who have pictured God as blind unconscious Will, unaware of what it was doing or any goal that it was bound for.

So far nothing has been said about the feeling-aspect of God, which Fawcett describes as bliss-consciring. Here again we have clues in our human experience from which we can reach out to an apprehension of the Divine. The moments in our lives when we are supremely happy, when for the time we are one with joy, are characterised by certain things. Firstly, the narrow bounds of self and self-interest are trans- cended: we feel that we have expanded into a wider and more vivid experience. The artist, the lover, and the mystic can all tell us of such moments. Secondly, conflict is absent, there are no restrictions, no unreconciled oppositions and no pressures from without—no sense that

> . . . . at my back I always hear
> Time's wingèd chariot hurrying near

for in such moments all sense of passing time has vanished. Thirdly, consciring is intensified. In those experiences we really live more intensely and deeply than we live at other times.

> And asking nought of God and life we bring
> The conflict of long days
> Into a moment of immortal poise.

In the Supreme One there are no bounds of self to transcend. He is the whole, and there is complete interpenetration through a limitless field. There can be no conflict, for there are no oppositions; and the intensity and breadth of consciring are beyond our conception. We can only surmise that for Divine Imagining with its infinite variety in harmony there must be also Joy and Delight incomparably greater than we can know or conceive. The truth of this is supported by the highest experiences of the mystics, but to say more of Divine feeling is as inadequate and futile as to speak of Divine knowledge. Our language is not big enough. There is a sentence in the Gita where the Divine Being is represented as saying, "I am Beauty itself among beautiful things". If to this we add, "I am Love itself among all who love", and "I am Wisdom itself among the wise", we cannot say more.

FINITE GODS: DIVINE SOCIETIES

Perhaps in millennia to come posterity will be able to read books on Cosmology and Theology written by men whose knowledge and wisdom are immeasurably greater than ours today. We have, however, made the daring if not impious leap of speculation as to the Divine Nature, and it can scarcely be regarded as more speculative or less possible to infer something of those great Beings who within the all-embracing grasp of Divine Imagining control and administer this vast Universe. It is strange that many good and intelligent people who lay claim to know- ledge about the Supreme Being regard as fanciful any suggestion of a hierarchy of conscious beings above the poor level of man's achievement, reaching out in an infinite vista towards the Ultimate. It is perhaps an unconscious legacy of the pre-Copernican outlook. It is true that St. Paul makes reference more than once in his writings to superhuman beings, archangels, thrones, principalities, powers, and ministering spirits, but I do not think it will be claimed that these conceptions are taken seriously in relation to modern thought.

On the other hand, modern thought takes astronomy and cosmology seriously. I do not think the ordinary man realises in what remote depths of space the planets swim, even in relation to our own sun. We can illustrate it by a model in which the sun is about 12 inches in diameter—say, the size of a large pumpkin. On this scale the inner planets Mercury, Venus, Earth, and Mars are about the size of lead shot at distances of 14, 26, 36, and 54 yards respectively, while Jupiter, Saturn, Uranus, and Neptune are about the size of marbles at 180, 340, 700, and 1,100 yards respectively. On this reduced scale the nearest star to our sun is another pumpkin 5,000 miles away. There are believed to be 100,000 million stars in our galaxy. The latest theory of planetary formation considers that planets may be quite a common feature of a star's evolution. Hoyle[1] remarks that the large 200-inch Hale telescope reveals between 100 million and 1,000 million galaxies, but that the number must be greater than these. We read also of an expanding universe. We ought to ask ourselves what all this means for our knowledge of God.

In trying to see meaning in the world we have adopted the only method (apart from the reception of revelation) which is open to us: the leap of inference from our own limited experience to the Divine heights. Following this method, what more can we infer? We have been driven to conclude that the reality outside ourselves is psychical: that the physical order is the lower region and the mental order the upper region of a psychical continuum. Beyond the psychical continuum are levels of reality which collectively we have called spiritual. Is it likely to be fundamentally different in any part of the universe? On the physical level we have direct evidence from spectroscopy that the same chemical elements exist in distant nebulae. These are present as the basis of whatever physical superstructure is built there. Astronomy discloses galaxies in all stages of evolution, some much younger and some much older than our own. Is it not reasonable to suppose that concurrently with physical evolution there are proceeding countless experiments with finite sentients for whom these lowest levels which we see through our telescopes are but a part of the setting of their evolving consciousness? If Divine Imagining is the supreme power from whose consciring the Universal scheme has come and is coming forth, it is well-nigh

[1] *Loc. cit.*, p. 274.

certain that it has lit up the intensity of consciring at innumerable points. In ordinary language there will have evolved in this universe beings of whose potentialities and capacities we can only form a very limited idea. We may surmise that if the springs of Divine consciring flow through some of them with great power, they will actively participate in the work of creation—directing, conserving, and adding novelty. The scale on which they work may be a planetary one, or a solar one, or for the highest beings it may be that of a galaxy or world-system. It seems to me naïve to assume, on the evidence of modern astronomy, that Divine Imagining finds pleasure in the infinite dispersal of physical objects in space, when the one planet of which we can claim any intimate knowledge has as its chief glory that it has been the setting for the evolution of self-conscious man. We should be wiser to assume that Divine Imagining finds pleasure in the evolution of centres of consciring akin to His own.

F. H. Bradley said, "Every fragment of physical Nature might, so far as is known, serve as part in some organism unlike our bodies."

E. D. Fawcett predicts, "Nature, psychical throughout, will be known as consisting not of mere contents, like the contents of our experience, but also of conscious powers, whose activity is the urge and drive of change."

We shall say something of these conscious powers and the mode of their evolution in Chapter 13. Here I want to say only this, that at a certain level of spiritual evolution such Beings are probably supra-personal, uniting in a closely knit society advanced individuals whose individuality is not lost but subordinated to the rich fellowship and purpose of a greater Being. It may be a single highly evolved Being or a supra-personal Group-Being who rules our own solar system: these are matters beyond our present knowledge. It does however seem probable that this galaxy or world-system, of which our sun is but one star, is governed by a vast hierarchy of such beings—a truly Divine Society at the apex of which, *primus inter pares*, is One whom we may properly and naturally call God. There is unity of purpose, of mind, of aspiration, and of fellowship throughout the Society, so that any member of it might say, "I and my Father are One". It is a One-Many.

Such a God whose rule and life run through our galaxy on all its associated levels must be very wise, very powerful, and very good—far beyond the highest imagining of man. Yet He is a finite God whose consciring may have in some degree the limitations which attention has for us, i.e. He may be able to conscire with high intensity only a part of the world-system at a time. Likewise His specious present may cover a time-span of many thousands of our years, and yet may not cover except as the equivalent of Divine memory and anticipation the vast stretches of thousands of millions of years which probably represent the physical life of our world-system. He may have to experiment freely in His exalted sphere, contending with evil on a great scale, scavenging, purifying, redeeming, planning, and exerting through the influence of the Divine Society that pressure which we describe in terms of evolution, while maintaining that controlling balance which the Greeks called the Divinity of Measure. He is not all-wise and all-powerful, only very wise and very powerful, and is perhaps the finite God which many thinkers have believed to be a necessity—among them John Stuart Mill, William James,[1] and F. C. S. Schiller.[2] He is active through the Divine Society striving to move the world-system onwards towards that perfection which was formulated in Divine Imagining for it, and which is apprehended in its completeness by Him. He is therefore the great ally of all aspiring souls. He is the Heavenly Father of whom Jesus said, "The Son can do nothing of Himself, but what He seeth the Father doing," for Jesus was Himself a member of this Divine Society.

It is of this God that we can say He is both transcendent to His world-system and also immanent in it, for He has partly sunk Himself in the life of the system, in its redemption and transformation into the perfect goal of Divine Imagining for it. We can say of Him what St. John wrote of the Greek Logos, "He was in the world, and the world was made by Him, and the world knew Him not." The deeper significance of the incarnation, suffering on the cross, and resurrection of Jesus on our planet is that they are presentations at one point of time and space of an age-long process of incarnation, suffering in, and re-emergence from the world-system which God Himself is undertaking. In so far as we are His co-workers we are all assisting in the evolution of God, which is the growth of the Divine Society—that "supreme love-lit society of which we are all potential members". Perhaps it was lingering memories of this Society which led Jesus to refer so often in His teaching to the "Kingdom of God".

When J. S. Mill contemplated the evil and suffering of the world, he was constrained to say that God could not be both all-powerful and all-loving. Recognising that God is finite, not *all*-powerful, although embodying power, wisdom, love, and goodness beyond our conceiving, we resolve Mill's dilemma. God Himself is contending with the evil, and in one sense suffering with the world. And thinking of our part in the world process perhaps we might adapt Browning's words

> 'Tis not what man *does* which exalts him, but what man *would* do:
> See the King—I would help him but cannot, the wishes fall through.

---

[1] *A Pluralistic Universe.* (Longmans, Green & Co., 1909.)
[2] *Riddles of the Sphinx.* (Macmillan & Co. Ltd., 1912.)

Could I wrestle to raise him from sorrow, grow poor to enrich,
To fill up his life, starve my own out, I would—knowing which,
I know that my service is perfect. Oh, speak through me now!
Would I suffer for him that I love? So would'st thou, so wilt thou!

Many questions may be asked about God which it is beyond our power to answer. We may speculate whether the Divine Society has *wholly* evolved within our world-system, or whether, since we know there are world-systems older than ours, it may not have had from its earliest beginnings the guidance and direction of advanced Beings from other systems. The latter may well be true, but these are matters far beyond us. We know that our world-system bounded by the Milky Way is one of innumerable millions of systems separated by incredible depths of space. Each may have its finite God—a Divine Society achieving a differently imaged goal of perfection within the infinite variety of Divine Imagining. Of Divine Imagining alone can it be said that it has no beginning and no end. Its infinite life is constantly flowing out into these temporarily insulated world-systems, and through each Divine Society it flows into every remotest part. This is the boundless Source of all to which such terms as omnipotence, omniscience, and omnipresence may be properly applied—though not the characteristics of an Absolute.

The two unreconciled groups of attributes in Christian thought about God can be understood if the one group refer to the Supreme Power—Divine Imagining—and the other group to the finite God of our world-system. Divine Imagining is immanent in the finite God, and He in turn governs and sustains with His imagining the world-system, leading it in the end to the perfection of the Divine Society which is one with Himself.

Of the possibility of a Society of Societies in union with the One Supreme, we can only think and be silent.

How shall polluted mortals dare
To sing Thy glory or Thy grace?
Beneath Thy feet we lie afar,
And see but shadows of Thy face.

Chapter

8

CREATION: THE BIRTH OF WORLD-SYSTEMS

God's great goodness aye endureth
Deep His wisdom passing thought:
Splendour, light and life attend Him,
Beauty springeth out of nought.
Evermore
From His store
New-born worlds rise and adore.

JOACHIM NEANDER (trs. R. S. BRIDGES)

Perhaps the conception of creation as a work of imagination, and God the Creator as the Poet whose works are universes, may take us further into the mystery than any other guide.

W. R. MATTHEWS

SOME IDEAS OF CREATION

ANYONE who thinks deeply about the physical world, no matter what his starting-point, soon finds himself involved in all the fundamental problems. We should expect this to be so in a Universe. The creation of the existing world-order is one such starting-point, and it raises for us questions such as these. If God created the world, how and why did He do so? What relationship of dependence or independence does it bear to Him? From what was it created? Was there any necessity about creation? Was the world created suddenly or continuously? Had it a beginning in time? It is appropriate to see in the first place what some of the best thinkers of the ancient world had to say about these issues.

There is an interesting passage in Plato[1]:

"Let me tell you why nature and the universe of things was framed by Him who framed it. God is good; and in a perfectly good being no envy or jealousy could ever arise. Being therefore far removed from any such feeling, He desired that all things should resemble Himself as far as possible. This is the prime cause of the existence of the world of change, which we shall do well to believe on the testimony of the wise men of old. God desired that everything should be good and nothing evil, so far as this could be. Therefore, *finding the visible world not at rest but moving in a disorderly manner*, he brought order out of disorder thinking this in every way an improvement. Now it is impossible that the best of beings should produce any but the most beautiful of works. The Creator therefore took thought and discerned that out of the things that are by nature visible, no work destitute of reason could be made

[1] Plato, *Timaeus*, 29, 30.

176

so fair as that which possessed reason. He also saw that reason could not dwell in anything devoid of Soul. This being His thought He put Spirit in Soul and Soul in Body, that He might be the maker of the fairest and best of works. Hence we shall probably be safe in affirming that *the Universe is a living creature endowed with Soul and Spirit by the providence of God.*"

The words which I have italicised will be immediately remarked by any critical reader. What was this disorderly world or chaos doing there at all? Are we to assume that this state of imperfection was initially created by God, but that, so to speak, on second thoughts He felt it could be improved? Or are we to assume that it was not created by God, in which case we become dualists? Dean Inge[1] has remarked: "The more dualistic view gained ground until Plotinus (A.D. 205-270) who rejected it. He repudiates the idea of a spatial chaos into which the higher principle descends with its Forms. But he seems to me to have been almost afraid to clarify what Plato had left obscure."

The dualistic type of thought among the Greeks drew strength from a widespread (and mistaken) tendency to associate the physical with evil. It is easy to see how this association comes about, for we recognise in our thinking two hierarchies, one of existence and another of values. The first of these covers degrees of reality from spirit to "matter", and the second of these ranges in its moral aspects from good to evil. If these two hierarchies are linked together, we can see how easily the association of matter and evil comes about. Origen, in attacking Celsus for this view, rightly recognised that evil did not have its origin in matter, even if its manifestations were most obvious to us on this level.

We should not, I am sure, wish to describe Plato as a dualist, but there can be read into the passage we have quoted the common Greek idea that the flux of change and decay was itself evil—a view which Philo shared and which the Buddha had proclaimed some centuries earlier. This state of affairs was to the Greek mind in complete contrast with the nature of the Absolute, perfect, immortal, changeless, and wrapt in contemplation beyond the arena of space and time. Because of this conception the Greeks had to invent a "Logos" who mediated the ultimate power and undertook the work of creation, while Plato spoke of a "Demiurge" who fulfilled the same function.

Plotinus thought of the world as existing on various significant levels, distinguishing particularly Spirit, Soul, and Matter. The first of these alone was absolutely real: each lower level was dependent for its existence on the one above it. Each level subserved its highest function in being ensouled or in-formed by the higher grade.

Traditional Christianity formulated its beliefs about creation in an atmosphere of conflict with the Gnostics who considered the physical

The Philosophy of Plotinus, Vol. I, p. 145. (Longmans, Green & Co. Ltd., 1929.)

177

order as evil, and with Manichaeism and Mithraism which were dualistic. The essentials of the Christian view are these:

(1) God created the world out of nothing. This means, on the one hand, that there was no pre-existing matter or chaos which was shaped and ordered by creation; nor was there any principle of evil responsible for such a chaos. Dualism is completely repudiated. On the other hand, it means that the world is not a part of God—a creation as it were from His own substance. Thus pantheism is equally repudiated. If it seems a strange idea that a sensible world should be made to appear where none appeared before, we may perhaps recall to mind that on a small scale both apparitions and materialisations appear where none appeared before, and these are attributed to the activity of finite minds. From the standpoint of Imaginism creation *ab initio* presents no problem. Conscita are both created and sustained solely in relation to Divine consciring. Scotus Erigena[1] (A.D. 800-877) came extremely near to the Imaginist position when he said that the world was the thinking out of God's thoughts; that God was the immediate creator of the Ideas which in their turn create the phenomenal world.

(2) While allegorical and mythical accounts necessarily picture creation as occurring at a particular point of time, there is nothing in Christian thought inconsistent with the idea of continuous creation. Indeed, if creation is regarded as appropriate to the nature of God at one point of time, it must be appropriate at any other point of time.

(3) God created the world freely as an act of will. Hegel's view that it was *necessary* for God to create a world would be unacceptable to Christian orthodoxy. The only sense in which necessity could be laid upon God would be that He must be true to His own nature. If, therefore, the nature of God is Divine Imagining, He must imagine, and when He imagines He creates. It need not be supposed, however, that the creation of a *physical* order was a necessity.

(4) While the created world depends absolutely upon God, God does not depend upon His creation. It is part of the Christian view that in spite of man's total dependence upon God, both as to his origin and his preservation, he nevertheless has a real measure of freedom, so that he can choose to aspire towards God or turn away from Him. The reconciliation of dependence and freedom in man, though it has its mysterious aspect, need not be impossible. We touched upon it in the last chapter, where it was suggested that the acorn, although separate from the oak tree which gave rise to it, continues in itself the common principle of oakness. In some such way man has (or rather *is*) within himself a germ of the Divine consciring with freedom to develop.

In thinking about the creative process we think perhaps too easily

[1] W. R. Inge, *Philosophy of Plotinus*, Vol. I, p. 146.

of the activities of the engineer, the chemist, or the craftsman who is constructing and shaping material already present. The fundamental type of creation with which we are concerned is more comparable with that of a poem by a poet, a musical work by a musician, or an apparition by a human mind. Here the basic activity of consciring is at work to create the new. The poem which a poet creates and holds in his mind, as Dr. Matthews has pointed out,[1] gives us a hint at the relation between immanence and transcendence. The poet's mind is immanent in his poem, yet it is at the same time distinguishable from the poem and transcends it. It has the power to become immanent in other poems. If we pursue the simile further, we might remark that the ideal way to know a poem would be to have a perfect telepathic rapport with the poet's mind. Then we should be able not only to enter into his thoughts but also into the ecstasy of his feelings. The poem would be as alive and meaningful for us as it was for its creator. Normally what happens is, that the poet translates his inspiration into the imperfect language of symbols. Then as a written document, or perhaps as a gramophone record, it acquires an inferior but a fixed form independent of its creator, and lacking the power of self-development. We must not pursue too far the analogy between the poet and his poem and God and His creation, but two observations may be made. If we could penetrate behind the symbol and achieve rapport with the poet's mind, we should find the living reality which the symbol so imperfectly represents, and this is what the nature-mystics frequently do with God's creation. Secondly, if the poet could impart some of his life to creatures or elements in the poem, so that they became capable of self-development, he would do what the Divine Creator has in fact done in His world.

An even closer analogy to the process of world-creation is found in the power of the human mind on rare occasions to create apparitions and even materialised forms. Here, the apparition is created and sustained by the co-operation of certain levels of the minds of an agent and a percipient. It has a certain apartness from these two minds, and some small degree of independence of action, although it is evanescent in character and soon fades out. It is possible that this form of creative activity bears on a small scale a very close relationship to the consciring of the Divine Being.

IMAGINALS

It is impossible to appreciate the Imaginist conception of Creation unless we clearly understand what is meant by an imaginal. This is the term used to correspond to the Platonic "Idea". Plato believed that

[1] *God in Christian Thought and Experience*, p. 218.

transcendental Ideas were the content or products of the mind of God (the Demiurge). They are reality itself, and all that we are aware of in the phenomenal world are imperfect instances or pale reflections of these. It was considered that the Demiurge created a World-Soul which ensouled the Universe making it an organism, and that the World-Soul contained the images of the Ideas. The World-Soul then fashioned the lower physical world as far as possible on these, but in the imperfect result we have only, so to speak, the shadows or pale reflections of these images. The Ideas themselves are unchanging, but are active and creative according to the *Sophist*.[1] We shall not enter into past controversy about their precise nature, but in so far as they are the causal fountains they are the direct ancestors of what we call Imaginals.

Imaginals are certainly not to be regarded as universal *concepts*, for concepts are *about* reality. They are reality itself: they are the permanent forms or prototypes of Divine Imagining which are the cosmic reservoirs from which everything originates on every level of existence. It may be asked why we need to postulate these imaginals: why cannot we look at the world as a great variety of related contents? We are forgetting when we ask such questions that content is content only for the consciring which conserves it in being. We may illustrate this necessity by the analogy of a game such as chess. Innumerable varieties of games are possible because of the conserved framework of chess which we describe as its conditions or rules. Again, innumerable varieties of pictures are possible because of the conservative framework of Divine Consciring which maintains the great primary imaginals of space, time, and colour in being. "No amount of creative innovation could produce red or blue if colour were not a basic conservative feature of the universe."

The scientist accustomed to measure frequencies is often content to describe light in such terms, but the truth is rather that when certain frequencies arise, conditions are favourable for the light-imaginal to manifest. Fawcett says of the light-imaginal[2]:

"It is a conservative feature of God, an eternal inexhaustible source of all the variations of light which occur in the indefinitely many world-systems. . . . It floods the time-process with itself in the form of a real multiplicity of instances which come and go. But it is changeless in the most important respect; it conserves always the unique qualitative character of light. . . . The imaginal is present not only in the light-contents of the sensible world, but also in the general idea or concept of light in the human mind."

It would be an impossible task to attempt to catalogue even the primary imaginals. Only some of these may manifest in our world-system, or

[1] W. R. Inge, *Philosophy of Plotinus*, Vol. I, p. 76.
[2] Z.D., pp. 360-2.

in our infinitesimal part of it. Furthermore, only the physical levels are familiar to us; none of us would claim to have sufficient knowledge of the more significant levels which lie beyond.

We are dealing with a subject of great complexity. A primary imaginal may comprise many sub-imaginals, as light itself does in the case of colours, or as living things do which may be classified into kingdoms, phyla, classes, orders, families, etc. Some imaginals appear permanently, as for example space, time, and the chemical elements. Others appear intermittently as conditions permit, as for example light and sound. New sub-imaginals are being created while others are disappearing altogether. The pageant of evolution affords many examples of this. There is conflict and competition between sub-imaginals, and a constant interaction which gives rise to novelty. Consider the panorama of Nature in which dominant imaginals act creatively upon groups of subordinate imaginals in ascending hierarchies. Specialised molecular sub-imaginals are subordinated to the use of cell-imaginals. Cell-imaginals are subordinated to the use of liver-, heart-, and kidney-imaginals. These organ-imaginals are in their turn used by body-making sub-imaginals which in their turn are used by the souls of men. Such biological sub-imaginals as we have referred to are all regions of both conservation and change.

We should not regard as sub-imaginals the products of man's imagining—beds, motor-cars, refrigerators, and razor-blades. It would be absurd to postulate an archetypal bed-imaginal of which all beds are particular examples. A particular bed is nevertheless a product of the relationship of many natural sub-imaginals such as metal, wood, fibre, etc., dominated by the creative imagining of man. It is obvious that there are many things within man's imagining, such as dragons and blue roses, which achieve no objectivity or general perception. When man imagines, he does not always create in the full sense of the word.

The pageant of the evolution of natural forms is a large-scale example of the activity of imaginals and sub-imaginals which possess considerable transforming power in bending lower sub-imaginals to their ends. "Variation" is the biological term for this. Some experiments as we know are fruitful, others are relinquished or destroyed in the conflict of sub-imaginals ("natural selection").

"Science talks of variations in very guarded language. But if we could become gods and become aware of the entire history of Nature and individuals at a glance, these variations would strike the mind very differently. We should contemplate a pageant created imaginatively in our very presence. But human beings bogged in the details of a process which seems to them monstrously slow, miss the revelation, save occasionally when stirred by the magic of sunsets or rapid transformations of the surroundings in which they live." [1]

There is another passage I should like to quote. This is from Professor William McDougall, and it points in the same direction.

"If heredity is conditioned, not mechanically by the mere structure of the germ-plasm, but by the teleological principle, it follows that the factors which have produced the evolution of species must have operated on and through this principle. Is it possible that the phrase 'the soul of a race' is something more than a metaphor? That all this wonderful stability in complexity, combined with gradual change through the ages, which Weismann attributes to the hypothetical germ-plasm [genes] is in reality the attribute of an enduring psychic existent [a sub-imaginal] of which the lives of individual organisms are but successive manifestations?" [2]

THE INITIAL SITUATION AND THE METAPHYSICAL FALL

We are now in a position to consider the process of Creation from the Imaginist standpoint. No conflict arises with the Christian conception of creation out of nothing. Everything that exists and persists in being does so because it is a conscitum for Divine consciring. The imagination of God is objective reality. Even on the human level the poem, the artist's picture, and the musical composition which appear for the first time in the world have as their essential and characteristic element an act of imagining. That which previously did not exist afterwards does so. Perhaps we should not say it has come out of nothing, but out of that fundamental mystery, a centre of consciring. Words, pigments, and musical notes are sustained by conservative sub-imaginals which for us are the raw material of expression of our imagining in permanent form.

We believe that the innumerable world-systems are different experiments of Divine Imagining, insulated from each other by the depths of space, and varying in their possibilities by reason of the different primary imaginals made available at the beginning of their evolution. The initial state of a particular world-system is conceived to be a perfectly harmonious and stable whole envisaged in the imagination of God. It exists as reality on the highest level; a unity of perfect beauty after its kind. This whole is conserved as content by God, and is not at this stage a domain of additive creation or novelty. It is a divine work of art present to God, and, within the limits of the imaginals initially present in its structure, it is perfect, that is to say, incapable of being improved upon. In this way a poem or a piece of music might exist in

[1] Z.D., p. 371.
[2] W. McDougall, Body and Mind, p. 377. (Methuen & Co. Ltd., 1928.)

the mind of its human creator for him alone. It endures unchanging as one whole, although it contains time-successions within itself. This archetypal world is not without perfect forms and beings as such, but they are not *sentients*. We may call them automata if we wish. They do not exist for themselves: there is no self-awareness in them.

God then imagined a process by which another type of perfection should ultimately come into being, one in which this archetypal world-system should come to exist as reality also for the beings whom He imagined within it. It is as though a poem or play should come to exist for characters in the play who are to become alive. With this decision the archetypal world-system passed as a whole into time-succession, the age-long process of Becoming as distinct from Being. We may call this feature the "Metaphysical Fall", for it may be regarded as the beginning of all evil. It was a step of tremendous moment which is to be justified by the end which will be achieved. This will be a world-system of perfect Love, Wisdom, and Beauty, existing for the Divine Society, fully conscious of themselves, of their relations to other world-systems, and to the Supreme.

How does the Metaphysical Fall come about? How does the perfect world-system which exists on the highest level of reality start to fall or evolve? The consciring which has hitherto sustained it conservatively now increases at selected points of the system until a new level is reached. So a wind blowing over dull charcoal embers may create glowing points of incandescence. This is the "breath of life" which creates innumerable primitive finite sentients which start to exist for themselves. Although Divine Consciring remains substantially transcendent, it now becomes in some degree immanent in these separate centres. These conscire irreflectively at first a fragment of their immediate environment. These fragments become the frontiers of the sentients, and might be called their bodies. It is understood that we are discussing a very early stage on the highest level of the world-system. The physical level is presumably the lowest and last to come into existence in the evolutionary process. This in its turn undergoes an evolution which is familiar to us, in terms of astronomy and biology.

I shall not enlarge here on the concept of degrees of reality or significance, which I believe to be a fundamental one in any attempt to understand the world. It is found in Platonism and Neo-Platonism, and I have endeavoured to interpret it elsewhere.[1] Evolution of the primitive sentients created on a high level by Divine Imagining involves a subsequent descent into levels of diminishing reality which are created by descending imaginals and sub-imaginals. There is a kind of creative downgrowth of themselves so that each level below is in some measure

[1] *The Imprisoned Splendour.* (Hodder & Stoughton Ltd., 1953.)

a pale and imperfect replica of the one above. This ladder of diminishing reality, with steps which we have labelled Intuitive, Mental, Astral, Aetheric, and Physical, corresponds to levels of differing breadth and intensity of consciring. It appears to be necessary for the evolution of sentients—which means their growth in consciring—that they should descend successively into these levels and emerge from them again. This process of descent and ascent, of evolution and involution, of incarnation and resurrection, perhaps several times repeated, is the basis of the development of individuality, of a permanent self, and of the growth of consciring. The involutional process or way of return carries with it a harvest of experience, and perhaps on the human level some measure of wisdom.

We can recognise at least two thresholds of consciring which the finite sentient must attain. The first step brings it into being as such, and gives it irreflective consciring. Degrees of this are found from the electronic level up to the higher mammals. There is then another level where reflective consciring begins (or, as some would say, where consciousness evolves into self-consciousness). Here there is an awareness of the self as knowing, as well as of the object known. Even in man, however, by far the greater part of his consciring is at irreflective levels. The reflective element is only the spearhead of his total consciring. Moreover, as we know well, this can only be maintained for some part of the twenty-four hours, after which, for an interval, it falls below the threshold. In so far as we can develop this spearhead and make it absorb the shaft, we grow in breadth and strength of consciring. For an advanced being there may be reflective consciring covering at will an appreciable time-span, some of which is past and future to us. It may include also some awareness of that sub-world of minor sentients of whose existence we know but into whose consciring we cannot enter. In an advanced man there need be no loss of reflective consciring in the sleep state; it can remain a continuous possession, being only transferred to another significant level.

There may be a case for introducing a sub-threshold at the point where the biologist finds it convenient to distinguish what *he* calls the living from the non-living, but I do not think this issue is of major importance.

Let us return to the Initial Situation when it falls into the time-process and becomes what Blake called the "disorganised Immortal". At first there is complete penetration without conflict. If space exists at this stage, as well it may, it is no separating barrier. As the level of consciring is raised at particular points, giving birth to a myriad sentients which descend through the significant levels of the world, conflict begins and interpenetration becomes less. The sentients tend to exclude each other. Strife, which Heraclitus called "the father of all things", begins. The harmonious balance is disturbed, and then its restoration is attempted by some imaginal solution, e.g. some added novelty in which a new sub-imaginal manifests. This again creates new disbalance and further transformation is necessary.

"Interpenetration, conflict, imaginal solution, these are the three aspects of the Imaginal Dynamic, the principle of movement which rules the manifested world. . . . The world-process is thus forced along the path of imaginal or creative evolution." [1]

On the physical level we have maximum separateness and minimum interpenetration, but there is still enough of the latter to keep us in touch with other sentients and with our environment. The organs constituting the special senses are just specialised points of ingress to provide interpenetration. On much deeper levels, one of the most characteristic elements of mystical experience is the lingering sense of a great unity. There, interpenetration is profound.

THE "DIVINITY OF MEASURE"

We remarked earlier upon the fact that we take for granted the persistence of things in being, a feature which should be regarded as the conservative aspect of Divine Imagining. There is another aspect of the world so familiar to us that we do not consider it to be remarkable, namely, that if the balance of relationships is disturbed, compensating activities arise to restore stability. It is natural to speak of phenomena on the physical level in mechanistic terms such as balance, equilibrium, compensation, etc. From the standpoint of Imaginism we regard this as evidence, on one significant level of the world of the activity of Divine Imagining. Thus Plato said:

"To do anything in excess seldom fails to provoke a violent reaction to the opposite extreme, not only in the seasons of the year and in the animal and vegetable kingdoms, but also especially in commonwealths. . . . Thus excessive freedom is unlikely to pass into anything but excessive slavery, in the case of states as well as individuals."

Greek thought had a concept of the "divinity of measure", which in the sphere of morality was symbolised by the figure of *Nemesis*, distributing fortune to men in due proportion and pursuing with retribution any violation of these proportions. Indian thought has the concept of *Sattva* which is a harmonising and balancing principle mediating between the creative activity of *Rajas* and the inertia of *Tamas*. [2]

[1] *O.D.*, p. 181.
[2] E.g. Radhakrishnan, *The Bhagavad Gita*, p. 317. (George Allen and Unwin Ltd.)

The Initial Situation of which we have spoken was a spiritual harmony characterised by "divinity of measure". Plunged as we are into conflict of a very marked kind, with evil and suffering among the most profound problems of the human lot, the persistence of this principle on the lower levels of the world is an assurance that however long the way and slow the progress, we are being impelled towards the best imaginable goal.

Nature is full of illustrations of the fact that whenever circumstances change to disturb the harmony, counterbalancing activities arise which tend towards a restoration. We have examples on the electronic level in electromagnetic induction and thermo-electric effects. On the biological level there are innumerable examples of the balance maintained within living organisms. We find the same is true of the closely interwoven activity of the sum of organic life on the earth's surface. We find it true on the psychological level where states of strain and stress give rise to mental adaptations in order to make things more tolerable. We find the principle at work on the sociological level where the pendulum swings often between anarchy and dictatorship, licence and restriction, *laissez-faire* and the welfare-state, between the extremes of socialism and conservatism.

Place plant-tissues in an acid medium and they will endeavour to restore the *status quo* by secreting alkali; place them in an alkaline medium and they will secrete acid substances. Plant two similar trees, one in the sun and the other in the shade; the latter will try to compensate for its lack of sunshine by growing larger leaves. The human body has an amazing variety of devices which act so as to restore with the minimum of inconvenience any disturbance of its satisfactory functioning. As one example we may refer to the volume, pressure, and chemical composition of the blood, which remain remarkably constant under a wide range of conditions. Suppose a severe haemorrhage takes place. The nerve endings in the carotid sinus cause the elastic walls of the blood-vessels to contract and so build up the pressure necessary if the heart is to maintain the circulation. Fluids from the tissues surrounding the blood capillaries, pass through their walls to help to restore the original volume. Reserves of red-blood cells are thrown into the circulation, while the bone-marrow will start to manufacture more of them. If for any reason, such as severe exercise, the carbon-dioxide in the blood increases, this excess stimulates a respiratory centre in the brain which accelerates and deepens respiration and at the same time makes it easier for the oxy-haemoglobin to part with its oxygen. If a man climbs at high altitudes where the pressure of oxygen is less, compensatory changes follow. His heart beats stronger and faster, his chest muscles develop, and the number of red-blood corpuscles considerably increases. Examples of adaptation in physiology are innumerable.[1]

In an interesting chapter on the circle of life on earth Kenneth Walker[2] says:

"Life feeds on life. Animals live on plants and in turn are eaten by animals more powerful than themselves, a certain mean being maintained between the eaters and the eaten. If there is a temporary upset of this balance in a particular locality, it is soon restored; a large number of some species of caterpillar appears in one part of this country and within a few days flocks of the very birds which feed on these caterpillars arrive to deal with the new pest. W. Aspden describes how when voles increased in a part of Scotland, short-eared owls flew from Scandinavia to restore the balance. By what means were the birds brought to the caterpillar-infested neighbourhood, and what prompted the owls to emigrate at that particular moment from Norway? Students of the science of ecology attempt to answer these questions, but it must be confessed that we know as little about the factors which regulate the balance between species as we do about those which control the growth of the various cells of the body."

Mechanical terms such as balance, equilibrium, and energy are used in speaking of physical and chemical change, but even here we should bear in mind that we are fundamentally dealing with psychical change and psychical harmony in the region of very primitive sentients. The building-up process (anabolism) so characteristic of plant-chemistry, means that greater psychic potentiality is created (energy is stored), while the breaking-down process (katabolism), where food is used as fuel by animal life, is the dispersal of this psychic potentiality accompanied by the fall of the minor sentients involved to a more harmonious state (CO_2 and water), where no further change is likely. On the chemical level conservative imaginal activity is dominant. On the biological as distinct from the chemical level we see clearly the inadequacy of mechanical symbolism, precisely because creative novelty plays a much greater part. When, for example, we try to account for the construction of an eye, which solves problems of great complexity for the organism, creative imaginal activity is obvious.

On the human level, whether dealing with individuals, groups, or nations, the language of psychics is the only appropriate one. In the story of human progression and regression we observe the historical equivalent of Natural Selection as civilisations have come and gone. Where life has been too easy, and the challenge of existence insufficient for too long a time, decay sets in, and a civilisation may perish in an emergency which it cannot meet, as did Rome and Egypt. Where life

[1] *Vide* Alexis Carrel, *Man the Unknown*, Chapter VI.
[2] Kenneth Walker, *The Circle of Life*, Chapter II. (Jonathan Cape Ltd., 1942.)

has been too difficult and the problem of survival all-absorbing, no great civilisations are to be expected. Progress is marked where the challenge has been sufficient but not overwhelming, so that the will to meet it is aroused. Comparing Sumer and Egypt, Stanley Casson says[1]:

"While from Sumer . . . we get the first form of defensive security, elaborate irrigation planned on a scientific basis, and a form of town architecture which is far more European in its manner than Egyptian, the contributions of Egypt are lamentably small. Perhaps the underlying reason is that the Sumerians faced problems that the Egyptians never had to consider. In the Mesopotamian plains flood and unequal rains . . . were factors. The imminence of barbarous mountain folk forced them to organise defence; the uncertainty of crops persuaded them to indulge in experiments which culminated in the science of mathematics, land-surveying, and astronomy. . . . Where Nature is against you your inventions have to be more fertile. But in Egypt Nature wore her most friendly guise."

In conflict and challenge as handmaids of the Imaginal Dynamic, forcing communities along the path of creative evolution, we have one of the clues to the problem of evil, which we shall consider in a later chapter. For the moment we shall merely remark that the Imaginal Dynamic makes use of evil and conflict for ends which we believe will finally be justified. Of this we cannot know in advance, but our immediate assurance is found in the constant operation of the "Divinity of Measure". The movements of events swing from one disharmony through temporary harmony to another disharmony, but let it be noted that they do swing about a norm, even though catastrophe, pain, and suffering are often involved in the processes of restoration. From the cosmic standpoint we must hold that this is inevitable and right, for the paramount consideration is that the world-system should be moved towards the goal of Divine Imagining, even though many finite sentients suffer on the way.

CREATIVE EVOLUTION

Reviewing the process of creation in broad outline: we regard the beginning of each world-system or galaxy as an act of Divine Imagining on the ultimately real or spiritual level. This perfect archetype has real existence, but only as content for Divine consciring. At a myriad selected points the intensity of consciring is raised, and finite sentients each having a small capacity for irreflective consciring are created as the system falls into the space-time process. There is now no longer interpenetration without conflict, as in the perfect archetypal order blended from the primary imaginals. The finite centres begin to act for them-

[1] Stanley Casson, *Progress and Catastrophe*, p. 124. (Hamish Hamilton Ltd., 1937.)

selves, and as the creative descent takes place into lower levels of the world-system, interpenetration diminishes as conflict increases. Harmonising imaginal solutions are found which reduce the conflict temporarily, but new stresses again arise and new solutions follow each other interminably. After many stages of activity on higher levels, the world-system finally descends to imaginal creation on the physical level, which, as far as we know, is the lowest level of existence. On this level we do understand a little, and can observe some of the steps of creative evolution.

The most primitive centres of irreflective consciring present on the physical level—electrons, protons, neutrons, mesons, etc,—remain very much under superposed imaginal control, as we know from the existence of statistical law. It is on the biological level of development that conflict becomes intense and many sentients run amok, i.e. they are concerned with their own advantage to the detriment of the greater whole. This is also part of the problem of evil discussed in Chapter 10.

Let us return to the most primitive and ubiquitous of imaginals, that which created and still creates hydrogen in inter-stellar space. The appearance of hydrogen made possible the appearance of the helium sub-imaginal, and in so doing started stellar evolution (on the physical level) on its way through an enormous release of energy. The variety of atomic sub-imaginals which followed made possible the appearance of molecular sub-imaginals. The appearance of certain complex nucleo-protein molecules made possible the descent of life-imaginals, and after innumerable experiments gave rise to that remarkable unit, the living cell. The aggregation of cells made possible the descent of other imaginals, and the whole pageant of plant and animal life came slowly into being. We must remind ourselves constantly that the "higher" is not adequately explained by the "lower". The appearance of higher imaginals takes place when conditions on a lower level make their manifestation possible. Greater sentient wholes arise because aggregates of lesser sentients become satisfactory content for the consciring of the higher sentient which descends into it and thereby has its own intensity of consciring raised. On the higher mammalian level we recognise the existence of experiments through millions of years before the ape-organism could be developed to a point where human sub-imaginals (i.e. human souls) could make use of it as a locus of consciring.

Observe that when a higher sentient uses a complex of lower sentients as its body it does not by that procedure acquire any awareness of the consciring of these lower sentients. A man knows nothing of the consciring of his muscle cells or brain cells, and they in turn know nothing of the higher ends which they are serving. It will be pointed out later (Chapter 13) that we human sentients are in our turn the cells or servants of higher beings—important sub-imaginals—of whose outlook and purposes we may have only the faintest idea. Perhaps F. H. Bradley had a suspicion of this when he suggested that "several bodies might be organs to a higher unknown soul".

It has been pointed out earlier that our consciring of the physical world (of which our bodies are a part) is extraordinarily limited, to a degree which appears simply to serve the practical ends we have referred to. We see a blade of grass, but what do we know of the myriad cellular and molecular processes within it? If we put yeast cells into glucose, they feed upon it and multiply. Now this feeding is not ingestion like ours. The yeast cell produces a chemical substance called an enzyme, which, fitting like a key into the complicated lock of the glucose molecule, opens it and releases its energy. If we now put these yeast cells into a different sugar, e.g. galactose, the key will not fit, and there is a period of quiescence. A little later the yeast cells will be found to have manufactured a new enzymic key which will unlock the galactose molecule. Are yeast cells highly intelligent? The mechanist should ponder this question. We prefer to say that the sub-imaginal which creates the yeast type of cell and maintains its function, interpenetrates the lower (chemical) sub-imaginals involved, and all the resources of its aeons of experimenting are conserved in it. We have here a simple example of creative imagining, but examples could be multiplied a thousandfold in Natural History. Thinking of these things Fabre was led to regard the wonder of instinct in animal life as "imagination governing matter".

While tracing directly *or indirectly* all the multiplicity of living things to imaginals and sub-imaginals in a descending and multiplying hierarchy of great complexity, we should not wish for a moment to assign every species or genus to a sub-imaginal. The latter supplies the dynamic for certain broad lines of development, but the consciring of finite sentients, both higher beings experimenting, and lower sentients with their limited local initiatives, together with Natural Selection, may account for much detailed variety.

SOME REFLECTIONS ON DESCENT

We have looked at a phase of the great cycle of Becoming, which has been regarded as the means by which a vision of Divine Imagining is ultimately to be realised. A perfect archetypal order is to become actual for innumerable finite sentients, the higher of whom will become a Divine Society. The process at which we have so far glanced is one of evolution or descent, and indeed we know very little about it except what may be inferred from the phase which we can study on the physical level. Of the involution or ascent, we shall say something in later chapters.

What do we conceive to be gained or achieved by the process of descent? Is its necessity clear? Could not Divine Imagining have created in its final and perfected form a Divine Society without the long and painful way of descent? Doubtless He could, and it may be that on certain high levels of our system, or in other world-systems such beings exist. We must start, however, at the point of which we have knowledge: that we are participants in *one* experiment in the evolution of consciring in finite sentients. Can we see how the cycle of descent and ascent, perhaps repeated several times, achieves this evolutionary growth? In a general way, I think we can.

We have found it convenient to recognise certain significant levels of existence, and have labelled them spiritual, intuitive, mental, astral (i.e. post-mortem), aetheric, and physical. We may suppose these world levels are created in succession by the gradual descent and activity of the imaginals. There is a certain threshold of consciring associated with each of these levels: it is highest on the spiritual and lowest on the physical level. If the consciring of a sentient rises in intensity above this threshold it becomes reflective (self-conscious) on that level. Suppose a finite sentient, say a bird, is created from a sub-imaginal of which it is an expression and to which it remains related. Its intensity of consciring may be so feeble that its appearance on the physical level, where the threshold is low, is associated only with irreflective consciring. Its intensity cannot rise above the appropriate threshold. When it dies, the finite centre of consciring is presumably withdrawn into the bird-imaginal or sub-imaginal which sustains it. The investment is presumably withdrawn with some interest on the capital, and higher types of birds may thereby be rendered possible. There may, however, be temporary existence of the particular bird on the astral level with feeble irreflective consciring there, but of a transient nature. When, however, a finite sentient of a higher order, such as a human soul, is involved in descent, its intensity of consciring might (let us suppose) be irreflective on the intuitive and mental levels, feebly reflective on the astral level, and more strongly reflective on the physical level. By its association with a physical body the soul's consciring is raised in its intensity. It is as though the process of limitation lifts its level, as the water of a stream rises when it is confined between narrow banks. Alternatively, we may visualise the consciring of the lower (physical) sentients as adding itself to the level of the soul's natural capacity and lifting it over the threshold. It certainly appears that if the physical life-span is used properly, then the process of involution or ascent which follows death of the body is accompanied by a raised level of consciring on the higher levels to which the soul withdraws in succession. If we admit re-incarnation (for which I think there is a good case), it seems likely that after a considerable time (perhaps hundreds of years) the descending process may again set in. Such a cycle of births and deaths may be repeated several times until the minimum level of consciring in the soul is raised to a point where advance can take place more effectively on higher levels than by further descent to the physical. There is, however, nothing mechanical or arbitrary about all this. We are not dealing with a set of rigid laws or with impersonal "forces". The human soul is a unit in a group of souls which together derive from and are sustained by a sub-imaginal. This not only nourishes and sustains its members but presses them along the evolutionary path in so far as it can do so while respecting their freedom. I shall have much more to say of this in Chapter 13.

There is obviously a point on the evolutionary scale where a permanent centre of individuality is acquired. It seems likely that this is not below the level of man, and that immortality is something that has to be won at man's level.[1] Whether all men have won it we do not know: I have been informed that the answer is in the negative.

The general view advanced of the appearance of man (or any of the key forms of life) on earth, is that it is a convergence of two evolving processes—a higher and a lower. On the lower level an adequate physical form must have been evolved, such as the hominids. This then made possible the appearance on this level of the higher imaginal of Homo Sapiens whose souls had made the descent through the significant levels of the world, and remained as waiting factors until the physical conditions were satisfactory for manifestation. We should remember that this is true not only of the first appearance of man on earth, but of every human being born into the world today. He is the meeting-point of two lines of development. One of these is the hereditary chain which interests geneticists and provides the physical vehicle: the other is the world-line of a soul in evolution who conserves on irreflective levels the experience, possibly of a long past. He appears

> Not in entire forgetfulness
> Nor yet in utter nakedness

for this experience will be available to him throughout his life as the intuitive promptings of his deeper self.

We have touched upon themes of which we have little knowledge,

---

[1] In the myth of Genesis iii. 22-23 the eating of the fruit of the Tree of Knowledge of good and evil may represent the passing of the threshold corresponding to the birth of *reflective* consciring. The myth says that Adam and Eve were subsequently driven out of the garden lest they should "take also of the tree of life and eat and live for ever". The myth indicates thus that immortality is something which has still to be won by man's effort, and that no short-cuts will be allowed!

and some of our speculations are necessarily fancies moving in a somewhat rarefied air. It has been suggested that just as a human sentient may appear in the interests of his development in a plurality of lives, so a finite god or supra-personal being might appear in a variety of world-systems in the interest of his fuller evolution.[1] It has also been pointed out that world-systems or galaxies which are separated by incredible depths of space on the physical level may be interrelated in a unity on the highest levels. These are matters far beyond us and likely to be so until we ourselves enter the Divine Society.

[1] *Z.D.*, p. 319.

Chapter

9

THE ADVENTURE OF BEING MAN

I am a child of Earth and of starry Heaven, but my race is of Heaven alone.

Orphic saying

I thought, beloved, to have brought to you
A gift of quietness and ease and peace,
Cooling your brow as with the mystic dew
    Dropping from twilight trees.

Homeward I go not yet; the darkness grows;
Not mine the voice to still with peace divine:
From the first fount the stream of quiet flows
    Through other hearts than mine.

Yet of my night I give to you the stars,
And of my sorrow here the sweetest gains,
And out of hell, beyond its iron bars,
    My scorn of all its pains.

A. E. (GEORGE RUSSELL), *The Gift*

WE proceed now to consider this "nursling of immortality"—Man. For the rest of the book we shall be concerned with his nature, some problems which are very close to him, and the long pilgrimage upon which his feet are set.

When young parents look at the child which they have brought into the world with affection, fascination, and pardonable pride, they are not as a rule greatly exercised by the problem of the child's nature and the origin of its soul. That it should have its mother's colour of eyes and its father's shape of nose seem much more noteworthy phenomena. Indeed, these are remarkable enough, even when considered with a full appreciation of genetics. If the colour of the eyes were fully understood, we should hold in our hands a clue to the universe. As it is, we merely say, in our ignorance, that a particular gene-grouping has made it possible for a particular colour sub-imaginal to manifest.

If we put to the young parents the question, "Who made the baby?" doubtless the mother could present a stronger claim than anyone. If we went on to ask, "And how did you do it"? we should risk being viewed with suspicion as either a philosopher or a lunatic. It is obvious that nothing the mother has ever learned, nothing of which any trace has ever arisen from the submerged depths of herself into consciousness, accounts for her ability to construct such a living organism. We need not labour this point, for every creature known to biology achieves in reproduction something scarcely less remarkable. When a seed is dropped into the ground, and a few months later a flower of exquisite colouring and grace delights the eye, we are not disposed to attribute scientific knowledge, craftsmanship, or aesthetic sensibility to the seed. To talk of a "life-force" tells us nothing.

If we pick up an artificial flower, a construction of wire, fabric, and pigment, often not without grace, we take it for granted that some purposive activity of a human mind has been responsible for its creation. Is it very unreasonable to suppose that high orders of intelligence, craftsmanship, and artistry lie behind the living panorama which we call Nature, and that sub-imaginals of almost endless variety are the "wire, fabric, and pigment" which the creative imagining of beings more advanced than ourselves, and higher sub-imaginals, mould slowly into new experimental achievements? We know little indeed about the psychical processes involved, but our general viewpoint is that even in the making of a flower there must be a science unknown to beings on our level, linking chemistry, genetic grouping, and aesthetics. When the conditions "from below" are appropriate (i.e. when chemical and biological sub-imaginals create specific molecules in a specific order of relationship), then higher sub-imaginals of specific form and colour can use these conditions to appear. There is a constant pressure of higher sub-imaginals to manifest, the higher always making use of the lower as vehicles. Instincts are the habits of biological sub-imaginals.

As we previously suggested, the highest sub-imaginals of which we have any real knowledge, those which we may call the sources of souls, found a satisfactory vehicle one or two million years ago for their manifestation in the Hominids. "Souls appear through, and not out of, the bodily events which limit them."[1] There is no sound reason for assuming that a soul has only one body—the physical one. It may create and use in its descent a body appropriate to each significant level, although it would seem that consciring can only achieve the reflective level of intensity in one of these bodies at a time.[2]

If the young parents to whom we referred could see behind the world of appearances, they would know their own contribution to the child to be significant but small. They provide the "model" cell with its genetic content, although they do not control the gene-grouping. The fertilised ovum then becomes the focus of innumerable waiting sub-imaginals drawing on the material supplied by the mother to carry out their habitual activities. Occasionally there is a failure in collaboration, but this is uncommon. Many of them continue in activity to promote and control the processes of growth which continue after birth has taken

[1] *Z.D.*, p. 383.   [2] *Z.D.*, p. 454.

place. Linked with genes which express the lower levels of a psychical field are of course specific aptitudes, capacities, and potentialities. This is what the parents have made possible—and this is all they have done. Into this vehicle has descended one manifestation of a waiting sub-imaginal, a soul in its own right. The parents have done nothing to create this being: they have only provided an opportunity for him (or her) to gain further experience of the special kind which terrestrial life affords. The soul may or may not have had such experience before. It may have in its treasury stores of gathered wisdom, some of which in after life will become apparent. It may on the other hand be a young soul adventuring forth for the first time.

With the recognition that children (so-called, because of their *physical* immaturity) are human beings in their own right, facing their own destiny and unfolding their own soul-inheritance within the limits of the psycho-physical vehicle the parents have partly provided, a new and wiser attitude to the younger generation might arise. It was surely with this insight that Wordsworth thus addressed the young child:

> Thou, whose exterior semblance doth belie
> Thy soul's immensity;
> Thou best philosopher, who yet dost keep
> Thy heritage, thou eye among the blind,
> That, deaf and silent, read'st the eternal deep,
> Haunted for ever by the eternal Mind,
> Mighty Prophet! Seer blest!
> On whom those truths do rest
> Which we are toiling all our lives to find. . . .

MAN AS A HIERARCHY

I hope I have been able to convey to the reader a conception of the human being as a hierarchy whose essence is a centre of consciring, which with its various vehicles or non-material bodies we may call a soul. The soul *is* the man; it is incorrect to say that he *has* a soul. Any soul is a particular expression of a sub-imaginal which sustains it, and to which it therefore retains an intimate relationship. It makes use of a physical organism created by lower sub-imaginals which conscires irreflectively on its own, although knowledge of this seldom arises into the soul's reflective awareness. The physical organism in its turn subordinates to its instinct of clinging to life and securing pleasure the still lower irreflective consciring of body organs. These in turn subordinate to their specialised function the constellations of cells, and so on. I draw attention to a suggestion of Professor William McDougall[1]:

[1] *Body and Mind*, p. 366.

"It may be that the soul that thinks in each of us is but the chief of a hierarchy of similar beings, and that this one alone . . . is able to actualise in any full measure its capacities for conscious activity."

There is a particularly interesting experience described by Sir Auckland Geddes[1] of a man who became acutely ill with gastro-enteritis due to poisoning, and was brought back from the portals of death almost at the last minute. The patient described an experience he had as follows:

"I suddenly realised that my consciousness was separating from another consciousness which was also me. These, for purposes of description we could call the A- and B-consciousnesses, and throughout what follows the ego attached itself to the A-consciousness. The B-personality I recognised as belonging to the body, and as my physical condition grew worse and the heart was fibrillating rather than beating, I realised that the B-consciousness belonging to the body was beginning to show signs of being composite, that is, built up of 'consciousness' from the head, the heart, and the viscera. These components became more individual and the B-consciousness began to disintegrate, while the A-consciousness, which was now me, seemed to be altogether outside my body which it could see. Gradually I realised that I could see, not only my body and the bed in which it was, but everything in the whole house and garden, and then I realised that I was seeing not only 'things' at home but in London and Scotland, in fact wherever my attention was directed. . . ."

In a very unusual study of his own dreams P. D. Ouspensky[2] came to certain conclusions which also support the view put forward. In the course of experimenting he discovered what he called half-dream states, in which he could observe critically the origin and construction of his dreams. It would seem that on the way to sleep he found a method of creating and retaining reflective consciring on levels of mind where normally activity is irreflective. In this state he found he could initiate dreams and to some extent control them. He says, "Usually I only gave the first impulse, and after that the dreams developed as it were of their own accord, sometimes greatly astonishing me by the unexpected and strange turns which they took." His customary repertoire of dreams was created and studied in this way, and led him to an interesting classification of dreams. We are only concerned here with certain conclusions at which he arrived. The reader will easily translate his terminology into ours—of reflective and irreflective consciring.

[1] *Edinburgh Medical Journal*, N.S. (IVa), Vol. XLIV, p. 365 (1937).
[2] *A New Model of the Universe*, p. 281. (Routledge and Kegan Paul Ltd., 1938.) It is a pity that Ouspensky's important contribution to our knowledge of dreams has never received the attention it deserves. His technique is one method by which we might come to know a good deal more about the structure of personality, although the method may not be without danger.

"We speak only of the head, brain thinking, and we ascribe to it the chie part of the work of creating dreams as well as all our thinking. This is utterl wrong. Our legs also think, think quite independently of and quite differentl from the head. Arms also think: they have their own memory, their ow mental images, their own associations. The back thinks, the stomach think each part of the body thinks independently. Not one of these thinkin processes reaches our consciousness in a waking state, when the head thinkin operating chiefly by words and visual images, dominates everything els But when the head consciousness calms down and becomes clouded in th state of sleep, especially in the deeper forms of sleep, immediately othe consciousnesses begin to speak. . . . These separate consciousnesses in u possess their own conceptions of many things and phenomena, for whic we sometimes have head-conceptions and sometimes have not. This is pre cisely what most prevents us understanding our dreams. In sleep the ment images which belong to the legs, arms, nose, tips of the fingers, to the variou groups of motor muscles, become mixed with our ordinary verbal-visu images. We have no words and no forms for the expression of conception of one kind in conceptions of another kind. . . . We remember and describ only head-dreams, i.e. dreams consisting of visual-verbal images."

There is no need to comment on these two very different sources o experience supporting the conceptions we have expressed. Ouspensky' experience is possibly the first recorded evidence of an experimenta kind, of the awareness of the imaginal activity of the organs of the body He makes another observation which we may mention in passing: tha it is impossible to say one's own name in a dream and continue sleeping We can appreciate the reason for this by recalling that the dream stat is one of irreflective consciring, i.e. the dreaming self is not aware o itself at the time as it is aware of its experience. A person's name is s intimately linked with reflective consciring that knowledge of the nam is apparently only possible along with the waking state.

BELIEF ABOUT THE SOUL

We have said that man *is* a soul temporarily using a physical body o one level of reflective consciring. It may seem odd, therefore, to discus beliefs *about* ourselves since there is a sense in which we know ourselve more intimately than anything else. Our standpoint for the moment is concession to the sceptic who does not doubt the physical world bu doubts everything else. His position is a strange one, for it is through hi mind that he doubts. Still, he may accept this and yet believe that hi mind will perish with his body. He would do well to weigh the opinio of Kant:

"I am much disposed to assert the existence of immaterial natures in th world, and to place my own soul in the class of these beings. It will hereafter, know not where or when, yet be proved that the human soul stands even in this life in indissoluble connection with all immaterial natures in the spirit world, that it reciprocally acts upon these and receives impressions from them."

It is desirable to attempt to define "soul" at least to some degree of approximation, for terms such as spirit, personality, and mind are clearly related and in some degree overlapping. We have previously referred to a number of different significant levels of the world, and this idea is helpful in trying to understand the different functions and "bodies" of man. By the term "body" we mean the form or vehicle in which the self functions on any particular level. By "soul" we mean the self or individualised being whose nature is a hierarchy participating in all these levels. It is the centre of consciring together with all its non-physical bodies. The "mind" is a level of the soul—a very extensive and important level, or group of sub-levels. Each mind emerges from, and remains related to, a greater mind (perhaps the collective unconscious of Jung) which is the instrument of the spirit which unites a number of journeying souls whose evolution and development are intimately related. Much more is said about this in Chapter 13. Souls, as we have said, are individualised, but the spirit which sustains the whole group is a unity. At this point I shall not do more than quote a few sentences from F. W. H. Myers' communications which convey what I believe to be the right impression:[1]

"A spirit . . . which nourishes a number of journeying souls with its light is a thought of God. This thought is individual in that it has a certain apartness from its Creator, the apartness of the created thing from the One who gave it birth. . . . These myriad thoughts, or spirits, begotten by the Mighty Idea, differ from one another; many of them, nearly all, before they control and manifest themselves in matter, are crude, innocent and incomplete embryos. They must gather to themselves numberless experiences, manifest and express themselves in uncountable forms before they attain to completion, before they may know perfect wisdom, true reality."

In many parts of these scripts Myers makes similar statements: for example,

"A spirit manifests itself many times on earth, and it is the bond which holds together a group of souls, who in the ascending scale of psychic evolution, act and react upon one another. So when I talk of my spiritual forebears I do not speak of my physical ancestors, I speak of those soul-ancestors who are bound to me by one spirit. There may be contained within that spirit, twenty souls, a hundred souls, a thousand souls. The number varies."

[1] From *The Road to Immortality*, by Geraldine Cummins. (Aquarian Press, 1956.)

In our terminology such a spirit is a sub-imaginal, and the "Mighty Idea" is Divine Imagining.

The term personality is a less definite one, but represents for me the more superficial aspects of the soul: those, for example, which are the fruit of any one life on earth and are the characteristics by which we are known to others. If a soul adventures forth into earth-life more than once, it will acquire on each occasion a new and distinct personality (although not necessarily a very dissimilar one). The views expressed seem to me fully in harmony with Neo-Platonic thought. Expounding the views of Plotinus, W. R. Inge[1] speaks of the soul as

"in the centre, not at the summit of Plotinus' philosophy. It stands midway between the phenomenal world, of which it is the principle, and the world of Spirit which is its principle. . . . It has its own centre, a life proper to itself; but it can expand infinitely in every direction without ceasing to be itself."

Porphyry expounding Plotinus says, "Particular souls are distinct without being separate; they are united to each other without being confused and without making the Universal Soul a simple aggregate." This is extraordinarily close to the description of the Group-soul nourished by a single spirit, of which Myers wrote.

The sceptic whose belief can stretch no further than that of Mind, so dependent on the physical body that it must perish with it, has much to consider and explain away.

First, I should put the experiences of the mystics, those moments of illumination, so life-giving, so powerful in their incidence, so amazing in their unfolding vistas of Love and Wisdom, that those who have had them claim that they have touched reality when the veils of appearance have fallen away. It should moreover be observed that of such revelation the mind is no more than a recipient or quiescent spectator.[2]

Secondly, I should put all that body of evidence where the soul behaves as "an agent in its own right, not as a psychic exhalation rising out of and wholly controlled by the physical body". Sir Auckland Geddes' case may be cited as a type of this, but there are innumerable examples of out-of-the-body experience.[3]

Thirdly, I should put all that body of evidence which is so familiar to us that we take it for granted. The lives of many men provide the strongest evidence of souls living their own lives. We see mathematicians living in a world of symbols, artists living to express their insights, reformers and philanthropists living to express their compassion, and martyrs dying to affirm their faith. None of these are

---

[1] *Philosophy and Plotinus*, Vol. I, pp. 203-5.
[2] *The Imprisoned Splendour*, Chaps. XIV and XV.
[3] *Loc. cit.*, Chap. X.

activities of interest or value to the physical body (except perhaps the latter, to which it must have a strong aversion). These strangely contrasting interests suggest that duality which Geddes' patient expressed in terms of an A- and B-consciousness, with the first of which he identified himself while the second he related to his body. We noted in this connexion how the consciring of *A* was widened and restored as it became free from the restriction of *B*.

Let us return now to the Imaginist viewpoint, to see if we can speculate further on the soul's origin and history. As we have postulated a perfect order existing in the Divine Imagination prior to the Metaphysical Fall, this implies that the sub-imaginal of a group of souls has within it on its highest level, prior to their evolutionary descent, the ideal forms or patterns of these souls. The sub-imaginal is in embryo a small-scale replica of the One-Many, the Divine Society, "a god though in the germ". Descent must, at least on the first occasion, be irreflective for the germinal souls. Reflective consciring should appear first on the physical level, where the threshold is lowest, and should be gradually carried higher in the ascent. Subsequent descents and ascents should diminish the irreflective phases and increase the reflective ones, the souls slowly growing in their range and depth of consciring.

> And I shall thereupon
> Take rest, ere I be gone
> Once more on my adventure brave and new:
> Fearless and unperplexed
> When I wage battle next
> What weapons to select, what armour to indue.

Since the initial level of the sub-imaginal is characterised by great interpenetration, the interesting question arises as to whether the soul is not always rich in content although it has no knowledge of these riches until its reflective consciring gives it the power. There may be initial capital to which the experience of souls bring their own earned riches, pouring them into the common treasury of the Group-soul to which they all belong. Some intuition of this may lie behind Plato's theory of reminiscence.

The truth behind the idea of Jung of the "collective unconscious" is that the sub-imaginal to which a group of souls is related creates this great common mind in its descent to the appropriate level. In this common soil those individual minds are sown and nourished which are used by the germinal souls of the group, as trees grow from the earth. "Inspiration", which is sometimes attributed to a "super-conscious" (a meaningless term), is the descent of latent treasure from the Group-soul to become conscita for one of the reflectively consciring souls. I believe that all inspiration has this origin, although it may be mediated through a more advanced soul of the Group to an incarnate soul, through their common collective mind.

Reference has been made to the probability that each human being regarded as a centre of consciring may have several bodies related to the possibility of living on different significant levels. Of these we can only conscire reflectively in one at a time, and the physical body alone is familiar to us. The aetheric body remains closely linked with the physical throughout its life. It never functions as a separate body, but constitutes the "husk", which is shed immediately or very soon after death (Chapter 12). If clairvoyant evidence may be taken as reliable, we may claim to know a little about it. The objective body of the after-death state, sometimes called the astral body, is known to us in some slight degree through those who claim to have had experiences outside their physical body, and otherwise only through communications from discarnate persons. I think there is good reason to suppose that the astral body bears a close resemblance in form to the physical body at its best. We shall leave these matters for the present, and merely say that we all possess this body in our earthly life, but seldom consciously use it.

The highest body of the soul had its origin in Divine Imagining in the Initial Situation. It was created for it, but with consciring initially at a low irreflective level. It has to be awakened from its sleep, and the whole process of descent and ascent normally leads to a rising intensity and breadth of consciring, so that in the end the soul, fully reflective, will normally use this body alone. It is this highest body which determines individuality and the ultimate differences between each of us. It has access to the treasure conserved for us in the Group sub-imaginal, and this treasure we appropriate as well as add to by our experience of ascent and descent. When we can conscire reflectively in the highest body we are perhaps ready to enter the Divine Society.

In regard to the process of birth on earth, the lowest level of the soul's descent, Fawcett has advanced an interesting and novel idea.[1] We know that the struggle for survival characterises the sub-human levels of Nature. We should describe this as rooted in the conflict of lower sub-imaginals. Fawcett extends the idea to a "struggle for manifestation of souls needing physical bodies whereby they can conscire reflectively on earth". He suggests that "it is this struggle in the background which supports instinct", and remarks that what we call the means of subsistence, climate, human and animal rivals, all exemplify groups of imaginals which limit each other and are sometimes the occasions of catastrophe and death when the "divinity of measure" has to operate in restoring too much divergence from the pattern.

[1] O.D., p. 255.

PLURALITY OF LIVES

Reference has been made to the possibility that in the course of their evolution the souls of human beings may manifest on earth in physical bodies more than once. It is an ancient idea which has had the support of many thinkers throughout man's long history. I shall not here present the strong case which I think can be made out for it: this I have done elsewhere.[1] It is scarcely necessary to say that corrupt forms of the doctrine implying transmigration of souls into and from animal life have no interest for us; nor have certain religious forms of the doctrine which affirm that human souls are caught in a ceaseless mechanical round of births and deaths, to escape from which is the chief aim of the wise man. We are concerned only with the truth in the view that excursus into earth conditions as a human being, in varied settings and widely separated centuries, furthers the evolution of most souls. Nor is it to be assumed that the *personalities* in such successive lives of the same being are identical. The *soul* is the same, the quality of its "mind" and "heart" are immortal elements, and the wisdom gathered though its past continues to be available to the new personality as intuition. Personality, as we have previously suggested, is the product both of these enduring elements and of the immediate setting—genetic structure, environment, opportunity, and challenge. The "heredity" of the soul will usually ensure that interests and proficiency which it has acquired in one life will appear easily in the next, but the new environment will generally secure that the scope of interest and opportunity is different in the interest of wider development.[2]

In the process of ascent following death of the physical body, the soul using its astral body lives a life of widened interest and satisfaction with expanded sensory and motor faculties available (*vide* Chapter 12). The ordinary person may ascend no higher than these astral levels, and finally (possibly after some hundreds of years) the intensity of consciring may fall to the irreflective stage in which no further progress for such a being is possible on those levels. The shallow expanded stream of life, scarcely moving, has to find new vitality and strength by confinement within the narrow banks of a physical body once more. By rebirth the soul becomes reflective on the physical level, and in the conflict, trial and stress of terrestrial existence a new intensity of con-

---

[1] *Loc. cit.*, Chap. XVIII.

[2] The student of *Oberland Dialogues* (p. 272) may be possibly misled by a statement that "as the Buddhists and Proclus urged long ago, the same self does not pass from life to life". I hope that the distinction we have made between personality and soul is clear. Fawcett makes this very clear on p. 295. "After one mortal life a Plato vanishes, though the soul in the background persists. . . . Plato for the soul is an incident or experiment; a new personality resembling but superior to Plato is to be made in connection with a new body. . . ." The essence of Plato endures.

sciring is built up. On its next ascent the soul may go much further on the astral levels, and even penetrate higher: much depends on the soul's attitude to terrestrial life. It seems likely that many souls who drift through terrestrial life benefiting little from the challenge and experience which life here is particularly able to provide may perforce return again and again. "Young" souls undertaking two, three, or four re-incarnations, we are told by Myers, may then acquire sufficient maturity to render unnecessary any return to physical embodiment. Wider experience and intenser consciring may then be acquired sub-jectively through communion with the group soul, and objectively through descent to the astral levels where in a more restricted environ-ment and by service to those less advanced than themselves they can fit themselves to rise higher.

There are no rigid laws about these things in an imaginal universe. Each soul makes its own bed, and can doubtless lie on it as long as it wants! No one is compelled to progress: there is always free-will. Nevertheless, the imaginal dynamic does endeavour constantly to move souls onwards, and so ministers to the evolution of spirit. Its goal is the re-creation of the Divinely imagined world-system with a fully reflective Divine Society. The individual soul's progress appears to be wrapped up in the great rhythm we have described: descent and ascent, restric-tion and expansion, service and aspiration, building up of consciring on a low level and expenditure of consciring on a higher level.

Many of the statements we have made appear to be *ex cathedra* and the critical reader has every right to ask, "What is your source of knowledge?" Part of what we have said may be regarded as a plausible deduction from Imaginism. Part is based upon the data of revelation— in this case communications believed to be trustworthy, from very able persons who once lived on earth. Certainly no one is invited to accept anything which his intuition does not endorse. But such an attitude is surely the only appropriate one in regard to truth whether in history, philosophy, or religion, and in regard to beauty and insight in all forms of art. No truth or insight of others is of value to us unless we see it to be true for ourselves. All discovery in these fields is ultimately a response of our own souls; even though it is but a distant echo, it reveals that somewhere in our own treasury it is an insight we already possess.

In certain automatic writings, believed to be from F. W. H. Myers,[1] he makes some interesting observations on the idea of rebirth. I select a few of these below. Myers classifies human beings broadly according to their development, as animal-men, soul-men, and spirit-men. He gives

[1] Found in two books of Geraldine Cummins: *The Road to Immortality* and *Beyond Human Personality*. I give my reasons in Chapter 12 for believing these are genuine communications from Myers.

no precise definition of these classes, but it is clear that animal-men are the type whose interests are centred largely on sensation and the things of sense; soul-men have some degree of appreciation of goodness, truth, beauty, and love; spirit-men are rare beings who incarnate only once except for special reasons. Of animal-men Myers says that they almost invariably reincarnate. Of soul-men he says:

"The majority of people only reincarnate two, three, or four times. Though if they had some human purpose or plan to achieve they may return as many as eight or nine times. No arbitrary figure can be named. . . . I do not write as one having authority. This little sketch of the soul's journey in relation to earth is written out of my own experience and knowledge. . . .

"There is no set law concerning reincarnation. At a certain point in its progress, the soul reflects, weighs and considers the facts of its own nature in conjunction with its past life on earth. If you are primitive, this meditation is made through instinct—a kind of emotional thought—that stirs up the depths of your being. Then the spirit helps you to choose your future. You have complete free-will, but your spirit indicates the path you should follow and you frequently obey that indication."

Of the nature of the related Group of souls to which reference has previously been made, Myers gives considerable information which we shall consider in detail later. He points out that the nature of this inter-relationship makes unnecessary more than a few re-births on earth of any one soul. My intuition, such as it is, accepts Myers' statements as plausible. I accept the likelihood of a plurality of lives, in the terms stated. Such a view illuminates much that I find obscure in the in-equalities of souls at birth, so that a Chopin or a Mozart at a childish age shows a degree of musical maturity and competence which neither heredity nor environment can account for. Nor is such precocity con-fined to musical genius: it is found occasionally in mathematics, in aesthetic sensibility, and in spiritual maturity. Moreover, I cannot dismiss as delusive the convictions of certain responsible persons whose subjective experience includes what they believe to be glimpses of previous lives.[1]

MEMORY[2]

It is difficult to think about the nature of man, and in particular the relationship between soul and body, without recognising the import-ance of memory. It is obviously in virtue of my memory of past actions that I can act intelligently today. If I had no memory, I should recognise

[1] Some interesting evidence is found in A. W. Osborn, *The Superphysical*, Chapter XV. (Nicholson and Watson.)

[2] This section is rather technical and may be omitted on first reading.

neither people nor things, including my own appearance. Yet it is one of those essential characteristics of man of which our ignorance is abysmal.

From the Imaginist standpoint we can assign memory a natural place. Divine Imagining conserves the pasts of innumerable world-systems as concrete, fully made reality, and this is presumably the Divine Memory. Individuals similarly conserve on a small scale the sum of their own experience. Personal memory, as we ourselves know, is a faint record, and we normally have access to only parts of this. The phenomenon of hypnosis points to the likelihood that no personal memory ever perishes but that under favourable conditions it can be conscired reflectively. The fabric of memory is normally sustained, except for a scanning-point, at irreflective levels. The recalling of a memory is certainly not a re-experiencing of the past any more than looking at a photograph is re-experiencing the person or scene. Recalling a memory is the consciring of a new construction in the present moment, which draws however on the past for its verisimilitude. This is saying very little, and leaves unanswered the question of what we envisage memory to be. Where is it located, in the brain, in the mind, or in both? Is remembering in the discarnate state similar to ours?

In 1896 Henri Bergson wrote a book *Matter and Memory* in which he dealt with some of these questions. He regarded the brain as an organ of attention to life, and as being primarily concerned with action, not with perception or abstract thought. In other words, brain states were regarded as corresponding to only a small fraction of the sum of mental states. He believed there was only a difference of degree between the (wrongly called) perceptive faculties of the brain and the reflex functions of the spinal cord.

"While the spinal cord transforms the excitations received into movements which are more or less necessarily executed, the brain puts them into relation with motor mechanisms which are more or less freely chosen; but that which the brain explains . . . is action begun, prepared or suggested, it is not perception itself."

As regards memory, Bergson distinguishes two kinds, habit-memory and memory proper. The first of these derives from motor mechanisms of the brain alone; the second, which is true recollection, is a function of mind, although in actually expressing memories motor activity in the brain is involved. Habit-memory is used, for example, when I repeat a poem by heart, or play from memory a piece of music. In contrast to those who consider both perception and true recollection to be brain functions, one being a weak version of the other, Bergson regards them both as mind functions, and points out that we never mistake the perception of a slight sound for the recollection of a loud one. Where a complex thought is being developed in the mind, Bergson would say that it is only that part of it which could be acted out or which could be expressed in terms of sensation which has corresponding brain states.

Bergson finds in the aphasias support for his views. Bear in mind his view that the recall of memories is a mental function and that their expression involves brain activity. In the true aphasias progressive deterioration arises in finding words to express recollections, and according to Ribot, proper nouns disappear first, ordinary nouns next, and verbs last. Those who think that memory is wholly brain function presumably believe that something corresponding to images of these is found in cells of the brain cortex. To these persons Ribot's observation must present a puzzle. On Bergson's view which would regard aphasia as an inhibition or impairment of mental function, we should expect verbs to be accessible longest, for they express action and therefore sufficient brain excitation may be associated with them to produce recall. Proper names are, however, remote from action. Where an aphasic patient cannot find the noun for which he is seeking, Bergson suggests that he may think of an action linked with the noun and thus stimulate the brain to provide the phrase which is a roundabout substitute for it.

When able men have given their best thought to the problems of mind and memory, we do not seem to have advanced much further in a real understanding of their nature. I suppose this is because we are trying to express in objective terms our subjective life. An intelligent discarnate person who has risen to a sufficiently high level may, however, be able to study more objectively that which remains essentially subjective to us. In anatomy and physiology we have studied the structure and function of our physical bodies: so he may be able to study the nature of his non-physical body. His difficulty is likely to be that of finding suitable descriptive terms to convey this knowledge to us. In the scripts which I have alluded[1] to, F. W. H. Myers has endeavoured to explain memory in both incarnate and discarnate beings, but remarks, "I have tried to explain to you what you cannot possibly conceive so long as you are in matter." In attempting to understand his views I have constructed the diagram shown on next page.

We have pictured a human centre of consciring, showing will as a function, and the individual mind as bounded by a full circle. Linked with it is a network of personal memories within a broken circle to suggest that it can be invaded by thought from without and from the Group-mind to which it is intimately related. The right-hand side represents the physical structures. The unifying principle of Myers is the same as the B-consciousness of Geddes (p. 197), which showed

[1] Geraldine Cummins, *The Road to Immortality*, 3rd Imp. (1947), p. 71, etc.

signs of being composite. The dotted part represents a pervading fluid essence of which Myers says it is "something far subtler than electricity and yet of the same nature". I identify it with the "psychic aether" of which much has been said earlier. It receives all the impressions of the senses and precipitates them in the network of memory. In terrestrial life something like a myriad aetheric spider-threads link latent images of the memory network with brain cells. A few of these are shown. Suppose we are trying to recall the name D of a person whose character image A we have access to. If I understand Myers aright, an act of will causes the mind to create B as a kind of temporary travelling image of

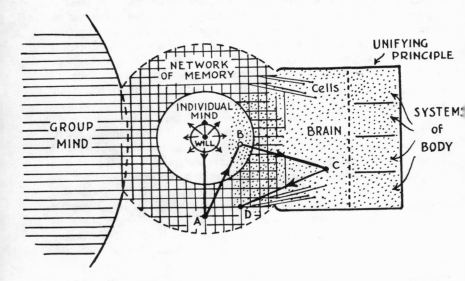

A which finds and may stimulate the particular brain cell C, which in turn is linked with D the lost name. Thus A and D are ultimately linked together.

In discarnate life remembering is a different process since the brain and the aetheric body have perished. The memory network remains associated with the mind, and direct access to it is possible by passing into a certain subjective state.

Myers describes the mind of man as a "power station constantly generating the fresh electric fluid of memory, constantly receiving, constantly giving out again". He says that thoughts imaged superficially and faintly have no length of life, but vehement and emotionally strong images may continue permanently. (This seems very relevant to the subject of haunting.)

For the sake of simplicity the diagram does not show the myriad connections of the body with the individual mind. Myers calls this a "nerve-memory" and describes the waking reflective mind (the full circle) as the product both of this nerve-memory, conveying the body's desires to it, and, most important, a reflection of the subliminal part of ourselves. These features I have not attempted to portray. The diagram is imperfect, but may help some who attempt to follow Myers' thought.

Since the "threads" which relate the memory network to the brain cells are a part of the apparatus of memory for incarnate beings, it is obvious that memories of prior lives, if any, should not normally be available. They are presumably stored in the subliminal part of ourselves and should only be accessible in unusual subjective states.

KARMA AND MORAL LAW

In the adventure of being man, one of the aspects of human life which presents us with a moral and intellectual problem is that of the great inequality of equipment, deserts, and opportunity with which people enter it. Some souls born into the world have healthy bodies, loving parents, an environment of culture and refinement, and opportunities which are the envy of their contemporaries. Others are crippled by disease or incapacity, lack the assurance of affection and security which are a child's basic needs, and find that life brings to them a succession of hardships, difficulties, restrictions, and disappointed hopes. The problem that arises for every sensitive person is a moral one: Is the world just to individuals? It may be that on the whole the verdict of mankind is for life rather than death, that on balance the happiness and satisfaction outweigh the suffering and dissatisfaction, but our moral problem remains. When we are considering human feelings, hopes, and longings, we must move out of the realm of statistics and recognise the worth and the value of the individual.

It is a very old problem, and some aspects of it are faced in the book of Job. It can scarcely be claimed, however, that the writer of this ancient book offers any solution. He dismisses several views that he considers untenable, and certainly helps Job to see his problem in perspective by reminding him that he lives in a world which is full of surprise and mystery. But the writer obviously stands baffled before the problem he sets out to solve, and loses sight of it in a magnificent flow of poetic imagery. Implicitly he says no more than any Oriental who proclaims, "The ways of Allah are inscrutable."

The Christian response to this problem is, I think, somewhat as follows. There are mysteries here which we cannot attempt to explain, but we believe that this life is not all, and that "our light affliction which is but for a moment, worketh for us a far more exceeding and eternal weight of glory". Difficulty, suffering, and hardship may be the soul's opportunity to rise to great heights; they are the refiner's fire which separates the gold from the dross. Perhaps Principal Oman sums it up in a sentence of faith and daring, "It is in this life that all things work together for good, but not as if this life were all."[1]

I also believe that this life is not all, but regard the assumption that the nature of the next life is compensatory to this one as no answer to the questions raised. I quite agree that suffering and difficulty provide the occasion by which *some* people make great spiritual advance, but is this true of the mental defective, or of the child whose personality and disposition have been warped and spoiled by cruelty and the wickedness of others before it could acquire any powers of resistance? Faced with such facts, we ask again how souls came to be born in such circumstances; is it just to them, and where does the responsibility rest?

These questions should not be evaded, but I can see no answer which even begins to look plausible, except in terms of the soul's pre-existence and the general truth embodied in the idea of *karma*. The materialist has no problem: his answer is simply in terms of poor heredity, poor parenthood, poor social conditions, and the laws of chance.

The views we have previously expressed picture the soul as generally entering on birth with experience behind it, but what do we understand by *karma*? It is the extension of the idea of cause and effect to the deeper levels of being, the idea that thoughts and actions create chains of consequence which sometime and somewhere will react upon their creator. It is a moral principle of justice underlying the world, because of which persons and events are drawn into our orbit of experience or repelled from it. If we are looking for the framework or means by which this principle operates, I think we must turn to the deeper parts of the memory network relating the individual mind and the Group-mind, where something akin to telepathy operates to attract and repel other minds. The seeds of past experience remain latent there until quickened by the right stimulus.

The earliest allusion to the doctrine of karma is found in two of the oldest Upanishads.[2] On one occasion King Pravahana teaches it to a Brahmin as the factor determining rebirth. On another occasion King Janaka says:

"According to his works, according to his walk, he becomes; he who works righteousness becomes righteous; he who works evil becomes evil; he becomes holy through holy works (karma), and evil through evil. As they

---

[1] *Honest Religion*, p. 128.
[2] *Brihad Aranyaka* and *Chandogya*.

say, man is formed of desire; as his desire is, so is his will; as his will is, so are his works (karma); whatsoever works he works, to those works he goes." [1]

The same teaching runs through both the Testaments,[2] from which I quote one instance, "For with what judgment ye judge, ye shall be judged: and with what measure ye mete, it shall be measured to you again."

There are some thinkers who criticise the doctrine of karma as mechanistic and deterministic, as though it leaves man for ever imprisoned in binding chains of consequence. This is a complete misunderstanding. At every stage of life up to complete maturity, sometimes called Enlightenment, determinism and freedom concur. The one certainly limits the other but does not eliminate it. The spiritually advanced man has a wide area of freedom, the restrictions of his karma are fewer, and his soul has very effective control over the body of sub-imaginals which it uses. The primitive man has only a little area of freedom, and his soul is to a very substantial degree influenced by the body sub-imaginals. His instinctual desires very largely rule him. If I play cricket, my freedom is limited but not destroyed by the framework of rules determined for me. It is so with human life. We are all sensible of the given-ness of very much of our living, but within this framework we have a limited area of freedom to choose and act. The use we make of it is all-important as by this we increase or diminish the freedom we *shall* possess. The determined area is that of karmic consequence, the area within which we are free is that of our reflective consciring. We suffer and enjoy today what our soul (or a closely related soul) has created in the past, and we shall tomorrow enter into a karma modified by our present action and motive. We are the masters of our destiny.

Gautama the Buddha made perfectly clear that he was no exponent of a mechanistic karma.[3] (His views, of course, have suffered at the hands of his followers.) He stated that the motive and spirit in which actions were performed were of determining importance, and specifically said that where deeds took their origin in covetousness, hatred, or infatuation —these were the deeds whose consequences would have to be met, if not in the same life, in a subsequent one.

The *Bhagavad Gita*, which deals at length with Action and its karmic consequences, recognises the same truth. It teaches that all deeds should be performed as an offering to God, that is, without concern for success or failure, praise or blame. "Therefore do thy duty perfectly, without care for the results; for he who does his duty disinterestedly attains the

---

[1] Charles Johnston has drawn attention to the likeness to Revelation xxii. v. 11-12.

[2] Matt. vii. 2, xvi. 27; Rom. ii. 5, 6; 2 Cor. v. 10; Gal. vi. 7, 8; Psalm lxii. 12; Prov. xxiv. 12.

[3] H. C. Warren, *Buddhism in Translations*, pp. 218-21. (Harvard Oriental Series.)

Supreme." It is repeatedly said that there are different ways to the Supreme, and no one should assume that withdrawal from life into meditation is a superior way. It describes as a "saint" and as "the wisest of men" he who whether acting or not acting in the world has his mind centred in God.

"The wise call him a sage; for whatever he undertakes is free from the motives of desire [i.e. selfish desire], and his deeds are purified by the fire of Wisdom.

"Expecting nothing, his mind and personality controlled, without greed, doing bodily actions only; though he acts, yet he remains untainted.

"Content with what comes to him, without effort of his own, mounting above the pairs of opposites, free from envy, his mind balanced both in success and failure, though he act, yet the consequences do not bind him."

The *Gita* clearly envisages that as we progress we cancel our karmic debts and cease to create fresh karma; we enlarge our sphere of freedom and push back the frontier of the determined; we become masters of life because there is no selfish desire in us to anchor us to it. There is nothing we want for ourselves.

There are some who criticise the doctrine of karma as leading to fatalism—the attitude in which a man says, "It is my fate: I can do nothing about it." This also is a misunderstanding of karma, for it teaches in the first place that there is no fate except that which we, in our association with others, have created. Moreover, by meeting every situation in the right spirit we can "cancel the debt" and need face it no more. In the second place it teaches that we are creators of the future, and it is a call to courageous living. An extension of the same misunderstanding may lead such men to suppose that they are not their brother's keeper—that compassion and the helping hand extended to a brother are a waste of time, for every misfortune is his "karma". This is a complete travesty of the doctrine. None of us live in isolation. Our lives are lived in association with others, and these associative links are frequently part of our karma. We fail most lamentably if we fail in love and compassion and such aid as we can give to our fellows. The karma of omission may be equally as grievous as that of commission.

What may be described as an individual's karma is intimately related to that of others in the Group-soul to which he belongs, and may also be linked with the karma of other interacting groups and more comprehensive wholes. It is important to remember this in the light of the concept of "Divinity of Measure" to which it is closely related. Indeed, karma might be regarded as the detailed mode of outworking in its moral aspect of the Imaginal dynamic which keeps unbalance within limits and moves us slowly forward towards the best imaginable end.

We return now to consider how the concept of karma bears upon the riddle of birth, with its widely different equipment, environment, and opportunities, sometimes apparently so unjust to the individual. Taken in conjunction with the assumption of prior lives, we have at least a plausible standpoint. These varying conditions are part of the karmic inheritance of the incarnating soul. The spirit which nourishes the journeying soul guides it to go forth again into circumstances which will re-awaken some of the seeds of its karma, knowing that by meeting these rightly, the soul will take a further step forward on the road of its destiny. We are presented again with fences at which we have taken a toss. We meet again situations calling for similar moral choice, and when we choose the higher way for its own sake, rather than the lower way we chose before, we have mastered and cancelled this karma. Thus suffering which we have merited may make us compassionate with those who suffer and teach us fortitude and courage. Even the person to whom life deals hard blows and brings bitter disappointments will meet them with more equanimity and resolution if he realises that these are not the blows of chance but part of his own destiny which he has sometime to meet, and moreover that his spirit led him to meet it now, knowing that he has adequate resources to triumph over it.

Let it be said, however, that here is no basis for judging others. To say to the poor cripple, "Thus you have earned", is utterly presumptuous. For one thing, our karma is by no means isolated from that of others—it may indeed be closely linked with it. This works both ways. For my own part, I believe there is redemptive activity on the human level as well as on those sublime levels of self-sacrifice which call forth the admiration and worship of mankind. Great souls may choose to incarnate into conditions of hardship, handicap, and suffering, in order to redeem and inspire, perhaps for the love they bear for another soul who can only be helped in this way.

Again, we should remind ourselves that in an imaginal universe there is no rigid "law" of karma, no mechanical sequence of events, no cycle of mere recurrence, no history repeating itself; always there is freedom to choose, always the new entering in, whether as the choices of others or as the descent of help from more advanced beings which we may call grace. We are all rich with treasure we have not earned, which others have earned for us.

As Rosenstock-Huessy put it: Man is primarily a loved soul.[1]

[1] Quoted from J. H. Oldham's *Life is Commitment*, p. 77.

Chapter

10

LIGHT ON EVIL AND SUFFERING

I have wept a million tears:
Pure and proud one, where are thine,
What the gain though all thy years
In unbroken beauty shine?

All your beauty cannot win
Truth we learn in pain and sighs:
You can never enter in
To the circle of the wise.

They are but the slaves of light
Who have never known the gloom,
And between the dark and bright
Willed in freedom their own doom.

Think not in your pureness there,
That our pain but follows sin:
There are fires for those who dare
Seek the throne of might to win.

Pure one, from your pride refrain:
Dark and lost amid the strife
I am myriad years of pain
Nearer to the fount of life.

When defiance fierce is thrown
At the god to whom you bow,
Rest the lips of the Unknown
Tenderest upon my brow.

A. E. (*The Man to the Angel*)

THERE is probably no problem which presses so constantly on the minds of men as that of evil, and particularly that form of it which leads to pain and suffering in man himself. Suffering may be physical or mental, and there can be few people who at some time in their life have not passed through such experiences and asked themselves questions about it. These questions may be pushed aside when the emergency passes, but they are persistent questions, and our philosophy of life demands the incorporation of some answer. They are, moreover, questions that thinkers seldom claim to answer completely or wholly satisfactorily. It is interesting, and perhaps significant, that we tend to be incredulous or even suspicious of any such claim. It is as though most men feel intuitively, however unwilling they may be to admit it, that within the span of human life we do not hold all the clues.

The philosopher is troubled by the origin of evil, its status, and its relation to God. The plain man has more immediate concerns. He sees people struck down by disease such as cancer—a hazard which no foresight on their part could have avoided, and to which no folly on their part has contributed—and he asks, "Is life just?" He reads of floods, of earthquakes, volcanic eruptions, and famine which may cause the deaths of thousands of innocent people, and result in injury or catastrophe to thousands who survive. He wonders, "Are we at the mercy of chance? What have these people done to deserve this?" He knows that war and unemployment are scourges of society which do not always bring suffering to the guilty men but involve millions who are innocent. It is estimated that in one visitation of the Black Plague in England over three million people perished, more than one-third of the population at that time.[1] Yet Gibbon's opinion is that "man has much more to dread from the passions of his fellow-creatures than from the convulsions of the elements". We need not enlarge upon the tragic spectacle of what a pessimist called "the martyrdom of man". It is only one aspect of life, but it is sufficiently oppressive to make many sincere people share the dilemma of John Stuart Mill. God cannot both be all-good and all-powerful. He may be all-good but not able to prevent things going wrong, or He may be all-powerful but not all-good. We shall look at this dilemma later. Our immediate task is to see what light is thrown on the problem of evil and suffering from the Imaginist viewpoint.

EVIL AND THE TIME-PROCESS

We shall not concern ourselves with definitions of good and evil, since we are concerned with the basic questions of their existence, not with ethical questions involved in the debatable boundary between them. We may take good to be that which the high-minded person regards as desirable, and evil to be that which he regards as undesirable. We saw in Chapter 8 that the process of Creation and the Metaphysical Fall gave rise to innumerable finite sentients whose interests started to clash. This conflict may be regarded as the initial evil, although it was the first stage of descent on the long road to a higher perfection. The lowest sentients such as electrons, atoms, etc., have very little initiative and remain under good central control, so that their behaviour may be statistically predicted. When we rise to biological levels, however, local initiatives start to run amok, and imaginal variations have appeared with no other consideration than that of forwarding the interests of their particular species. Consider such creatures as the python, the scorpion, the red-back spider or the taipan. The natural sub-imaginals from which

[1] Quote from *The Human Situation*, by W. Macneile Dixon.

these derive, create entirely for their own ends, in order to gain an advantage over others. We must not blame Divine Imagining for these unpleasant growths of free local consciring. The risks associated with freedom and chance had to be taken on this, the only road which leads to the end to be reached. The soil which grows flowers will also grow weeds.

If, as we suggested earlier, intelligences higher than man may experiment psycho-kinetically in genetics, we may also have to face the possibility of miscreations and undesirable products from this source. These intelligences may not always be dominantly wise or good, and ugly and virulent creatures may arise either accidentally or deliberately from their experiments. If imagining in the corrupt human being may give rise to ugliness and horror in art and letters, its counterpart in more powerful discarnate beings may give rise to some of the unpleasant types in Nature. Against these features good intelligences may have to contend with their ingenuity and resources. On such a view, "Nature, red in tooth and claw" may not wholly be the product of conflict on its own level, but may be partly the outworking of conflict on higher psychical levels.

Another source of evil in the world lies in the failure of higher sub-imaginals, which descend so as to manifest through lower ones, failing adequately to control the latter. Such anatomical failures in development as the patent inter-auricular septum or ductus arteriosus, the cleft palate, and so on are examples of this. Prior to modern surgery, how many mothers must have lost their life in child-birth due to cephalo-pelvic disproportion. Another aspect of failure on the part of descending sub-imaginals is their inability to remove vestigial organs such as the vermiform appendix. The genes responsible for this organ in man apparently show such strong conservative tendencies that the power of the unifying principle has not yet broken them up. Lower sub-imaginals, such as those of organs, occasionally do a disservice to higher descending sub-imaginals (such as human souls) by their excessive and resistant conservatism, so that defects like congenital deafness, night-blindness, and insanity are preserved by heredity. We must face the obvious fact that souls are sometimes too weak to compel lower sub-imaginals to serve their ends satisfactorily.

Another source of what we are disposed to call evil is found in the operation of the great over-ruling principle of Divinity of Measure. This sometimes involves suffering for some in the interests of the whole. Suffering may arise through the surgery which removes a growth or an organ from the body, in the best interests of the latter. From the standpoint of the tumour or organ this is evil, for the process will lead to its death, but from the viewpoint of the body which is a greater whole, it is good, for it will prolong its life.

We must not overlook the fact that, in our world, pain and suffering are among the most potent stimuli of effort. They promote the desire for change, and then there may result research, struggle, and enterprise which are essential to progress. As long as things remain comfortable, man is not a creature likely to make any great effort, or have any great aspiration to go forward. W. R. Matthews expresses this[1]:

"No reflective person who has grasped the conception of the development of free personalities, a good greater than any degree of satisfactory feeling, would desire that existence should be freed from all obstacles, that everything should be given without effort, or that man should be endowed with happiness in such a way as to deprive him of his status as a self-determining being. As J. S. Mill remarked, no one would really choose to become a cow, even if he would be a perfectly happy cow: still less would anyone really wish to become an automaton however contented."

I think this thought lies behind A. E.'s poem *The Man to the Angel*. It is conceivable that there are other world-systems in which the suffering and conflict characteristic of physical existence do not arise, and that these lead ultimately to Divine Societies which are different from ours. We cannot tell: but we know that we are committed to *one* great adventure in this imaginal universe, and that our finite God is Himself involved deeply in it.

We have mentioned some of the sources of evil and suffering in our world. The price to be paid by human beings may seem very high, and the way may seem very long, but this can only be rightly judged in the light of the end to be attained. When we have reached the level of the Divine Society we shall know what the vision is, and looking back over the long vista of the past we may expect to be immeasurably grateful for the best imaginable consummation. Principal Oman said with great insight[2]:

"If . . . the sole perfect order is knowing God's truth of our own insight and doing God's will of our own discernment and joyful consecration, and what distinguishes children of God from mere works of God is just search for truth however imperfect, and aspiration after righteousness however inadequate, we can have some understanding of the need for the painful and wandering way man has had to travel, with its errors and its sins, its divisions and its conflicts."

THE EVILS WE SUFFER BUT HAVE NOT CAUSED

We may summarise the sources of what *we* call evil in the world as follows:

(1) Creative initiative, i.e. freedom to conscire, may be abused.

---

[1] *God in Christian Thought and Experience*, p. 237.   [2] *Honest Religion*, p. 18.

It may be abused for mere self-interest by (a) sub-human sentients, (b) human sentients, (c) super-human sentients.

(2) Higher sub-imaginals may fail to control adequately the lower sub-imaginals through which they manifest.

(3) The great principle of Divinity of Measure must operate in the interests of the whole, and in doing so must sometimes disregard the immediate interests of a part.

It is obvious that what is called evil depends on one's standpoint, i.e. upon the breadth of one's range of consciring. When a starving man has caught a rabbit, *he* thinks it is good, but the rabbit would not share that view. What is called evil depends also on the standard to which judgment is referred. A surgical operation may at the time entail the evil of suffering, both physical and mental, but it is considered good in relation to the end of greater health to which it leads. A man who rescues a child from a burning house may suffer the evil of burns and disfigurement, but the courage manifested and the end achieved lead us to acclaim the act as supremely good. Even if he had failed in the rescue and lost his own life, the judgment of the best of men would be to praise the act as good. This is because in the scale of value-judgments the revelation of these higher imaginals—courage, heroism, and compassion—is assessed more highly than the entailed evil of physical suffering, or even of a life cut short.

It is important that we should exercise the same kind of judgment and adopt the highest vantage-point to which our minds can rise when we express our views on the world process. It would be unjust to the author of a play to condemn him as a blackguard, or as a weak person who has lost control of it, on the strength of a passing glimpse of the stage. We should require to know what went before and, more important still, what will come after the fragment we observed. This is why an *adequate* philosophy of life is so important, and by this I mean one which places the span of an individual's life in the setting of a vastly greater whole. This is also why I attach importance to the data of psychical research and the far-reaching inferences which may be made therefrom, living as we are in an age which demands evidence but is prone to assume that the data of the senses are all there is to be known. In the absence of a perspective which can see the individual's life as a fragment of a continuous and greater whole, it must often seem meaningless, tragic, and unjust.

Let us turn to look at the catastrophe which follows from flood, volcano, earthquake, lightning, and tempest. These sometimes lead to suffering and death under circumstances with which man has had little to do, and which in most cases it would have been difficult for him to avoid. It is obvious that these are hazards which are unavoidable by living creatures on a planet such as ours. On another planet at a different stage of its evolution some of them would be unknown, but so would life as we know it. Moreover, other hazards for other forms of life would be inevitable. The occurrence of flood, volcano, earthquake, lightning, and tempest are but extreme instances of processes which are constantly in operation, which we can express in terms of habits of Nature, and which maintain our planet in its present condition. What should really call forth our wonder is not the occurrence of these catastrophic occasions, but their comparative rarity, and that over-ruling stabilising principle to which we have frequently referred as the Divinity of Measure.

If we turn to the other and greater natural hazard of man, disease, we face an essentially similar situation. The fact at which we should wonder is the normal harmonious working of our complex organisms, and not that sometimes they work imperfectly. Consider some of the types of disease to which we are prone: infections, degenerative diseases, tumours, metabolic upsets, and psychosomatic disorders.

It is familiar knowledge today that infectious disease is due to the invasion of micro-organisms, and these have tended therefore to acquire a bad reputation. The kinds responsible for disease are, however, a very small fraction of the total and, taken as a whole, micro-organisms are of the greatest benefit to mankind. Indeed, they are indispensable to human life on the planet, and play as important a part in the economy of Nature as animal and vegetable life. Let us remember that essential parts of the bodies of all animals contain proteins. Now, proteins are derived from plant life which synthesises them from nitrates in the soil. There would be no continuous supply of nitrates in the soil if it were not for micro-organisms, some of which break down animal tissues and excreta while others extract the nitrogen of the air for this purpose. Our body surfaces, both internal and external, swarm with bacteria fighting for existence. From the great majority of these we suffer no ill, we may even gain some advantage. It is only a minority of micro-organisms which run amok in the sense of unscrupulously attacking the tissues of their host; moreover, if these go too far they will pay the price and perish with their host. When we look at the whole picture of micro-organisms in perspective there is no ethico-philosophical problem. That a few should run amok, using their creative function at the expense of higher sub-imaginals, is always a hazard connected with freedom however limited. It is an unavoidable risk, and, given time, the resources of the higher sub-imaginals are generally equal to an effective counterstroke.

Perhaps it is not too sweeping to say that all other kinds of disease are due to a loss of effective control, i.e. higher sub-imaginals lose the power to keep the lower subservient to their ends. This is obviously so with degenerative diseases such as arterio-sclerosis. It is notably illustrated in the case of tumours. We ought to wonder at the normal control of growth, whereas we find a vexing problem in the comparatively uncommon phenomenon of uncontrolled growth. The possibility of running amok is inherent in the freedom of finite sentients: a risk that was taken in our kind of world. As the power of those sub-imaginals which give rise to souls grows with their evolution, increasing control may greatly minimise the occasional tendency of the lower to run amok.

This suggestion leads us naturally to those diseases characterised as metabolic, where some disturbance of the hormone system takes place. The reader is aware that there are a number of glands in the body which secrete chemical substances as required, that these are carried by the blood stream, and that they control processes in distant parts of the body. We shall not enlarge on the part played by the endocrine system, but merely remark that it is intimately related to certain irreflective levels of the mind. The mind can effectively influence this system, and in its turn it is influenced by it. The higher sub-imaginals (souls) and the lower sub-imaginals (glands) show marked reciprocal effects.

Finally, in psycho-somatic disease it is not the lower sub-imaginals which run amok but the higher. That part of the higher sub-imaginal which we call mind exercises control of the lower, but it is a perverted control.

We must admit that pain may sometimes be a useful signal that something is wrong and may lead the human sentient to take action to prevent more serious damage. This is a useful form of sensation, just as are the special senses, and we can scarcely call it evil just because its feeling-tone is unpleasant. The end would not be achieved unless it were unpleasant. The real mass of pain and suffering arises through the misuse of creative freedom, the running amok of lesser sentients, and the loss of higher imaginal control.

It is not necessary to dwell on those balancing activities of the Divinity of Measure which result in the suffering of some in the interests of the whole. If it were not for the conflict of sub-imaginals, cod-fish might fill the Atlantic and locusts might eat all vegetation. This might seem a most desirable end from their standpoint, but from ours it would be counted evil. So Fawcett remarks[1]:

"What you name 'the means of subsistence', 'climate', human and animal 'rivals', and so forth, all alike exemplify groups of imaginals which by limiting

[1] *Z.D.*, p. 473.

one another and other imaginals, secure the proportions most favourable to the world-plan. The seemingly banal pressure of populations against the 'means of subsistence', as noted by Malthus and others, is the outward and visible sign of a balancing process effected through struggle."

From one standpoint it is an evil that malnutrition and consequent disease should take heavy toll of life in over-populated countries, but must it not be admitted that the progress of the whole is more favoured by living under conditions where the struggle for mere existence is not all-consuming and where some energy and enterprise can be devoted to higher ends?

THE EVIL WE CAUSE

After facing the evil in the world from which man suffers, but which he has not caused, we must freely recognise that by far the larger part is caused by man himself through the misuse of his freedom. It is analagous to the running amok of lower sentients when higher control has broken down. There is this important difference, however, that when reflective consciring is attained at man's level, he must accept moral responsibility for his actions. He makes conscious choices, he acts with motives and intentions and the operation of karma begins. It is important to distinguish between acts and intentions, for, as the Buddha pointed out, it is the latter which have karmic implications for the character of the person.

We do not propose to enlarge upon the evil which man has directly or indirectly caused. It is a vast pyramid with which it is his responsibility to deal. I do not wish to imply that he is without higher help in this task. On the contrary, he may count on the aid of his elder brothers on higher levels of existence; but without man's own co-operation they are impotent. Grace, which is unmerited help, derives from God but is mediated in its descent through the hierarchy of beings devoted to His service.

The evil caused by man may be classified as follows:

(*a*) Moral evil, an offence within the compass of man's free choice, against Goodness and Love.

(*b*) Error, ignorance, and faulty judgment, an offence against Truth and Wisdom.

(*c*) Ugliness, an offence against Beauty.

There is scarcely need to delineate moral evil: pride, anger, deceit, cruelty, lust, greed, all forms of egotism—the assertion of self-interest and the disregard of other's welfare. Their strength derives partly from the instinctual tendencies of lower sub-imaginals which constitute the body, and partly from the soul's own past attitudes. It may perhaps be the recognition of these truths which lies behind the idea of "original sin", a concept unfortunately named and commonly misunderstood. Once reflective consciring is attained, man has his destiny in his own hands. He must then start to contend with the egoistic tendencies which have arisen through conflict and learn that his future evolution is through love. It cannot be claimed that this truth has yet been learned or extensively practised by mankind. The great convulsions of our time —war, economic distress, and social disharmony—are evidence of the long way man has still to go in dealing with those moral evils of which they are the manifestations.

The evils of error, ignorance, and faulty judgment, are a consequence of the immaturity of man. His ignorance is great; his imagining frequently has no correspondence with reality. Truth, which is the substitute for reality in our thinking, is "menaced always by error which is revealed as an aberration due to finite fancy". There is no need to remind the reader of the strange things which men have believed and erroneously called truth, nor of the intolerance and persecution by them of others who did not accept their beliefs. We should also have to place in this category of evil those errors of judgment which lead to accidents and physical catastrophes on land, sea, and air.

Finally, there is the evil of ugliness. Some features of the animal world are products of the war of sub-imaginals, and possibly of superhuman sentients. But man has added much to the world that by no stretch of imagination can be called beautiful or even pleasant. It is another aspect of his immaturity and limited vision. It has been said of man that he "needs must love the highest when he sees it". The trouble is that the highest he has the capacity to recognise may be low, for it is determined by his development.

GOD AND EVIL

We turn to look briefly at some of the philosophical issues associated with the existence of evil. In particular we return to the propositions of J. S. Mill's dilemma referred to earlier.

(a) *The proposition that God might not be wholly good.* The common sequence of thought probably runs as follows: Man does evil things because his nature is partially evil. This is presumably because of the influence of heredity and environment. Each generation may therefore blame its predecessors: but from where did the first men derive their evil? Even if it was only a potentiality of evil, must not this be attributed to the Creator?

I think it will be clear to the reader that a world-system cannot embody two contradictory goals. If the sentients within it were to possess some degree of *real freedom*, then they were *free* to misuse it for evil ends or to use it for good ends. Two things may then be claimed. Firstly, if God being omniscient foresaw how men would misuse it, is He not to that extent responsible for allowing it to appear? Secondly, if He was aware of the possibility of evil, is He wholly good? The answer to the first question is surely yes, but this does not mean that God is not wholly good. All evil is relative to some viewpoint. If freedom granted to finite sentients could lead only to evil or to a lesser good, it would stand condemned. In as much as it can lead to a vastly greater good it is fully justified. This vastly greater good is no less than full communion with God in and through the Divine Society. The second question is answered by Dr. W. R. Matthews,[1] who stresses the distinction between "knowing" by directly experiencing a thing and "knowing about" which is indirect. He points out that while a patient alone has intimate knowledge of his pain, the doctor who attends him may have knowledge about it, although it is not a part of his direct experience. So it may be with God and evil; he has knowledge about it, but stands opposed to it.

(b) *The proposition that God might not be omnipotent.* The implication is that if He were, He would destroy evil or prevent it. This deduction is not justified for reasons we have discussed above. The possibility of evil is the only way through to a vastly greater good. To prevent evil would be to abrogate the real freedom of finite sentients. As a proposition, however, we accept its truth in relation to the finite God or Divine Society of our world-system. We ascribe omnipotence to the supreme power alone: Divine Imagining.

(c) *The proposition that evil is an illusion.* Faced with the dilemma of Mill, there is another way by which some people have sought mental satisfaction. They have in some form denied the reality of evil. The extreme position claims that evil is an illusion: it does not exist. We only think it does, and such thinking is itself delusive. Such a view held by Christian Scientists is in such notable contrast with common sense and with rational judgment based on observation, that if it were true, *all* rational judgment would be suspect and might well be delusive. Furthermore, such a claim leaves unexplained the cause of this widespread delusion. We should be driven to a kind of pantheism in which there is one reality which is equally present everywhere, an impossible position.

(d) *The proposition that evil is the absence of good.* This view, supported by Scholastic philosophers, is an equally strange one. Apart from the existence of logical objections to it,[2] it is a view which must

---

[1] *God in Christian Thought and Experience*, p. 240.
[2] C. E. M. Joad, *God and Evil*, pp. 83-6. (Faber and Faber Ltd., 1942.)

appear to most people completely inadequate to the facts. When we consider some of the expressions of evil which have occurred in our time, of Dachau and Belsen, of Hitler's gas-chambers, of all the cruelty and torture which some men have inflicted on others, of the greed and cynicism which exploit human lives for profit, of the conspiracy of evil which led Christ to His cross, who but very academic philosophers could entertain for a moment the view that "evil is nothing positive" but only the absence of good? We dismiss it without further comment.

(e) *The proposition that evil is entailed by good, which is its opposite.* If this were true we should be driven either to the view that God is not wholly good, or to a fundamental dualism such as that of Zoroaster, or to the view that He was neither good nor evil. None of these conclusions being acceptable to us, we must repudiate the proposition that the existence of evil is the necessary consequence of good's existence. Sometimes a rather different statement is made: that we would not know or recognise good, apart from the evil with which we are able to contrast it. I think this must be admitted, but I think the distinction made previously between "knowing" which is experiencing, and "knowing about" may be relevant. We could presumably have used our freedom to know good while only knowing about evil (assuming that there was some evil to know about). In fact, we have all misused our freedom to know, that is to experience both good and evil. It is perhaps not without significance that knowing the latter has not helped us to know the former.

We have frequently expressed the view that there are different significant levels of reality in the universe. It seems to me a most significant thing that the mystics, in their penetration to the higher levels, return to tell us of the all-pervading sense of unity. They speak of Peace but not of Strife, of Joy but not of Sorrow, of Beauty but not of Ugliness. These observations are possible, because in ordinary states of awareness the mystics have experienced like the rest of us the clash and strife of the opposites. It is satisfying to know, on their testimony, that the higher levels of the universe are free from such conflict. It is the things which we in our most exalted moments call good which are found there. But we must finish where we began—that what we call good and evil depend on the quality of the observer. On very high levels conflict may exist between the good and the not-so-good, although to mortal eyes both lights may be so bright that we cannot distinguish between them.

DOES GOD SUFFER?

The reader is quite justified in saying, "How can *we* know?" Any answer can only be speculative, and it implies that we have in some sense tried to think and feel our way into Divine experience which is so vastly beyond our own. It is however a question which is asked, and one to which theologians have presented no united answer. On the one hand we have the view of which I may take Dr. Leslie Weatherhead as a spokesman[1]:

"We are driven to contemplate a God who carries our sorrows in a sense that is overwhelming and awe-inspiring. . . . In a sentence it comes to this, that the sufferings of men are the sufferings of God. Indeed it cannot even be put like that. The sufferings of men are a shadow. The substance is an anguish, poignant and terrible, which only the heart of God could bear."

Arguing from the immanence of God, he believes that God is hurt and injured when the sparrow falls to the ground, and therefore can no longer be the medium of expresssion of His purpose. On the level of man, Weatherhead says, "the suffering which is ours in terms of pain, is His in terms of something which is much more intimate than sympathy". G. A. Studdert-Kennedy[2] passionately supports this in his verse written under the stressful conditions of the First World War. It is a viewpoint which popular Christian thought probably endorses.

At the other extreme, the Greek element in Christian theological thought places God above change and the things of this temporal sphere. He is transcendent: and since to Him the whole of time is an open scroll, He can neither be surprised nor sorrowful. Possibly the weight of theological opinion takes this view.

Perhaps Dr. Matthews may be quoted[3] as holding an intermediate opinion when he says:

"It is not necessary to hold that suffering is the predominant note in the life of God, if we assert that God suffers. Pain may, even in our human life, enter into an experience which, taken as a whole, is triumphant and joyous."

Dr. Weatherhead would agree, for he says, "Underneath the terrible anguish of God which none can fathom, there is the deep sentiment of joy, because . . . He knows the end to which the universe is tending." Christian theology, holding a Trinitarian doctrine, would probably also support the view that the sacrificial life and death of Jesus revealed in Time the eternal nature of God. To this it might be replied that the essential nature was revealed in the love, not in the suffering. On the human level doubtless there cannot be love without the willingness to sacrifice the self, and to suffer for the beloved, but how far our human terms and attributes are applicable to God is a question to which no answer seems possible. We know a little of what love is, but we do not

[1] Leslie D. Weatherhead, *Why do Men Suffer?*, pp. 141-4. (S.C.M. Press Ltd., 1935.
[2] *The Unutterable Beauty.* (Hodder and Stoughton Ltd., 1927.)
[3] *Loc. cit.*, p. 248.

know what it means to have Love combined with immeasurable Wisdom and Knowledge.

Of Divine Imagining, the supreme frontal Power, I should claim that He is beyond suffering. The issues which we are discussing therefore refer to the finite God of our world-system, the Divine Society. I am myself disposed to say that suffering is not the right term to apply to God. He feels love, He knows *about* our suffering, and He feels that pity which is moved to succour it, which is best called compassion.

I am helped in this perplexing issue by a simple human situation, although I should not wish to claim it as an analogy. A child breaks her doll and is overcome with grief. Her feelings are deep and her suffering and distress are touching to the mother. The mother feels compassion for the child and tries to comfort her. I do not think it is true to say that the mother suffers with the child, for she cannot enter into the limitations of the child's outlook and feel the same concern about the doll. Her wider knowledge of life and values forbids it. She feels sorry, however, at the child's grief, and at the limitation of outlook which makes it so intense, and her love and compassion flow out towards the child. Perhaps God looks at us and says

I will be sorry for their childishness.[1]

I wonder if the root of all mental suffering is not to be found in isolation and separation from God—in confinement within the prison walls of the separate ego? I judge then that there cannot be any suffering for those, the Divine Society, who are one in their communion with Him.

Rabindranath Tagore, whose saintliness and wisdom have been an inspiration to many in both East and West, wrote thus[2]:

"The barrier of Self is *maya*. When it is dispelled, then we in our suffering have tasted the draught of sorrow that wells up from the heart of creation, flowing out to be merged and transformed into the sea of endless joy.

"When we do not see ourselves in the Infinite, when we imagine our sorrow to be our very own, then life becomes untrue and its burden becomes heavy. I understand more and more the truth of Buddha's teaching, that the root of all our miseries is this self-consciousness. We have to recognise the consciousness of the All before we can solve the mystery of pain and be free.

"Our emancipation lies through the path of suffering. We must unlock the gate of joy by the key of pain. Our heart is like a fountain. So long as it is driven through the narrow channel of self it is full of fear and doubt and sorrow for then it is dark and does not know its end. But when it comes out into the open, on the bosom of the All, then it glistens in the light and sings in the joy of freedom."

[1] Coventry Patmore's poem *The Toys*.
[2] C. F. Andrews, *Letters to a Friend*, p. 80. (George Allen and Unwin Ltd., 1928.)

TIME, CAUSATION, AND FREEDOM

Here at the roaring loom of Time I ply
And weave for God the garment thou see'st Him by.

GOETHE

Onward the chariot of the Untarrying moves;
  Nor day divulges him nor night conceals;
Thou hear'st the echo of unreturning hooves
  And thunder of irrevocable wheels.

WILLIAM WATSON

His life and work were based on a reasoned philosophy of conduct. Its
corner stones were humility and discipline. The life of man was difficult but
not desperate, and to live it worthily you must forget yourself and love
others. . . . He believed that in the world as it was created there was a
soul of goodness, and that, in spite of evil, the inward frame of things was
wiser than its critics.

JOHN BUCHAN (on Sir Walter Scott)

THESE three topics have already been approached in Chapter 2 and
again in dealing with precognition in Chapter 4. Each of them has been
the subject of much discussion among philosophers, and into this it is
not proposed to enter. We shall here review the attitude of Imaginism
towards them.

THE NATURE OF TIME

There are some aspects of time which are strange, yet familiar to
everyone. We all live in, and order our lives by clock-time, which is
derived from some periodic natural process—the rotation of the earth
on its axis, or the revolution of the earth round the sun. Time is believed
to "flow" independently of observers' wishes or inclinations, and it is
the same for us all. We cannot arrest its flow, still less can we travel
through it into past or future. We can act only in that vanishingly small
interval called the "specious present". All this is commonplace.

On the other hand, human minds appear to be related to time in
certain rather extraordinary ways. I shall give some examples. (1) Even
though our reason assures us that clock-time flows uniformly, our *sense*
of the passage of time is very variable. If I am waiting impatiently for
the kettle to boil, with nothing to engage my interest, time appears to
pass slowly. If I am interested in a book, it appears to pass speedily.
In pleasant company we say that the hours pass with inconsiderate

haste; with those who bore us the hours drag interminably. It is clear that our *interest*, and the degree of our detachment from the observation of time's passage, affect our sense of it considerably. (2) To a child, time passes slowly; with advancing age the years seem to pass with increasing swiftness. This sense may not be directly connected with age (which is a condition of the physical organism); it is probably associated with breadth of interest. There is a sense in maturity of so much to do and to learn, and this contrasts with the brevity of incarnate life. Lecomte du Nouy[1] has suggested that for a child "the time that elapses between the third and seventh years represents a duration of fifteen or twenty years for a grown man". (3) Some people have the ability before going to sleep to determine with considerable accuracy the time at which they will awaken. (4) Closely related to this, it would seem, is the precision with which a post-hypnotic suggestion will be carried out at a stated future time. This can be done even though the person has no access to clocks or watches in the interval.[2]

These examples suggest that the relation between the human mind and time is a peculiar one. Some thinkers have suggested that we should recognise the existence of psychological time, but if so, its relationship to clock-time must vary with the individuals' subjective states, and such a concept is not going to be easy to handle or develop. I confess I have often wondered whether there is not some fundamental relationship between the sense of time's passing and the breadth of consciring. Hints of this come from many directions, but I think one of the most consistent sources is that of mystical experience. One mystic writes of a profound experience which "must have slipped into the interval between two demi-semi-quavers" so that the "swiftly flowing continuity of the music was not interrupted". Another says that "only a few minutes could have been occupied by an experience in the spirit, of which the incidents were so vivid and the details so numerous that my memory still fails to exhaust them". To very limited conscring a few hours may seem an age; to very profound conscring a few centuries may seem a moment. To the may-fly its few hours may seem a full lifetime of experience; to the great Being who rules our world-system one of the Ancients said, "a thousand years in thy sight are but as yesterday when it is past, and as a watch in the night".

There are three characteristics of time which are generally regarded as fundamental: duration, simultaneity, and succession. It is of the last of these that we commonly think in connexion with change and the "flow" of time, but all of them find a natural explanation in Imaginism.

---

[1] Lecomte du Nouy, *Biological Time*. (Macmillan & Co. Ltd., N.Y., 1937.)
[2] T. W. Mitchell, *Medical Psychology & Psychical Research*. (Methuen & Co. Ltd., 1922.)

Duration, the continuing of things in existence, is the conservative aspect of Divine consciring. Succession is the condition of the additive or novel aspect of Divine consciring. Because Divine Imagining is the foundation principle, its nature is revealed in change, and time-succession is therefore a real thing. Simultaneity is but another facet of the activity of consciring which grasps things together, so that we may at one time experience colours, sound, smells, ideas, emotions, etc.

As we have said before, Divine Imagining leaves no place for the "Absolute" which has attracted philosophers such as Parmenides and Plato, Hegel, Bradley, and Bosanquet. Bradley frankly said, "If time-succession is not unreal I admit that our Absolute is a delusion." It is quite understandable that, sailing on the restless seas of change, men's hearts have craved for the landfall of reality—perfect, finished, and changeless. Our confidence is, however, securely based in Divine Imagining, the Eternal Creator, Lover and Artist, revealing Himself in the reality of the time-process. With an Absolute, as Bradley realised, the whole of Becoming would be only an appearance of what is eternally present in the Absolute, much as we might look at one cinematograph film after another taken from an inexhaustible film library. With Divine Imagining as our world-ground we are relieved from the incubus of contemplating that all the evil and suffering of the world are part of the revelation of the Absolute. We are relieved also of the burden of trying to explain what purpose is served by this cosmic picture-show which conveys to us so painfully the illusion of reality! It is satisfying also to reflect that reality need not for ever be stained even by the memory of evil, and that by His ceasing to conscire it, or any part thereof, Divine Imagining can allow it to disappear as though it had never existed at all.

This leads us naturally to consider what is the status of the Past. It is *made* reality, which normally endures unchanging (as far as we know), because conscired conservatively by the Divine. In some similar sense a piece of written music is *made* reality: that is, it contains succes-sions within itself but remains unchanged as a whole. The Past is deserted by all the finite sentients which once were active in its making, so that only the empty forms remain. Fawcett uses the simile of a coral reef in process of building. It remains unchanged, and constitutes evidence of past activity by myriads of creatures: but it is only that part of a reef which is still being made which is inhabited by living creatures. (The phenomenon of retro-cognition may be an unusual displacement of human consciring on to this unchanging past sustained by the Divine, or more probably it may be temporary rapport with memories sustained in the Group-soul.) The Past has been described by Bergson as "that which acts no longer". In so far as the past may be said to affect the present it can therefore do so only indirectly through the gathered experience or memory of those finite sentients which are active in the present. Perhaps it would be better to define the Past as "that which *we can act upon* no longer".

The status of the Future from the standpoint of Divine Imagining is to be regarded as tentatively planned reality which will be subject to modification and change by the consciring of the indefinitely many sentients, sub-human, human, and super-human, which will participate in it. From the viewpoint of these finite sentients it is still reality to be made. In this sense it is a plastic future, as we described it in Chapter 2. We might liken it to an unrolling canvas on which the Divine pattern is faintly outlined; the many-coloured threads which will give substance to the tapestry are contributed by the finite sentients. The intended pattern will, in the weaving, sometimes be distorted and unrecognisable, but God the Divine Society is active amid the disorder to re-create that which in the end will lead to perfection. In automatic scripts attributed to F. W. H. Myers,[1] he says:

"The future of the earth is imaged already in the imagination of God. It has happened because He has already thought it. But what has not happened is the change in the individual soul, the manner for instance in which it reacts to the trials and joys of life."

A little later the impression is conveyed that the imaged pattern may be adapted to circumstance, so as best to move events forward to the imagined goal.

"God watches over the cosmic life of the group-souls. And, according to their growth, He plans or designs the future of the life of mankind. But because it was all imaged by Him at the beginning so is there little to change in the vast cosmic picture which lies in His imagination."

There is one concluding observation which I desire to make before leaving the problems of time. There is an ancient idea, which may have originated with Pythagoras, that time follows a circular or cyclic path of progression; briefly, that history repeats itself. Nietzsche popularised the idea and P. D. Ouspensky[2] has been the most recent writer to whom it has appealed. It is, I am convinced, a completely erroneous view, certainly incompatible with Imaginism. The underlying element of truth in it is that our spiritual progress depends on facing again hurdles similar to those where we have failed, in meeting new situations involving moral choices similar to those in which we have let ourselves down, until the choice of the higher way becomes, as we say, second nature.

[1] Geraldine Cummins, *The Road to Immortality*, p. 71. (L.S.A. Publications, 1947, and Aquarian Press, 1956.)

[2] *A New Model of the Universe*, Chap. XI. (Kegan Paul, Trench, Trubner & Co. Ltd., 1938.)

Time-succession is not repetitive or cyclical: it is the manner of additive creation rooted in Divine Imagining.

WHAT CAUSES EVENTS?

Let us consider the nature of three different events which will illustrate the problems inherent in causation:

(a) Two billiard balls collide with each other and rebound with changes of speed and direction.

(b) Two volumes of hydrogen and one volume of oxygen are ignited and give rise to a few drops of water.

(c) Wordsworth creates the *Ode on Intimations of Immortality*.

It will be remembered that J. S. Mill defined "cause" as "the assemblage of phenomena, which occurring, some other phenomenon invariably commences or has its origin". This does not in any way penetrate below the surface and offer us a reason why "some other phenomenon" should occur at all. Why do events continue to happen? It is a question not unlike an earlier one: Why do things continue in being? Our answer is a similar one. It is because of the ceaseless pressure of the imaginal dynamic moving things onward in time towards the far-distant goal. No event is "invariably and unconditionally" (to use Mill's expression) consequent on its physical antecedents, but there always enters into events the activity of imagining—whether it be Divine Imagining, or human imagining, or that of myriads of sub-human sentients. *All causation embraces freedom*, even though in the extreme case this freedom is that of a myriad lowly sentients, so that we call it chance, and predict mass behaviour by statistical means.

The part which imagining or consciring plays in causation is obvious in the third example. Where human agency is involved it is a factor which cannot be ignored; it is indeed so important that no one has ever dreamed of framing a law setting out "that assemblage of phenomena, which occurring", an Ode on Intimations of Immortality invariably commences! It may seem that in the second example there is little room for imagining. Even here, however, on the level of chemical change where conservative factors are apparent (as in the conservation of mass), there is qualitative novelty to be accounted for. Certain qualities have disappeared and some new and very different qualities have appeared. We say that waiting sub-imaginals are able to manifest as a consequence of physical change. We must not lose sight of the fact that the whole stream of events is psychical, and that with deeper understanding we may some day see a habitual if not a necessary connection between the lower (chemical) levels and the higher (qualitative) levels of the one continuum.

In the first example of billiard balls in collision, the whole energy interchange is predictable because we are dealing with myriads of lowly sentients whose initiatives are at that level of freedom which we call chance. Here the part played by imagining is minimal, and for practical purposes negligible. The first two examples illustrate Mill's two types of solution of conflict. In the first, which is an unsuccessful attempt at interpenetration, the solution is a conservative one: no change in the nature of the balls results from their penetrating fields, and a redistribution of energy, i.e. of lowly consciring, is all that happens. In the second example a considerable measure of interpenetration results in conflict and a new harmony through the creation of water molecules. The solution of conflict is here transformative: creative novelty from waiting sub-imaginals enters into the situation. That which appears to be a mechanical sequence on physico-chemical levels (but which should be regarded as the habitual behaviour of lowly sentients) obviously merges into change on the biological level where local initiatives cannot be ignored. As we rise higher still to consider the causation of works of art, of the Renaissance, of the world wars, of the economic depression of the 'thirties, we see human initiatives playing a dominant part.

Philosophers who hold a different view of time to ours naturally differ in their view of causation. Kant, for example, considered time to be only a form of *finite* experience, and he regarded causation as a "judging concept" by which we try to unify and explain our experience. In contrast, we are not concerned with concepts at all, but with the dynamic behind the succession of events in the world. For Bradley, to whom change was unreal, there was no need to discuss causation at all.

Imaginism sees time rooted in the Supreme Being as the form or condition in which duration and succession are possible. Events take place not merely because others have gone before them but because the imaginal dynamic is using the endless process of inter-penetration, conflict, and reconciliation to move the scheme of things forward to its goal of perfection. The causal process is not just a stream of events. Events are conscita for consciring!

HOW FAR ARE WE FREE?

For a long time there has been an old controversy between protagonists of determinism and freedom. The latter have claimed for the human sentient *some* measure of real freedom (usually ascribed to the will); the former have denied he had any, and claimed that man's feeling of being free to choose is illusory. I may fancy that I am quite free to think of any number I want, but I am quite deluded, they say. Somewhere in my "Unconscious" are those factors which have determined my choice! On the basis of occasional evidence of such factors operating, the determinist makes a sweeping and unjustified generalisation.[1]

All that we have said about causation is relevant here. We say that there is no rigid determinism anywhere. Even in the domain of physics and mechanics there is *some* degree of freedom, but on this lowly level it falls off into chance. The electron which revolves in a hydrogen atom is sustained conservatively in a Bohr orbit, but it has enough freedom to make a quantum jump to another Bohr orbit. Chance is the term we apply to the measure of freedom to conscire which these lowly centres possess. A certain amount of awareness is appropriate to the term freedom, so that the dividing-line between what is properly called freedom and what is called chance is ill defined. Rising up the scale of finite sentients we can see ever more clearly that the imaginal harmonisation of conflict is introduced as a response to the conditions: it does not emerge out of them.

Let us look in more detail at the case of man. We claim that in spite of all the influences which play upon us from our environment, from our bodily inclination, and from our memory, the final choice is always ours to make. In this, Imaginism insists that we are right. Undoubtedly, for many people, the degree of freedom to choose is much less than they suppose, but it is always there. *The physical levels of the Universe are those of greatest restriction, and the highest levels are those of greatest freedom.* It follows that the man who has little development on the higher levels is the most restricted. His soul's freedom to conscire is still there, but it is a small voice amid the clamour of the lower sentients which constitute his body, and he easily persuades himself that this clamour is all his own voice. Conversely, the man who has the most freedom is the spiritually developed man. For him the various bodies he possesses are vehicles of effective action on the levels to which they correspond, but they are not the determinants of conduct on those levels.

Because we are Man we possess that chief treasure—a centre of consciring which is God-like in its character. It is

> The hold that falls not when the town is got,
> The heart's heart, whose immurèd plot
> Hath keys yourself keep not!

> Its keys are at the cincture hung of God;
> Its gates are trepidant to His nod;
> By Him its floors are trod.[2]

[1] E.g. Ernest Jones, *Psycho-Analysis*, p. 41. (Baillière, Tindall and Cox Ltd., 1920.)
[2] Francis Thompson, *A Fallen Yew*.

The hold is a gift, but the town has to be made our own. Wider freedom has to be won. All that was said about karma in Chapter 7 is very relevant here to the limits of our freedom. To this I shall add the following thought in conclusion.

I recently put the following questions to a wise man whose friendship I had the privilege of enjoying before he died some twelve years ago—and whose continued friendship I still recognise, although our lives are lived on different significant levels. "Is there accident or chance within the pattern of life for each individual? How far can one frustrate the pattern? How far are we free?" These are the answers I received through the automatic script of a sensitive: "Yes, so far as my knowledge goes, there is chance within the pattern of life for each individual. Banish from your mind the false superficial idea labelled determinism or fatalism. Within limits each human being has the choice. Only the Spirit of the Group-soul knows from weighing and balancing his character what choice he is almost certain to make. Secondly, your past life and your progress in it determine some of the conditions and events you meet in your next life. Through your failures you sow the seeds of certain temptations you have to meet again, often in very different guises and circumstances. But always there is the element of free-will. It depends on your spiritual and imaginative progress in that particular life what material is necessary, not merely to you but to those in your pattern in the following life. Sometimes there are innocent victims of ghastly tragedies on earth. These are occasionally caused by others in your pattern who have not made progress, who have gone backward. 'We are members one of another' is indeed a true saying."

Chapter

12

THE NATURE OF THE "NEXT LIFE"

> To all who wait, blindfolded by the flesh,
> Upon the stammered promise that we give,
> Tangling ourselves in the material mesh
> A moment, while we tell you that we live,
> Greeting, and reassurance; never doubt
> That the slow tidings of our joyful state,
> So hardly given, so haltingly made out,
> Are but the creaking hinges of the gate . . .
> Beyond, the garden lies; and as we turn,
> Wond'ring how much you hear, how much you guess,
> Once more the roses of glad service burn
> With hues of loving thought and thankfulness;
> Once more we move among them, strong and free,
> Marvelling yet in our felicity.
>
> PAMELA GREY
> (Sonnet obtained by influenced writing and
> attributed to the inspiration of F. W. H. Myers)

No echo comes from behind the dark curtain which will even faintly convey the music of that other life, yield to man the strange rhythm of a universe within a universe, a life within a life, and all lying as ships in harbour, within the infinite imagination of God.

GERALDINE CUMMINS
(Automatic script attributed to F. W. H. Myers)

FOR some time it has been my belief that the evidential case for man's survival of death is a very strong one. More recently I have had communications through the automatic writing of a friend in London which have transformed this belief into conviction. My communicator has been the close personal friend referred to in the last chapter, a very gifted and remarkable man, unknown to the sensitive.

In this chapter I desire to present a constructive picture of the life after death. The sources of information are necessarily communications through various sensitives by persons who have passed on, and the writer's judgment has had to be exercised in estimating the reliability of the sources. In what are believed to be good sources there is a remarkable measure of general agreement, and the picture which I proceed to draw is one which I believe can be trusted. My foundation sources are the communications from F. W. H. Myers through the automatic script of Miss Geraldine Cummins as given in two of her books,[1] and

---

[1] *The Road to Immortality* and *Beyond Human Personality*. (Psychic Press Ltd., 1952.)

235

of these I wish to say a little here. The careful reader very rightly asks, "How reliable is this source?"

It is well known that the automatic scripts of some sensitives give no clear indication of activity other than that of the subconscious levels of the writer's own mind—although this may include evidence of the exercise of ψ-faculty. On the other hand, it becomes clear to those who have studied them that a few sensitives have a sustained capacity for reproducing a quality of thought, and even at times a mode of expression in striking contrast with their own normal capacity, and in the opinion of those competent to judge, characteristic of the person from whom they claim to originate. The scripts through Miss Cummins, we are told, were received in the periods 1924-5, 1927, and 1931. Miss Gibbes, who was Miss Cummins' friend and collaborator, wrote of them, "At the time of the first indication of his presence Myers was entirely unknown to us personally, and we knew very little about him. His death occurred in 1901, when, in fact, the automatist was a small child. We did not endeavour to get in touch with him, neither had we read his famous book *Human Personality and its Survival of Bodily Death*, nor any of his other works."

There are a number of other interesting features. We are told that the speed of the automatic writing is remarkably high in contrast with Miss Cummins' normal rate of composition, which tends to be slow and laborious. This suggests an external control. I should not wish to draw any inferences from the character of the automatic script, because the process involved is complex and little understood. It may be mentioned as a matter of interest, however, that the handwriting of different communicators is different but self-consistent, and that it is different from the sensitive's own normal hand. In the two cases I have examined the script differs from the earthly handwriting of the communicators.

Secondly, Miss Gibbes claims that Miss Cummins has reproduced in various scripts "a number of different personalities, all differing in character and style" and says that "some were of people whom she had never met". This is, in my opinion, a very subtle test indeed, and I am in a position to lend my support to her claim.

Thirdly, Sir Oliver Lodge sought independent corroboration through Mrs. Osborne Leonard of the fact of Myers' communications through Miss Cummins. Sir Oliver wrote, "His reply was to the effect that he had communicated through her, and that in a general way he had managed to get through what he wanted; though he admitted it was difficult, and he couldn't be sure that it was always exact, but still on the whole he was willing to pass it as fairly representing what he had intended to say."

Fourthly, Miss Gibbes pointed out that Myers used unusual words in the scripts, such as polyzoic, polypsychic, metetheric, etc., of which neither she nor Miss Cummins knew the meaning, and which she found at a later date had been used in his volume *Human Personality*.

I should like to add to this evidence another interesting fragment. In *Beyond Human Personality* Miss Gibbes gives as an example of Myers' procedure, the following:

"Frederic Myers. Good evening, ladies, I must introduce the theme 'Love enclosed in Wisdom is the energy of integration which makes a cosmos of the sum of things'."

The sentence is not by any means commonplace, and Miss Gibbes remarks facetiously, "I am not a bit surprised that Myers wanted to put that down quickly."[1] I was recently turning the pages of Myers' classic work *Human Personality*, etc. and found the following sentence which Myers wrote when alive on earth:

"Love is the energy of integration which makes a cosmos of the sum of things."[2]

Such evidence as this, together with the total impression which the scripts make, reminiscent as they are of the poetic quality of his thought and style, give me very considerable confidence in them.

I do not propose to enter into any discussion of the mechanism of communication to which Myers makes several allusions in these scripts. It is by no means the simple, straightforward "telephone" type of activity that many people naïvely assume to be the case. Myers prefers to call the sensitive an interpreter and says, "It is an interpretation, not a literal statement, that is conveyed to you through him."[3] He also says of the sensitive, "What that mind cannot conceive or apprehend it cannot translate. It receives our thoughts not in words but as thoughts. We can on occasion, if we are clever, give to these thoughts the very definite stamp of our style." On the other hand, Miss Gibbes mentioned that a few words were written which were not understood by herself or Miss Cummins. The truth would appear to be that the process of communication is far from simple, and that while broadly speaking it may be telepathic in its character, it seems also in some measure to be a motor-control. If this were not so, the changed but consistent handwriting characteristics of different communicating personalities would be difficult to account for.

Perhaps I may quote from the description furnished by another

[1] Appendix II, *Beyond Human Personality*; also p. 162 of the 1952 reprint.
[2] *Human Personality*, Longmans, Green & Co., 1903, Vol. I, Section 335, p. 112.
[3] *The Road to Immortality*, 3rd Impr. 1947, p. 106.

sensitive, who is speaking to her communicator and describing her subjective state as a sensitive[1]:

"It is as though a ball is tossed to me. I receive it as a whole and then unwrap it and put it into words. But I suppose that you also supply suitable words sometimes, because as I unwrap my ball, the words come so much more easily and cleanly to hand than when I am working alone."

To this the communicator replies through her automatic script:

"That may be so, but I don't supply the words myself. I only select from those I can find in your mind, and this is why your limitations affect the giving of the thought. It is very seldom that I can make you use a word with which you are unfamiliar. With great difficulty I have sometimes made you spell out a word you do not know, but your faith isn't very strong and you usually hang back and make it very hard."

There is one further consideration which must occur to everyone who has made a study of trance communications of whatever kind. The prevalent trivialities and banalities arise, as we might expect, from those whose outlook continues to be attached to earthly things, and whose environment continues to be that of near-earth conditions. Communications from those who have advanced to higher levels probably involve difficult procedures not easy to control,[2] and it is because this seems to have been achieved by Myers that these scripts appear to me particularly valuable.

FALSE IDEAS OF THE NEXT LIFE

It has always been to me a matter of surprise that people, who on religious grounds claim to believe in their survival of death, are apparently content to hold vague and unsatisfactory views about the nature of the life they will then confront. If they knew that in a few years' time they would be going to live permanently in another country, they would take an intelligent interest in learning what they could of that country. I incline to think that the reasons for this prevalent attitude are psychological and rather deep-seated. Some may assume that there is no reliable information to be obtained, but it is an assumption seldom put to the test of serious enquiry. The real ground of this indifference is probably often a repressed aversion to consider this irrevocable event. As Bacon said, "Men fear death as children fear to go in the dark, and as that natural fear in children is increased with tales, so is the other."

When we consider some of the tales for which corrupt forms of

[1] Jane Sherwood, *The Country Beyond*, pp. 38-9. (Rider & Co. Ltd., 1945.)
[2] *The Road to Immortality*, 1947 Impr., p. 43.

religion have been responsible, it is not surprising that intelligent men have turned away in disgust. There has been the tale that a man's earthly life sets the unalterable pattern for all eternity: the sheep and goats conception leading to heaven or hell. It is a tale obviously designed to foster morality by the use of the weapon of fear.

There is the fantasy that death changes John Smith's character and interests in a most surprising manner, so that endless praises are thought to be his constant and satisfying occupation. The fantasy may indeed extend to the assumption that if he has "faith in Christ" he may find himself after death in that sublime presence. Popular hymnology has done a lot to maintain these ideas in currency.

> There is the throne of David,
>   And there, from care released,
> The shout of them that triumph,
>   The song of them that feast;
> And they who, with their Leader,
>   Have conquered in the fight,
> For ever and for ever
>   Are clad in robes of white.

It may be urged that these thoughts go back to Bernard of Cluny in the twelfth century, and that we have advanced a little since then, but it should be recalled that although this is a translation of the nineteenth century it still appears in hymn-books in the mid-twentieth century. Illustrations could be multiplied. It may well be that in an imaginal universe each person attains the heaven of his desire, but it is tragic to confuse local habitations in the hereafter, of limited even though sincere souls, with the infinite realms of Divine Imagining.

Another of the foolish tales which has had a long and dishonourable currency is that, following death, the souls of men have a long sleep until some distant day of judgment, when the worthy will undergo "the resurrection of the just", presumably in their re-assembled bodies, and the unworthy be condemned for ever. One has only to wander round old country churchyards or investigate popular hymnology to discover the extent of this fantasy.

> Wondrous sound the trumpet flingeth
> Through earth's sepulchres it ringeth
> All before the throne it bringeth.

Trumpets must have caught even the imagination of St. Paul when he wrote:

"We shall not all sleep, but we shall all be changed, in a moment, in the twinkling of an eye, at the last trump: for the trumpet shall sound, and the dead shall be raised incorruptible, and we shall be changed. . . ."

It is doubtful, however, if the trumpet would have had such popularity in this celestial rôle had it not been for the musical possibilities found in it by a most distinguished and exuberant composer, who we must assume was more concerned with an artistic triumph than the dissemination of theological truth. Words, to the thinker, are the vehicle of truth: to the musician they may be no more than a skeleton to be clothed with form and beauty. But the latter may give spurious life to the former. Perhaps some day there may be established a concordat between the Royal College of Music and Lambeth, so that no words of scripture may be set to music (which might become immortal) without the authority of, at least, a bishop.

It is tempting to pursue these thoughts, but we must refrain. It would be comforting for us if we could look back and see in these "tales" just the childish imagination of the race, as now in our maturity we put away childish things. Perhaps, however, they will at least serve to remind us that we are not necessarily servants of the Truth when we repeat and perpetuate thoughts, however ancient, or harbour ideas however august their origin. There is no greater or more responsible task facing this generation than an honest and fearless search for truth, and Browning very helpfully reminds us where the only touchstone is to be found.

> Truth is within ourselves; it takes no rise
> From outward things, whate'er you may believe.
> There is an inmost centre in us all,
> Where truth abides in fulness; . . .

This is the spirit in which we should face all enquiry, and not least the important issues of our destiny. I do not for a moment suggest that the fantasies and tales I have referred to are accepted by intelligent churchmen today: they certainly are not. I doubt, however, if the average churchman holds any clear views of the next life. I rather suspect that he believes that after death we become formless spirits floating about in a pleasant but indescribable heaven, or temporarily accommodated in doubtfully pleasant but necessary purgatory. If so, I can understand the source of funereal gloom.

SOME GENERAL CONSIDERATIONS

One of the basic difficulties with the "next world" is that of forming an intelligible conception of it. *Where* is it? Existence in a physical world is familiar to us through our senses: but when we have no longer physical senses, what will existence be like? There are two clues to the resolution of this problem which should be constantly borne in mind.

(1) The physical world which we feel so sure about, and which we

consider to be real and dependable because of familiarity, from the scientist's standpoint is not at all what it appears to the ordinary man. The latter says it is solid, for he can touch it; it is visible, for he can see it. The scientist says that physical objects are aggregates of molecules, which are built from atoms, which in turn are built from positive nuclei with electrons in rapid motion around them. The whole structure is almost empty space, and the plain man's experience is due to electromagnetic fields between the objects on the one hand and his finger and eye on the other (which, incidentally, are also nearly empty space).

(2) It is always the mind which interprets these sensations. It has become *adapted* to interpret them in the familiar way. We are unaware, for example, of the radio waves all around us, but if we had a special sense excited by these, the mind would adapt itself to perceive a *different* world. Moreover, the light waves by which I do see the world, and the radio waves to which I do not respond, intermingle and coexist without any interference. This is all commonplace, but we easily forget its implications. If, as many communicators claim, they live in, and respond to, a world of higher frequency than ours, there is nothing impossible or unreasonable in their claim. The mind which interprets is capable of perceiving another world, and doubtless many other worlds, every whit as real or every whit as illusory as this one. The answer to "Where is the next world?" must therefore be, "It is where the mind has the ability to perceive it". It may quite well coexist with this one in space without any interference arising.

It is helpful also to remember that the mind has a life *of its own* apart from the interpretation of physical sensations, and we sometimes become aware of this clearly. We may experience this in a dream or under anaesthesia. Under the influence of the drug mescalin two different worlds may coexist, both equally real to the perceiving mind. It is usually assumed that one of these worlds is subjective in its origin, in the sense that it is created by a level of the self. If it were claimed that both were objectively real, I suppose the only tests which might discriminate would be the extent to which both worlds could be shared by other observers. It is noteworthy that communicators claim that for many people who, after death, live on lower levels of experience, there is a large subjective element in it. It is the equivalent of a private dream-condition, but this is generally thrown off with their growing awareness of the existence of an objective world to which others are in relationship.

Those who desire to have a carefully developed account of the plausibility of such a world should read an article by Professor H. H. Price entitled *Survival and the Idea of "Another World"*.[1] I take from it a few significant sentences.

[1] *Proc. S.P.R.*, Vol. L, p. 1, January 1953.

"An image-world such as I am describing would not be the product of one single mind only, nor would it be purely private. It would be the joint product of a group of telepathically interacting minds, and public to all of them. Nevertheless one would not expect it to have unrestricted publicity. It is likely that there would still be many next worlds, a different one for each group of like-minded personalities. . . . If I may put it so the 'stuff' or material of such a world would come in the end from one's memories, and the form of it from one's desires."

We shall later find interesting support for Professor Price's surmise.

We must be careful whenever we are disposed to say (as we might do of two coexisting worlds in a mescalin vision) that one is real and the other an illusion. The facts are that one is familiar and relatively permanent, while the other is unfamiliar and transient, but this is no satisfactory basis for a judgment of reality. We should not be prepared to say on these grounds that the plain man's view of an object was real and the scientist's view of it an illusion. We should rather say that these are two views from different standpoints. The plain man's limited range of consciring only permits him to perceive one aspect, but a god would perceive both. So a discarnate being and an incarnate being might from their respective standpoints attribute to that state with which they were the more familiar the greater reality. If their consciring were wide enough, they would be equally aware of both states, and the only useful sense in which more reality could be ascribed to one state rather than the other would be in so far as one was causally prior to the other.

In one of Raymond Lodge's conversations with his father (through Mrs. Leonard) he describes how through the power of their minds they create the setting of their life—their homes, gardens, etc., as we do in the physical world. They do it for the same reason, namely, to provide a suitable and harmonious environment for their souls to live and work in. Raymond describes this as "one of the necessary illusions of our life", and the conversation proceeds:

"*Sir Oliver*: Then you live in a world of illusion?

"*Raymond*: So do you, father; in the right sense of the word you do. We live in what you might call an extension of the illusory world in which you live. The outer rim of it. We are in touch with a world of reality because we are in the outer rim of the world of illusion. We're more sure of the world of reality than you are. Father, the spirit-universe is the world of reality. Spirit and mind both belong to the world of reality. Everything else, that is external things, are necessary for a time, but superfluous and only temporary in existence as far as the world of reality goes—which is eternal and indestructible. Spirit and mind belong to that world. The world of ether is only created by the power of mind. We are not entirely free from your world of matter, we are more independent of it but are still concerned with it."

This conversation supports the general viewpoint, several times referred to, of a universe existing on different significant levels, all with degrees of reality. The physical is the least real in the sense that in the causal series it has been the last to proceed out of Divine Imagining. The same conception is used by F. W. H. Myers in an attempt to convey an ordered impression of man's future destiny. The term "plane" is used, for want of a better, to suggest different levels of consciousness, or worlds whose inhabitants enjoy widening and increasing intensity of consciring. Myers' classification will be introduced here: his descriptive terminology is of course no more than a symbol or distinguishing name.

(1) *The Plane of Matter.* This is experience of the physical form, whether on Earth or on any other celestial body with comparable conditions.

(2) *An Intermediate State*, sometimes called Hades. Our "aetheric level".

(3) *The Plane of Illusion.* More usually called the "astral" plane. It is the "summerland" of spiritualists and the "heaven" of ordinary folk.

(4) *The Plane of Colour.* The highest plane of existence in human form, of which it is the sublimest expression. It remains in the terrestrial "zone".

(5) *The Plane of Flame.*

(6) *The Plane of White Light.*

(7) *The Final State.* Awareness of Ultimate Reality. Communion with the Supreme.

In the present chapter we are concerned with the consciousness and life of the second, third, and fourth planes. It may be of interest to the reader to know that both Myers and the personal friend to whom I previously referred are said to be on the fourth plane.

THE SECOND PLANE OR INTERMEDIATE STATE

The phenomena which follow immediately after death occur on this plane, and to understand them we must refer to the structure of the human being. The physical body throughout life is interpenetrated by another vehicle which has been called the unifying double. This is a duplicate in appearance of the physical body. It is itself made up of two parts. The outer is a kind of "placental" structure made out of what we have called the psychic aether, and this part remains inseparable from the physical body during the latter's life. This aetheric husk (as Myers calls it) nourishes like a womb the inner vehicle which is the astral body, and this latter is the normal body of the soul on the third or astral plane. The astral body for all practical purposes is a duplicate of the physical body, but it does not participate in disfigurement or other defects which the physical may possess. It develops to maturity during physical life. In sleep, the astral body containing the soul is commonly displaced to a greater or less extent from the aetheric husk. The soul may or may not conscire reflectively on the third plane, but even where it does, memories of this are seldom retained on waking. In so-called astral projection or out-of-the-body experiences which are by no means uncommon, reflective consciring may be achieved in the astral body[1] and the experient sometimes notices two thin and very extensible silvery cords which link the cerebral and solar plexus regions of the astral body with the aetheric husk within the physical body.

Death involves not a mere projection of the astral body but a withdrawal of the unifying double as a whole, with gradual severance of the links which have bound the aetheric husk to the physical during life. Subjectively, the soul is then resting in a quiescent, sleepy, detached state within the aetheric husk. It is stressed by all communicators that circumstances differ for different individuals. We shall therefore describe average or typical experience, making a few comments later about unusual cases. An average time spent in this state may be two or three days. The process which takes place during this time is a severing of the cords joining the aetheric husk and the astral body, and a loosening and casting off of the former which is no longer required. The astral body frees itself and grows in strength. One might almost compare it to the emergence of a butterfly from the chrysalis stage. At the termination of this phase, the dreamy state of the soul changes into one of clear and growing awareness of the beauties of the astral plane. Dreamy restful phases apparently alternate with sleep, and as the process of sloughing off the aetheric husk proceeds, the soul may experience what Myers calls the "Play of the Shadow Show". Fragments of the memory of his past life float before the mind. The "brain-memory" which is associated with the aetheric vehicle is being discarded. Memory proper is recovered in the astral body. During this period the soul may have glimpses of his friends and spiritual kindred who "journey" from the astral plane to give him help and welcome.

Myers says of his own passing[2]:

"Pray do not conjure up unpleasant associations with Hades. I died in Italy, a land I loved, and I was very weary at the time of my passing. For me, Hades was a place of rest, a place of half-lights and drowsy peace. As a man

---

[1] The term "astral body" is not a very happy one, but we shall use it to avoid unnecessary confusion. It is important, however, to note that Myers in the Cummins' scripts unfortunately uses the term "etheric body" where we keep to the more general usage of astral body.

[2] *The Road to Immortality*, pp. 25-6.

wins strength from a long deep sleep, so did I gather that spiritual and intellectual force I needed during the time I abode in Hades."

In another book which I commend to the reader an account is given[1] by two communicators of their very different experiences in Hades. One supports Myers' own experience. The other person who passed over with an attitude of blank unbelief in survival, with strongly repressed emotions, and through a sudden and violent death describes an unpleasant phantasmagoria. He afterwards blamed himself entirely, and regarded it as a purgatorial experience made necessary by his "wilful ignorance and scepticism". He says that help was offered to him, but his pride and prejudices made him a difficult person to help.

Sudden death combined either with ignorance or gross scepticism apparently often lead to the strange situation in which people do not know that they have died. Where egoism prevents others enlightening them, they may wander for a considerable time in a fantasy world on the borderland of the second and third planes until they are willing to learn. The thoroughly selfish or egotistical person may wander in purgatorial misery and loneliness until he is concerned to be different, but these are lower astral plane experiences rather than those of Hades.

The ordinary average person with many weaknesses, faults, and failings has no ground whatever for approaching death with fear or trepidation provided he has some love in him. In characteristically felicitous phrase Myers has given us this message[2]:

"Beyond ambition, beyond any human forms of selfishness, beyond the struggling scarcely leashed desires, are affection, love—the drawing intangible force between kindred souls. It is stronger than death, it conquers despair and may conquer on all the finite levels of existence. It must be reckoned as a cosmic principle, and is known as 'the power behind the pattern' which is being woven for you as long as time for you exists.

"Death seems terrible to the average man because of its apparent loneliness. If he but knew it, his fears are vain; his dread of being reft from the pattern—that is to say, from those he loves—has no foundation, has no real substance behind it. For, wherever he may journey after death, always will he be caught again into the design of which he is a part, always will he find again, however deep his temporary oblivion or however varied his experience, certain human souls who were knit into his earth life, who were loved deeply, if sometimes blindly or evilly, by him in those bygone days."

GENERAL CHARACTERISTICS OF THE ASTRAL PLANE

Those who have followed the arguments of this book appreciate that in every act of perception on the physical plane there is something

[1] Jane Sherwood, *The Country Beyond*, pp. 24-7. (Rider & Co. Ltd., 1945.)
[2] *Loc. cit.*, p. 66.

given by the great Architect, but that there is also much that we create for ourselves. We carve it out of the presented world, and how much we perceive depends on our breadth and intensity of consciring. It is much the same on the astral plane, except that the part played by the individual is greater. The stuff or substance of this world (if these terms may be permitted) is malleable by individual minds to a degree which is far greater than anything we experience here.

The first need of the average person awaking from the dream-like experience of the second plane is to find himself with friends in an environment which is at least of the familiar kind. (It must be stressed again that experiences differ with the development of the individual. Perhaps it is best to conceive the astral plane as having sub-levels on the lower of which conditions are more *given* and earthlike, and on the higher of which individual creativity can play a greater part.) The ordinary person awakens therefore in surroundings which give him friendly welcome, in a country not unlike his own but more beautiful than he has ever seen before. It is in fact the product of the creative imagining of beings on higher planes, whom Myers calls the "Wise". From *their* point of view this environment would be counted an illusion: from the point of view of the astral plane dweller it is as real as trees, flowers, and houses are to us. In this setting he finds himself with some of the persons he loves, who have passed over before him. Their local environment is modified, though not always consciously, by the deeper minds of this community of individuals. In the case of those who are a little more advanced, the surroundings may be consciously modified, and some people take great delight in creating (through the fundamental activity of imagining) their ideal gardens and homes.

The essential naturalness of all this is perhaps best conveyed by a few extracts from a communicator[1]:

"To me it seems as if I left you only four weeks instead of years ago. That is because, when one is happy, time flashes by like a falling star. Also it may be because there is nothing to catch here—no trains or buses, and no income tax collector and other nuisances. Here our only currency is our own efforts. Our love of beauty, our thoughts for others and our willingness to work and create, are our pounds, shillings, and pence. I admit that I have had my bad, depressing, and painful hours since I left the earth, but out of them bloomed flowers of lovely life, and these have given me a joy, an ecstasy, I had never experienced during my journey through the world. For (on earth) it is a journey in which we travel faster and faster as the years go by. Our worries and anxieties seldom allow us to have a rest on the road and hardly ever

---

[1] Geraldine Cummins, *Travellers in Eternity*, pp. 146-7. (Psychic Press Ltd., 1948.) This little book gives a simple account of the communications between members of a family, some of whom were incarnate and some discarnate.

permit us those wonderful times we know here when, after contemplation, we reach up to God and enjoy the peace everlasting. . . .

"There are great cities over here for people who like cities. Harold has taken me on a short visit to Purgatory, which is another London. . . . But this etheric London isn't all purgatory. There were some lovely people living contentedly in small houses in rather grubby streets. They were good souls, but such streets were their idea of heaven, so they found it. . . . They will gradually be weaned from this shabby idea of paradise when they learn to throw themselves more outward, when they use the wings of their minds and visit other people's worlds."

The picture presented in such communications as this may seem to some readers very materialistic. If such criticism has weight it is presumably because of some higher ideal of formless existence. It is quite certain, however, that the ordinary person is not prepared intellectually or emotionally for such a possibility, and that his need after the transition is for a state not too unlike the world he knew. This he will find on the astral plane. There are, however, important differences from the world left behind. For one thing, food is not necessary. The astral body absorbs from its environment all that is essential for its health and well-being. Furthermore there is no need of money, for it has no value. People create what they want for themselves or for others. Relieved of the body's relentless demands people can now live creatively; they can enjoy what they desire, they have time to learn about the universe they inhabit, they have leisure to explore the fascinating powers of the mind, they have time to serve the light.

As for clothes, our natural instinct is to appear to those we love as we dressed on earth. In the early stages the production of clothing is unconscious, the deeper mind imaginatively creates it. Once these possibilities are realised, individuals consciously create for themselves that which they consider favours their figure and expresses their personality.

There is on this plane something of the nature of psychical gravitation which draws together into communities those who love each other and are akin in interests, provided their spiritual development is comparable. These things are more significant than blood-relationships, which may or may not concur with spiritual affinity. Groups of people with much in common therefore tend to share to a considerable extent their mode of living, their locality, their dwellings, their type of service, and so forth. Because these affinities are operative, the tensions and disagreements and also the challenges of earth-life are largely absent. To most people such a world would indeed be heaven, for their ideals, their dreams, and desires can within very wide limits be realised without frustration. From the point of view of spiritual progress all this has its dangers. With the creation of idyllic surroundings, the fellowship of delightful friends, with infinite leisure to create and to enjoy creation, and to explore the fascinating world around, there is no great stimulus to spiritual endeavour and questing. Such groups tend in the end (sometimes after hundreds of years) to disintegrate. Some members feel the call of their souls to prepare themselves spiritually and by service to others for advance to higher levels of the astral world or to the fourth plane. Others with increasing disinclination for effort come to know that if they are to make progress, it can only be by first travelling back, and they ultimately enter that subjective state which leads to re-birth on earth. The souls who desire to progress, frequently develop greater awareness which makes them able to find and visit other communities linked with that Group-soul to which they belong. They may discover communities perpetuating the life and traditions of seventeenth- or eighteenth-century England, or others of varying nationality, all deriving their spiritual sustenance from the one Spirit of the Group-soul (see Chapter 13). Myers says:

"Perhaps he finds the life of the Victorian era as it existed in London in the eighties, or the social conditions which prevailed in Devonshire during the Napoleonic wars, or the peasant life of the Highland crofters during the seventeenth century. But all have one characteristic in common, all are subliminated: that is to say, suffering, toil, and sorrow are absent from each fantasy. . . . Such a condition is suggestive in its aspect of the peaceful character of a still Summer day. . . . Eventually the collective desire for progression shatters this community life. The units that sustain it seek either the way back to the earth or choose the more difficult path which leads to Eidos, the fourth level of consciousness."[1]

It may be asked, Have dwellers on the astral plane access to the earth they have left? Can they "see" and be aware of the geography of the earth, and the lives and doings of people there? The answer is that while such awareness is possible, it is not a normal state of experience of the astral plane dweller. "This life," says Myers in picturesque phrase, "flows through their (earth dwellers') crowded streets, over their mountains, passes above and within solid ground and remains apart, aloof from all that material existence, as if indeed it did not exist at all."[2] On the other hand, there are some who acquire the faculty of contact with earth conditions through an act of imagining which is most simply expressed as a controlled reduction of the normal astral rhythm towards the lower rhythm of earth. Where there are strong bonds or ties of affection, it appears that there may be communion at will on a subjective level between the deeper minds of those who are on different

---

[1] *Beyond Human Personality*, p. 34.
[2] *Ibid.*, p. 66; also *The Country Beyond*, p. 34.

planes. In sleep, astral projection is not uncommon and may lead to communion with discarnate friends, although it is very rare for the waking memory to retain any knowledge of it. It is nevertheless registered in the memory of the astral body, and thus when a person dies he may meet those to whom he is bound by affection not as a stranger with many years of separation between them but as familiar friends.

Reference has been made to the power of the soul, consciously or unconsciously, to modify its surroundings. This invariably happens also in relation to the astral body, so that dwellers who have been on this plane a sufficient time assume the appearance which they conceive to be that of their best years. The old person usually reverts to a more youthful appearance, while those who die young grow to such maturity of appearance as they desire. These zones of the astral world, as we have said, are very much the setting in which dreams may be realised. Orientals have named it the "Lotus Flower Paradise" providing for joy and contentment but not for evolution. It is because of these features which perpetuate the thoughts and wishes of the limited human personality that Myers described it as the plane of illusion. To those who inhabit it it is real enough, but to those who have advanced further it appears largely to be pleasant stagnation.

There are no hard and fast rules, no rigid patterns of experience on the astral level, for those who pass through the portals of death differ so widely in their interests, character, and development. Some souls tarry on the plane of illusion until their comrades on earth join them. Others press forward to the fourth plane of being. They can return from higher planes to commune for short periods with those they love on the astral plane, and there is therefore less separation than on earth between persons who live in different towns or countries and visit each other occasionally.

So far, what we have said has related to the average person. Something may be added to indicate the kind of experience of those below this level. After awaking from the experience of Hades in which the aetheric husk was discarded, the condition of the astral body may vary considerably. The astral body of an undeveloped soul may be weak and ill-formed, so that for a long time it has to be tended before it can live a normal life on this plane. Alternatively, it may be developed, but marred by many defects due to fear, anger, greed, selfishness, cruelty, jealousy, and hatred, which in earthly life battered and warped it. These are equivalent to diseases of the astral body, and healing and help are necessary if a normal life is to be possible. There are some souls who devote themselves to this work.[1] There is no question arising of punish-

[1] *The Country Beyond*, pp. 48-50.

ment for sin: we are discussing the sequence of natural events where negative emotions have ruled earthly life. Moreover, that principle of psychic gravitation which draws like to like may draw such souls to the twilight waste-land of the lower astral levels. There, what may be called hell is a condition mutually created, not imposed. Souls on these tragic lower levels cannot be helped against their will, nor can they always be approached by those who try to do the work of rescue. Progress has to come through suffering, and when suffering has done its remedial work of opening the eyes to even a glimpse of truth, the soul's cry is not unanswered by those who are ever trying to help. "The history of the cruel man in the hereafter," says Myers "is a book I am not permitted to write." It is hinted that on the lowest levels the cruel man has to be purged and purified by entering into the sufferings of his victims.[1]

PERSONAL RELATIONSHIPS ON THE THIRD PLANE

We turn back in our description to the lot of the average person on the astral level. Innumerable questions arise and a few of these will be dealt with here. It has been said that souls often live together in communities in the same locality, sharing common interests and activities: are there relationships of the nature of marriage? The statement attributed to Christ[2] that "They which shall be accounted worthy to obtain that world, and the resurrection from the dead, neither marry nor are given in marriage" is said by Myers to refer to higher planes of being. On the third plane sexual love and marriage are possible for those who desire them, although there is no childbirth. Prior earthly relationships resolve themselves, for no pretence is possible. Relationships which are grounded in mutual love are known and apparent as such, while those which have not been matters of the soul perish with the physical body. Pure and passionate love may on both the third and fourth planes provide two souls with a harmony, ecstasy, and creative vigour inconceivable in the limitations of the lower rhythm of earth. On the fourth plane where conditions are substantially different from those of earth the expression of love changes its character. As there are here those to whom personal relationships mean less than their devotion to some particular pursuit such as science or the arts or discovery, so there is a wide variety of types of experience on the astral level.

We have previously mentioned that emotional pretence and dishonesty are impossible: this follows from the nature of the astral body itself. In terrestrial life it is assumed that the obvious separateness of physical bodies is associated with a corresponding privacy of individual

[1] *Beyond Human Personality*, pp. 38-9.
[2] Luke xx. 35.

thought and emotion. This is a wrong assumption, and it is no longer tenable on the astral level where emotional tones create an atmosphere which each person radiates around him. The astral body appears to be the generator and vehicle of emotions which are literally perceptible and objective to those around, and this creates a situation very different from the terrestrial one. Faults of temper and disposition, fear, greed, anger, and jealousy are viewed as diseases of the astral body: they are unpleasant in their quality and may even be harmful to the bodies of others. Cure is therefore important and often possible; if it is not, such persons inevitably find their way to lower levels where their unpleasant state is more tolerable to others. On the other hand, we are told that love is the natural atmosphere and radiation of the healthy astral body, that it is fascinatingly beautiful in its appearances, and that it is one of the chief instruments of healing.

One communicator very cogently says[1]:

"Never condemn selfishness or even malice as pure vice. They are the signs of a tormented and frightened soul which has recoiled upon itself and can only be helped by being set free from fear.

"I myself think that the discipline of earth is specially important for the following reasons: the actual emotional pressures are masked by the physical, and the strength of the sensations is dulled by it; hence, although fear of injury to the physical body is added to the dangers to be faced, yet the conditions do make it possible for each to fight his own fight while maintaining a bold face to the world.

"Here, no concealment is possible and the keenness of the emotions makes it a far more serious and dangerous matter when anything is radically wrong with them. . . . I think that the task of building up a healthy and happy emotional body is peculiarly the mission of one's earth experience."

This is far removed from the misguided ascetic advice "Kill out desire."

A very natural question is the possibility and the method of finding others in the astral world. The communicator from whom I have just quoted says of this[2]:

"I can't even find M now, because she is content to stay in the initial stages. This partly because she wants to wait for F, but also because she is still matter-bound. I can find her thought; yes, in much the same way that I can find yours, and we often talk together. . . . It is difficult to get in touch with those with whom one has had no earth connection. You must remember that distance depends for us on affinity, that we are separated into planes of being, and that unless we happen to be close confederates here, the only way of finding a person is by tracking down his thought. This can only be done if one knows what lines of thought to try. Urgent thought of the personality of the one you want often attracts his attention and then contact can

[1] *The Country Beyond*, p. 50.   [2] *Loc. cit.*, p. 76.

be made, but if one does not know the person, it becomes very difficult to send out the right thought or to recognise a response if one gets it."

So far as perception of incarnate persons by astral plane dwellers is concerned, we have indicated that this is not normal experience, but can be realised. The astral bodies of *incarnate* persons are tuned down in their rhythm when associated with the physical body so that they are not normally visible to astral dwellers. Thought has the freedom of both worlds. Myers remarks that the process of seeking to communicate with earth involves a conscious slowing down of *their* normal rhythm so that it is like entering a drowsy state from a vigorous and active one.

THE SIGNIFICANCE OF THIRD PLANE EXPERIENCE

There are a few further reflections on the character of experience on the astral plane which may assist us to grasp its nature. When we have any experience on earth it leaves its memory-record on all the various levels of ourselves. A detailed memory-record is made on the aetheric vehicle, a corresponding record in so far as it has emotional implications is made in the astral vehicle, and memory proper is in the mind. One of the experiences of astral life when spiritual progress is sought is said to be a gradual process of recollection in their full emotional significance of the events of the past earth life. It is, however, a recollection far more complete and heart-searching than normal memory has accustomed us to, for it includes an awareness of the emotional reactions of all who were affected by our thoughts, words, and deeds. Their feelings become ours for the time and we know intimately and often poignantly what others' suffering (as well as joy) has been. It is a purging and cleansing kind of suffering which awakens new insight, understanding, and humility. I cannot do better than quote from a communicator[1]:

"You must realise that all this recollection does not take place in a void; it is the subjective side of life, and the ordinary objective life goes on with it side by side. Of that exterior side we have spoken before. It is a full and happy one, or may be so when the retrospective process is not too fraught with suffering. . . . There is remorse and plenty of it, even for a man who led a short and fairly blameless life. It is not often possible to make amends here when one finds out how one has injured others; the opportunity has gone. Most earth connections have to be loosened or dropped for the time being. . . . Anger against oneself is useless, and shame and guilt come to be known as false attitudes due to pride. There is nothing for it but to accept the thing and recognise one's full responsibility. Sorrow must be curbed for the sake

[1] *The Country Beyond*, pp. 74-5.

of others around who would have to share it with one, so that all one can do is to be humble about it. In effect one says 'Yes, I did that. I am like that, more's the pity. I am not the fine fellow I once tried to think myself, but now I will eradicate that fault, strengthen that weakness, clear out that anger.' It becomes a process of stripping off all the pretensions with which one deceived oneself and others. . . . The last stages of retrospect fittingly close with the innocence of childhood. . . . It is rather like coming to the end of a long tunnel and suddenly finding an extensive view opening out beyond. For now beyond birth the great perspective of many past lives begins to open up."

This all rings true, and with this catharsis behind, and a survey of the self's progress, the soul may then move forward in peace, and with humble desire.

The above communicator has drawn attention to the quality which "sight" may have on higher levels of the astral plane. It is not only that there is an outward seeing with the eyes of the astral body, but that along with it is a far keener understanding of things. An intuitive faculty may indeed almost replace that of vision.

There are two themes, space and time, basic to our scientific outlook. They are both real products of Divine Imagining, and not devices of finite minds or illusory. What is the relation of space and time as experienced by dwellers on the astral plane, to the space and time which we experience? For my own part I have no confidence in theories which invoke more dimensions than three to account for the astral world; the explanation will not be found in a fourth spatial dimension (whatever that means), but in the nature and range of consciring, corresponding to the different "frequency rhythms" of which we have spoken. Certainly Myers located the astral world within our three-dimensional space, and the communicators in *The Country Beyond*[1] have many interesting things to say which fully support this. The experiments and observations which they made are worthy of study by those who wish to relate these two worlds together in their outlook. I shall mention with the briefest of comments some of these observations.

There is marked interpenetration of the two worlds or planes. From our standpoint we are not surprised, for both are psychoid.

The two worlds have different groups of images. There is no identity of these and apparently no causal or other relationship known between images or objects of the one world and of the other.

Astral cities appear to correspond in general location with waste or lonely places on earth, and busy terrestrial cities are avoided in the astral world.

The light which appears to pour "down" upon the astral plane is

[1] *Loc. cit.*, Chaps. IV and VII.

said to be life-giving and nourishing. The same might be said of ordinary sunlight of course.

The specious present of astral dwellers is stated to cover something of both the past and future of ourselves.

A number of experiments, surprising in their results, were made on the comparative passage of time on the two planes, but I shall refer those who are interested to the book mentioned. This kind of information must properly be treated with considerable reserve, but it is this sort of experimenting which, if substantiated, could provide us with clues of enormous importance in trying to understand the structure of the world. It is premature to speculate upon these matters, but they suggest the possibility of a new Theory of Relativity which will do for human beings on different levels of consciousness (or consciring) what Einstein's theory did for incarnate observers moving with different speeds in space-time.

THE FOURTH PLANE (THE PLANE OF COLOUR)

It appears that most souls, excepting only a few rare beings, spend a considerable time on the third or astral plane. Myers called it the plane of illusion, for such it must seem to those who are higher. To them in turn, we incarnate souls must appear to be living in a prison of grievous limitations and illusions. We have mentioned that sooner or later the third plane dweller is no longer content with its summerland, but desires to progress. According to his soul's development a choice now lies before him. He will know intuitively either that he must face the way leading to re-birth if he is to rise higher, or he will know that the way to the fourth plane is possible for him and that he should undertake it.

The transition from the third to the fourth plane is not unlike that from the second to the third plane, a sloughing of the astral body which releases the finer body within. This is different in many respects from the human form. Myers,[1] struggling with the inadequacy of language, describes it as "apparently a compound of lights and colours unimaginable. This coloured compound may be grotesque, bizarre in form, may be lovely beyond words, may possess strange absurdities of outline, or may transcend the loftiest dream of earthly beauty." It is a level on which souls experiment with form, learn how to control it, discover that the mind's imagery of a form is not necessary to the functioning of the self, and learn that it is possible to live in greater freedom without it. This kind of experimenting is described by Myers as the "breaking of the image". The fourth plane is nevertheless that

[1] *The Road to Immortality*, pp. 39-44.

in which the beauty of form reaches its zenith. Here the finest dreams of artists, sculptors, and visionaries are realised in reality. It is said to have colours, sounds, and scents of endless variety not known to the earth. "This vast region of appearances is gigantic in conception, terrifying and exquisite according to the manner in which it presents itself to the soul-man," says Myers. The scenery of earth at its best is to be regarded only as a very dull and imperfect copy of selections from this level of existence.

The power and sensitivity of mind are now vastly increased so that the depths and heights of emotional experience are greater. Joy and sorrow are part of the soul's lot in an intensified and rarefied form, and the zest of living is far beyond the pale conceptions of earth. There appear to be sub-levels on this plane also, so that the body of the soul increases its sensitivity and power as it climbs higher in the scale of being. Myers suggests that the fourth plane is the highest which the incarnate human soul in its loftiest mystical experience has been able to penetrate. It is a general principle associated with progress, that souls normally only have awareness of other souls who are on the same level or sub-level of development. It is possible for the more advanced soul at times to reduce his "rhythm" in a subjective state, and descending the ladder of being, to make contact with others who are on lower levels.

It is on the fourth plane that the soul learns to transcend the bounds of human personality. The Group-soul, to which we have referred, provides the common mind and intuitive centre from which spring and to which are related a number of journeying souls on the various planes of being. This is the larger self to which all these individual selves are related, and it is nourished by one Spirit. Myers called it a "thought of God", or, as we might say, a sub-imaginal. The soul on the fourth plane becomes increasingly aware of all those comrade-souls who are thus linked with him in his evolution. He attains a conscious awareness of this larger self, and begins to understand something of the richness of this communion, and to share the emotional and intellectual experience of the past lives of these his spiritual kindred.

COSMIC LIFE: GROUP-SOULS

O mighty river! strong eternal Will,
Wherein the streams of human good and ill
Are onward swept, conflicting, to the sea!
The World is safe because it floats in Thee.

HENRY VAN DYKE

For we are members one of another.

ST. PAUL

WE have made reference in the preceding chapter and on several earlier occasions to the Group-soul, a term used by Myers. I now propose to gather together all the information he has communicated on this theme and to supplement it from another communicator. Without an appreciation of this topic it is impossible to convey any conception of the further progress of souls beyond the fourth plane of consciousness.

Myers speaks of myriads of Spirits begotten of God, each of which "nourishes a number of journeying souls with its light". In the terminology of Imaginism each of these Spirits is a sub-imaginal field giving birth to the souls which it nourishes. He speaks of them as at first "crude, innocent, and incomplete embryos". Each of them grows and evolves through the souls associated with it, which adventure forth and gather experience by descent and ascent through the levels of being. These souls or centres of consciring remain related to the one Spirit in a way which is perhaps conveyed by saying that the individualised minds have their roots in a collective mind which the Spirit illuminates from above. The souls are the gatherers of experience which they bring to this common treasury. It is as though a Spirit realises that part of the pattern which Divine Imagining gave it birth to achieve, and the created souls are the workers which weave the living tapestry through long ages. It is said that the number of souls in different Groups varies. In some Groups there may be a score, in others a thousand souls. Moreover, the number is not necessarily constant, but may be added to by activities of which we are told very little (probably activities by some of the most advanced souls of the Group on the fifth plane). The souls of a Group are in general at varying stages of development, and if so are dispersed on some or all of the first five planes of being.

It is usually on the fourth plane that souls become aware of the Group-soul to which they are related and start to share the emotional and intellectual experiences of their comrade souls. With this development, the outlook widens and deepens greatly, and the soul discovers the reality and joy of communion with others to an extent which it can never do on earth.[1] At this stage the soul has consciously two aspects, one objective in the world of form and the other subjective in the Group-soul to which he belongs. "The interesting feature of my state here," says Myers, "is that I am within a larger mind which is not a collective one, but which is rounded off from many others."

Each stage of development has its peculiar temptations or dangers, and it appears that where a soul gathers intimate knowledge of the experience of a section of the Group-soul, he may sometimes adopt the "thought-mould" of this particular section to the exclusion of a wider outlook. All limiting barriers, whether racial, religious, philosophical, or otherwise, have to be broken down before progress to a higher level can take place. This larger self or mind has stored within it knowledge of all the previous life-histories of all souls in the Group. Before a soul can leave the fourth for the fifth plane it must have come fully and consciously to realise its oneness with this greater Being. Prayer and mystical experience on this level are, in the first instance, communion with the Spirit which enlightens and nourishes the Group.

Myers says a number of interesting things about the re-incarnation of souls. Where the soul is primitive or bound closely to the things of earth, re-incarnation is generally the rule. Such souls need to travel back, and in the earthly setting where their desire is centred, discover the necessity for something bigger. His own experience of the majority of people he has met leads Myers to suggest that two, three, or four earth-lives are the usual number undertaken. For special purposes there may be more, but the teaching of certain oriental religions that there is a long succession of lives until emancipation from the "wheel" is attained is not borne out by his experience. He points out that with the attainment of the fourth plane, and the power to enter subjectively into knowledge of the lives of comrades in the same Group-soul, there can be gained breadth of experience and wisdom which would otherwise only be possible by many more lives in a physical body. Thus says Myers:

"Through our communal experience I perceive and feel the drama in the earthly journey of a Buddhist priest, of an American merchant, of an Italian painter, and I am, if I assimilate the life thus lived, spared the living of it in the flesh. . . . [The soul] perceives all the consequences of acts, moods, thoughts, in detail in this life of a kindred soul and so it may . . . win the knowledge of all typical earth-existences." [2]

[1] Cf. Matthew Arnold's poem *To Marguerite*, which begins, "Yes, in the sea of life enisl'd".
[2] *Beyond Human Personality*, pp. 69-70.

Reference was made in Chapter 9 to the idea of *karma*. The relations at their deeper levels of the souls within a group are so close that the karma of one may sometimes considerably affect that of others. Myers states that in entering upon his last life on earth (which closed on January 17th, 1901) he entered into the karmic inheritance of another soul of his group who had left the earth before he was born. He informs us that he will not again return to earth, but that the karmic framework that he left behind would be the inheritance of a younger soul of the same group.[1] In an earlier chapter we described a human being as the meeting-point of two streams of heredity, one is physical and represented by the body which he receives from his parents, the other is his soul's heredity. We now see that the latter is partly his own creation and partly that of his spiritual kindred whose evolution is so closely linked with his own.

While individual souls may and do attain the fifth plane of being, it is not possible for the Group-soul as a whole to evolve further along the road of its destiny until all its members on the lower planes have attained to the level of the fifth. More advanced souls who achieve the fourth plane and choose not to return to earth enlarge their experience within the Group-memory, and also at times through a close bond with a younger soul who may have entered upon *their* karma on earth.

Occasionally, it happens that a soul is quite incapable of immortality and quite unworthy of it. In this case it may cease to be conscired by the sustaining Spirit of the group and will fall out of existence. All that is of value in its experience is, however, conserved for the benefit of others.

Myers says that occasionally there is created by Divine Imagining a Spirit which remains in close and direct contact with its source. It does not separate itself and proceed along the evolutionary road we have outlined. It finds the fulfilment of its being in producing on earth a single spirit-man, who after death rises swiftly through the planes of being to resume an immediacy of communion with God in the Divine Society. It seems clear that Jesus was such a one.

THE FIFTH PLANE (THE PLANE OF FLAME)

From a full experience of living on the fourth plane, it is very exceptional to find a soul undertaking re-incarnation, for he has already experienced "the height and the depth and the fulness of life" in form. The soul is beginning to realise that form itself is not essential and that the most advanced souls of its group are "calling it to the Flame-world, to that level of consciousness whereon perception, insight, and imagination extend mightily, slowly and surely gathering within them knowledge of the inter-stellar spaces, knowledge of the third disguise, of the

[1] *The Road to Immortality*, pp. 45-6.

starry raiment, and of those (to us) blazing fires that light up the heavens when day has died".[1]

Myers is referring to the physical body as the first disguise of the soul, and to the body of the third and fourth planes as the second disguise. These are human in form, but on the fifth plane the soul lives in what may be described as an outline or a "flame". Human language is clearly showing its limitations in describing these conditions. At this stage the soul is aware of all the souls which constitute his group; their emotions and intellectual achievements as well as their wisdom surge through his being, so that he has an immediate experience of what it means to be one and yet many. Most of the souls who constitute such a group are found on the ladder of consciousness whose foot rests on the earth, although there are sometimes those who have had experience on other planets. The great experience of the soul on the fifth plane is the extension of its knowledge beyond that of the Group-soul to that of the Psychic tribe (to use Myers' term). In other words, within his Group-soul he has acquaintance with all that the earth and possibly other planets of the solar system can give him; he now has to enlarge his horizon incomparably, to enter into the range of experience which is offered by the whole galaxy—this world system of which our sun is but one star.

One of the first steps to be taken is to seek stellar incarnation for a time. This is a type of experience remote from our own of which Myers has attempted to convey a general conception. I shall not attempt any summary of it here: the interested reader should refer to the book mentioned below.[2] We are told that those who incarnate in this way experience an intensity of life in vast stellar societies quite beyond our grasp. For them the conception of the cosmos is vastly greater, and "when they worship they draw nearer to the reality of His pervading presence". It appears that their life also has its objective and subjective aspects, and there is something corresponding to sin and suffering on their high level. Sin is there described as failure to progress towards a still higher level of consciousness. "There is," says Myers, "an Eternal Law which compels the seeker after Beauty and Truth to endeavour with all his might to reach the plane from which, mounting still higher, he may draw near to God. . . . Always the soul has the power to choose, and if the soul is deficient *in imaginative power and in faith*, he will have no desire to go forward."

At the close of a stellar life the ways that lie before the soul are many, and his choice, guided by the Spirit of his Group-soul, is determined by his success or failure to advance. Those who are conscious of

---

[1] *Beyond Human Personality*, Chap. XI.
[2] *Beyond Human Personality*, p. 100.

failure may decide to return some distance along the road and perhaps resume life on the fourth plane again. Others who have enriched and widened their experience may resume the closeness of their relation with the Group-soul which has had to be in abeyance during their stellar life. An incalculable variety of experiences await them on the fifth plane, in the form of knowledge of the Psychic Tribe and through it of the variety of life throughout the galaxy. Still other souls, perhaps through love of comrades or through knowledge of their weaknesses, or for the joy of such experience, seek further and more intense stellar life on stars with different conditions. We are told that even on the dark stars, which cannot be seen by telescopes, manifold intelligences seek embodiment and experience a life which brings riches to their common treasury. The experience of stellar incarnation is regarded only as introductory to the vast horizon of the fifth plane. In spite of its intensity, ecstasy, and wonder, it is an intermediate phase of experience bridging the transition from the highest form of human personality on the fourth plane to what may be called cosmic personality on the fifth plane. It is through this last experience in a body of "flame" that he comes to know that form is unnecessary. It is only then that he can begin that communion with the Psychic Tribe—those Group-souls in all parts of the galaxy which have risen in devious ways to the fifth plane and find there a higher unity. The enormous broadening of consciring on this level is suggested by some phrases which Myers uses.[1]

"He perceives and registers instantaneously numerous thoughts, feelings and fields of vision, whereas a human being only registers one at a time.

"He scans the past experiences that were the lot of his many comrade-souls; they make for him a present."

Service on the fifth plane is correspondingly on the grand scale. It has been stated that a Group-soul cannot go beyond the fifth plane except as a complete unity when all its souls have attained this level. Sometimes a section of a group may attain the plane together and become members of the Divine Hierarchy or Divine Society who direct and control the affairs of earth, the other planets and myriads of stars. These supreme artists, whom Myers calls the "Wise", control the mighty processes of Nature, the duration of life, and the complex moral pattern which has been collectively described as karma. They are the agents through which the Divine plan is being forwarded in each part of the galaxy. Their organisation and activity proceeds downwards to the smallest detail. The Divine Society includes all those who thus guide every part of the galaxy—the star-sown fields of heaven and all the higher planes of being linked with these physical manifestations.

[1] *Beyond Human Personality*, pp. 119-20.

It is strange to reflect that when puny man looks up on a clear night at a thousand steely twinkling points of light, there may be comrade-souls on some of those blazing orbs enjoying an ecstasy of life beyond his imagining, yet making the same long journey towards the goal. These comrades of man differ vastly from him in their outlook and knowledge, and not least in this, that he, an earthly pilgrim, cannot see the plan. He thinks he may live in a lonely universe alien to his dreams, where in a sceptical philosopher's phrase "omnipotent matter rolls on its relentless way". Did he but know it, could he but see for a moment with the vision of stellar man, he would become aware of his spiritual kindred throughout the galaxy all travelling the road of life and all moving slowly onward to that consummation pictured in the infinite imagination of God.

THE SIXTH PLANE AND BEYOND

In making any statements about this level of consciousness we are moving so far beyond human conceptions that they can scarcely be regarded as more than extrapolations of a very speculative kind. Myers has informed us that his awareness is of the fourth plane and that he has only had glimpses of the fifth in a subjective state. He does not give us the source of his further information and it may perhaps be regarded as teaching handed on to him.

To the advanced soul on the fifth plane, this world-system of ours is an open book, some little fragments of which are his own past and present experience, and other large tracts of which he has come to know intimately through sharing the memories contained within the Psychic Tribe. These comprise not only physical life in many parts of the galaxy but of life on those planes of being within and above the physical.

When all the souls of his group have reached the fifth level, the experience necessary to the Spirit which nourishes them is complete. It is a mature One-Many when all this experience is shared and sifted. With a new and complete sense of being, this member of the Divine Society may decide to go forward to experience on the sixth plane of consciousness. If they do so they pass through an intermediate phase which exists between all the planes, and they emerge into a state of consciring which Myers symbolises by the description "the plane of white light". They may now live without form. "They are lords of life, for they have conquered," says Myers. The last voyage of discovery of which we are told is that they may proceed to gather knowledge of world-systems external to our own.

Divine Imagining, by its very nature, is always creating. Astronomers inform us that beyond our galaxy, remote in the depths of space, there are others. I recall that thirty years ago text-books of astronomy informed us there might be as many as half a million galaxies beyond the Milky Way which is the fringe of our own. It was at the time suggested that these might be "island-universes" in evolution. Mr. Hoyle has informed us recently that the 200-inch telescope combined with modern photographic technique discloses between a hundred million and a thousand million galaxies.[1] Our own galaxy is apparently one member of a "local" group of nineteen to which the great nebula in Andromeda also belongs.

Do not let us forget that what the astronomer observes is only the outer physical garment—the lowest of the significant planes. Each galaxy is an Imaginal experiment of the Fontal Power, a dream of the Divine Being in process of realisation. Each may well begin with different initial conditions, a different group of imaginals entering into its being and evolution. Each is striving to realise the supreme beauty of the pattern imaged for it. Does the Group-soul or does the Psychic Tribe of which it is a part set out on this great adventure of surveying the experience of other galaxies? Does it find in other galaxies other Tribes to which it is akin? Is there any limit at all to the experience of the sixth plane? Is there a "far-off Divine Event to which the whole creation moves" when those world-systems which have attained perfection come together in a higher enriching synthesis? These are questions so far beyond an answer in human terms that even to ask them is rather fantastic.

Myers[2] suggests that there is a final leap beyond the sixth plane into immediate communion with the Supreme Power, the Creative Source. "Many are called, but few are chosen." In this final state of ultimate reality there is formlessness with the possibility of form, and timelessness with the possibility of time. This sounds paradoxical, but I think we can see how it arises. We must realise that there is (1) The conception of the Eternal Plan in the Creative Imagination (timelessness), (2) The continuous fulfilling of this conception (time-succession). The dream in the Supreme Artist's Imagination of the picture of all time is static and in this sense timeless: the execution of the picture involves the succession of events (which sometimes differ from that originally planned). In this sense we have a duality of time and timelessness. The dream of the Eternal Plan is the world of the Absolute which has appealed to many philosophers. But they have declined to admit the additive process in the life of the Supreme. Here they are wrong, for the fulfilling of the Eternal Plan is continuously enriching the very nature of God.

[1] Fred Hoyle, *Frontiers of Astronomy*, p. 274. (Heinemann Ltd., 1955.)
[2] *The Road to Immortality*, p. 53 (1947 reprint).

F. W. H. MYERS AND IMAGINISM

I do not know what impression these disclosures of Myers have made upon the reader. Some may echo the sad words of Thomas Hardy, "hoping it might be so". Some may feel that human imagining has run riot. Indeed, it must always be a bewildering experience when our finite imagining tries to grasp Divine Imagining. Whenever we are presented with data of revelation, we can only satisfy ourselves that they are not inconsistent with reason's claims, and having done this we shall doubtless react to them according to the intuitive light which we possess. For myself, I can only say that after a very close study of Myers' scripts I think they present an outlook which is reasonable (as far as reason can be applied to it), attractive, and sublime in its conception.

If I approach the meaning of the Universe from the observational background of astronomy, should I not ask myself what kind of a Being He is who has created this? I find it inconceivable that the Supreme Power finds peculiar pleasure in dispersing physical objects in space-time, even if they are very large ones! This being so, I must then ask for the meaning and purpose behind the appearances. Secondly, I find it inconceivable that Man on this little planet called the Earth is the crown of creation,—God's most advanced experiment with conscious beings. On the contrary, I find it reasonable to suppose that, wherever physical appearances are manifest to our senses, it is an indication that another imaginal experiment in consciousness is proceeding. From such premises the disclosures of Myers seem to me plausible, and even persuasive.

One of the impressive features of the Cummins-Myers scripts is the constant reference to the faculty of imagination, and the Divine Imagination—an insight which is in full support of Fawcett's philosophical outlook.[1] I shall give a few examples of this. (Two quotations made in Chapter 11 may also be referred to.)

"The great picture of all creation has been conceived in the imagination of God before ever the babe has evolved out of what we call the void." (*R.I.*, p. 71.)

"Many of us sorrowfully close the Book of Life when we have thus gazed into a future that is not yet for man, sprung out of the Unknown, out of the boundless sea which, I must again remind you, is the creation of the all-pervading imagination of God." (*R.I.*, p. 93.)

"Bear in mind the power behind each human being is imagination. It preserves the past in the form of memory, and unless temporarily fixed in a

---

[1] It should be said that these scripts in *The Road to Immortality* were obtained in the periods 1924-5, 1927, and 1931. Those in *Beyond Human Personality* came for the most part in 1933-4. Miss Cummins informs me that she first met Mr. Fawcett in the late 'thirties, and *subsequent* to this made some acquaintance with his *Dialogues*.

mould of its own making, is creating the present, adding to itself, taking away from itself." (*B.H.P.*, p. 71.)

"It is the artist's imagination rather than that of the mathematician which creates and maintains the visible universe; the created thing itself becomes creative, and therein lies one of the secrets of life and destiny." (*B.H.P.*, p. 95.)

[Writing of the planets] "All have been, or will be, the home of ensouled beings who, during a brief span of existence upon them are controlled by centres of imagination, who possess imaginal characters." (*B.H.P.*, p. 99.)

"I would describe in a phrase the creative basis of life in connection with the inhabitants of earth and the inhabitants of the stars. In each case the Inspiring Principle is a centre of imagination. That collaboration of soul and spirit which lies behind the physical body and the body of solar man may be summarised in a sentence 'limited focus of imagination which is connected with an imaginal field'." (*B.H.P.*, p. 114.)

The similarity, indeed the identity, of thought here between Myers (per Miss Cummins) and Fawcett, is quite remarkable, and strongly supports the Imaginist outlook. I should like to give some further examples of the striking similarity of outlook between Myers and Fawcett. In an essay on *The Subliminal Self* (*R.I.*, p. 82) Myers is writing of the evolution of man.

"The larger mind has been there in a state at times unformed, from the dark ages. . . . At first this mind found it could only at times send faint reflections to primitive people, whom it had gradually evolved, created as a sculptor creates. But in time the form of man developed and was the more easily able to receive the image. The Word was made flesh with greater and greater facility.

"You may ask in connection with mind why it thus sought to express itself? It desired individuality; it too desired form; and form and individuality were to a certain degree achieved through this constant interchange between mind and matter."

Compare in detail these ideas with a few sentences of Fawcett (*O.D.*, p. 247), allowing for the difference in terminology.

"The divine imaginal field . . . was originally one of *mere content*; a conscitum constructed as home of a nascent world-system. . . . But this divine imaginal field is to be lit by finite centres of consciring who will exist not only for God *but also for themselves*. At first the regions in which these centres will arise are only tracts of content, some more or less simple, some complex, all under the central divine control. . . . Among these regions is that of the imaginal which is to be the seat of the permanent human souls. . . . The imaginal just mentioned is conscired more intensely until that degree of strength which constitutes a 'threshold' is passed. Beyond this 'threshold' a tract of content, once only conscired, becomes one of consciring at first irreflective, and a finite centre or agent is born. . . . The content ever aglow for Divine Imagining has now become aglow for itself."

The reader will perhaps excuse this digression for it illustrates the striking consonance of Myers' outlook with Imaginism.

We have said a good deal in this chapter of the Group-soul, a key-concept in Myers' exposition of man's destiny. We have mentioned also the Psychic Tribe—a higher synthesis. Compare these ideas with Fawcett's statement[1]:

"Human individuals allied with physical bodies may well belong to a common imaginal, though they retain perhaps distinctiveness within it. The complexity indeed may be such that sub-imaginals within wider sub-imaginals, and these again within yet wider, exist in a hierarchy."

I give one concluding example. The reader should compare Myers' account of the work of Group-souls on the fifth plane who control the affairs of earth "down to the last decimal" (*B.H.P.*, pp. 94-5) with the following quotation from Fawcett:

"Men of science have credited even the humble germ-cell with trying experiments which we call variations, and seeing that this organism is of psychoid character they may be right. But far more efficient experimenters may be at work, including in their sphere of operations both the germ-cell and the soul. I refer to the group-souls and those powers whom Plato referred to as minor gods."

CONCLUDING REFLECTIONS

The vastness of Creation is inconceivable. We have been given the impression of worlds within worlds, and systems within systems: of a universe full of life, climbing what Tennyson might have called

> the great world's altar-stairs
> That slope through darkness up to God.

We must remind ourselves that the altar-stairs start everywhere, and that darkness only surrounds the lower steps.

We have had glimpses of a great principle of integration running through the universe, "sub-imaginals within wider sub-imaginals, and these again within yet wider, existing in a hierarchy". Those sub-imaginals which are Group-souls constitute for us, as human beings, the clue to much that is mysterious in our life.

I conclude with a reflection which may be of interest to the student of Indian religious thought, if not to the general reader, and I shall state it very briefly. It is well known that the great affirmation of

[1] *Z.D.*, p. 523; *O.D.*, p. 352.

Vedanta is "That art Thou." There is one Self in all, or, expressing it otherwise, the essence of individual man is identical with the Supreme Spirit. Thus the Upanishads say

"This is my spirit within my heart, greater than the earth, greater than the sky, greater than the heavens, greater than all worlds.

"The all-working, all-wishing, all-smelling, all-tasting one that embraceth the universe, that is silent, untroubled—that is my spirit within my heart; that is Brahman. Thereunto when I go hence I shall attain."

This affirmation, which holds such an honoured place in Vedanta, must have been the fruit of profound mystical experience by the ancient sages of India. I want to suggest that the profoundest mystical experience of which any incarnate human being is capable is communion with the Spirit of his Group-soul, that "Light from above" which Myers spoke of as a thought of God, and as having "a certain apartness from its Creator, the apartness of the created thing from the One who gave it life". I suggest, with great respect, that it was such mystical experience that led to the great Vedantic affirmation, and that it would be truer to say "Of That art Thou."

Chapter

14

FINAL REFLECTIONS

What needest thou?—a few brief hours of rest
Wherein to seek thyself in thine own breast;
A transient silence wherein truth could say
Such was thy constant hope, and this thy way?—
    O burden of life that is
    A livelong tangle of perplexities!

What seekest thou?—a truce from that thou art;
Some steadfast refuge from a fickle heart;
Still to be thou, and yet no thing of scorn,
To find no stay here, and yet not forlorn?—
    O riddle of life that is
    An endless war 'twixt contrarieties.

Leave this vain questioning. Is not sweet the rose?
Sings not the wild bird ere to rest he goes?
Hath not in miracle brave June returned?
Burns not her beauty as of old it burned?
    O foolish one to roam
    So far in thine own mind away from home!

Where blooms the flower when her petals fade,
Where sleepeth echo by earth's music made,
Where all things transient to the changeless win,
There waits the peace thy spirit dwelleth in.

             WALTER DE LA MARE (*Vain Questioning*)

IN his book *Process and Reality*, Professor A. N. Whitehead says, "There remains the final reflection, how shallow, puny, and imperfect are efforts to sound the depths in the nature of things. In philosophical discussion, the merest hint as to finality of statement is an exhibition of folly." With such a view we must cordially agree.

It does not matter from what vantage point we start out in our enquiry, provided we think fundamentally and relentlessly, we touch a core of mystery which reason and the scientific method are unable to resolve. Fawcett has remarked, "For each level of our conscious life, knowledge is bounded. And our level is a low one."

When we look at a field of grass we are aware of the greenness and perhaps of a few blades in slight movement. But how minute a fraction we conscire of the total processes taking place. We have no awareness of the subtle chemistry in a myriad molecular changes, of the cell-metabolism and the cell-division, of the flow of sap, and of the vast life of micro-organisms and insects which weave their lives with the field.

We see a group of dragon flies hovering and darting over it, but we do not conscire the process which brought them into being and sustains their "crowded hour of glorious life", nor do we know where the life which animates them will be tomorrow. Of the external world which enters through the gates of our senses, only the smallest fraction which is essential for practical purposes rises above the threshold of our reflective consciring. When we perceive the green grass, the physiological processes which occur in our brains themselves never rise above the threshold. Our eyes, remarkable instruments as they are, respond to light frequencies of only one octave out of a very large number. They are sensitive, but only enough to register the light from one star in every twenty million in our galaxy. In relation to the universe around us, we must face the fact that we are restricted to a remarkable degree. Our direct acquaintance with it is minute, and much that we often describe as knowledge is inference.

If our outward view is so restricted, what shall we say of the "inward" view along a dimension of increasing reality? Perhaps the most significant comment we can make is that many people are not aware that there is such a view. It is at this point that psychical research or parapsychology (which sounds academically respectable) has significance for our day. It has taken the fringe of phenomena which are so close to the physical norm that scientific methods can be used to demonstrate them, and in so doing has shown this new dimension to be there beyond any doubt. This is an important step forward in our emancipation from the limited philosophical outlook of scientific materialism.

We are digressing, however, from the point we wish to stress. This is that although we have some awareness of a physical universe vast beyond our imagining, and of levels behind the physical which await our exploration, these are only faint glimpses which our restricted consciring makes possible. It is perhaps not surprising that the Orphics looked upon the physical body as a tomb, and those buried in it as practically dead. Yet all such judgments are relative only in their truth. Every penetration to a higher level of reality tempts an advancing being to look back upon the lower as a level of illusion from which he has become emancipated. Here we must be careful in forming our philosophy of life. Every level of existence from the physical upwards is a level of outworking of an imaginal pattern, and is therefore playing its part in the long process by which our world-system is finding its way to the sublime goal of Divine Imagining.

In this concluding chapter I propose to do two things. The first is to review the plan which Imaginism envisages by which the human soul makes its long pilgrimage to eternity. The second is to suggest how we can best use our terrestrial experience to facilitate this plan.

THE PLAN

Each world-system, of which a starry galaxy is the temporary manifestation on the physical level, is an experiment of Divine Imagining in which probably different initial conditions obtain. Groups of imaginals interpenetrate and make the world-system a perfect work of art, a perfect whole within the limits of the imaginals supplied. It exists as a poem or a work of art may exist for its human creator—perfect within the limits of the theme prescribed. This perfect world-system exists at first only as content for Divine consciring. The content includes soul-imaginals, comprising perfect beings, but they have no self-awareness, no consciousness of existence; they are not sentients or centres of consciring. They exist only for their Creator. He imagined, however, a higher type of perfection in which they should exist for themselves, and with this began the metaphysical fall into time-succession. At the very outset of this world-process, what Fawcett calls the permanent souls or highest bodies of souls were formed, but they had no centre of reflective consciring to light them. The first step in descent was to create these centres by augmenting the intensity of consciring in local regions. Myriads of finite sentients were thus given independent existence. The vast societies of natural agents, those sub-imaginals, which ultimately manifest on the physical level as atoms, molecules, cells, and plants, never appear to rise above the irreflective level. The higher animals certainly achieve some measure of reflective consciring, but possibly never achieve *permanent* centres or souls. The age-long journey of the human soul has never been, as some have suggested, an evolution which has proceeded through various levels of the animal kingdom to man's estate. It has been a process of slow growth in intensity and range of consciring. The Permanent soul or highest body born in the initial process of Divine Imagining has to be raised from its level of irreflective consciring to the reflective level of man, and far beyond this to that quality of consciring characteristic of the Divine Society.

Let us return to the early stages where certain regions of the field of content are conscired more intensely. The bodies of these sentients are insulated from each other by tracts of content conscired at a lower level. At the same time they are related in groups, each nourished by a sub-imaginal, a "Spirit" or individualised thought of God. Within this group there is greater interpenetration than with the outside, but initially interpenetration is marked throughout the whole system. It is when Divine consciring sufficiently raises the intensity in limited centres that overflow results in conflict, and the imaginal dynamic starts to impel the world-system along the evolutionary road from level to level. A soul "descends" (in Platonic language), having built for it on each level, by lower sub-imaginals, a vehicle or body which imperfectly images the higher. It gains more significant consciring as it descends because the reflective thresholds are lower. The soul is lifted above these critical thresholds by penetration of content from without, through the senses of the body it has appropriated. The physical body of man is built by a lower body-making sub-imaginal, which cannot however raise its products above the animal level of reflective consciring. When one of these is annexed by a descending soul, the latter, in Fawcett's words, "is awakened by the physical body and then uses it". The brain, which Bergson regarded as an organ of limitation, certainly restricts the range of the soul's consciring, but in so doing lifts its apex well above the reflective threshold. But, as we all know, much of the soul's activity remains continually at the irreflective level (the modern "unconscious" mind). We shall not here repeat the story of man's further development which we have told from Chapter 9 onwards. It is a long journey which we believe will take him through types of all the vast range of experience which this amazing universe can offer.

Perhaps the evidence which we have on the physical level of an expanding universe is an indication that through untold aeons of time there are those who are attaining to union with the Supreme, who are admitted to the last secret, and share with the Fontal Power the joys of creative imagining.

LIVING: HERE AND NOW

From the cosmic panorama it is fitting in conclusion that we should bring our thought down to the business of living and ask ourselves how we can best use the here and now to advance the purpose of our being. In a tribute paid after his death to that remarkable and lovable Irishman George Russell (A. E.), mystic, poet, and artist, someone said, "A. E.'s life had a single objective—the objective was not supremacy in a particular craft, but as complete a perfecting of the self as was possible in the circumstances which destiny had decreed. . . . He might have said with Epictetus 'Material things are indifferent, but how we handle them is not indifferent. My business is to use what does turn up with diligence and skill.' " To this wisdom I should like to add a fragment from another wise man: this deals with personal relations. "What matters is not one's self, but the influence of one's self on other people's selves."

Most people who look at the setting of their life, and at those many apparently chance events which have determined their present situation, are usually impressed by the given-ness of things. To a far larger extent than we often recognise, we find ourselves presented with an environment, with personal relationships, with problems, and with work which we had only a little part in determining. Especially when faced with frustration and adversity, we are prone to wonder how far there is any higher directive, any "Providence" such as our fathers trusted, or whether we are just corks tossed about on the restless seas of change. I ask the reader to look again at the end of Chapter 11. There is a limited but important area of freedom preserved to each of us, but it is within a pattern—that pattern which the Group-soul of which we are a member is weaving in the great tapestry of Divine Imagining. I have been assured on several occasions that there is design and purpose behind human events, and that *at the right time* those threads are placed in our hands which it is our duty to weave with our highest skill and utmost devotion. We may sometimes think we are isolated: the truth is that we are bound on a great co-operative adventure with comrade-souls which will last for us as long as time exists.

It appears that terrestrial experience with all the restrictions of a physical body offers us a special opportunity to develop. One of the characteristics of the after-death state (Myers' third plane) is its congeniality, and the comparative ease with which our hopes and dreams may be realised. This results in lack of challenge to serious endeavour, to effort, struggle, and self-discipline, which are the conditions of the soul's growth. Earth is the place of challenge, and according to the effort we make in response (not according to the success which the world considers us to have achieved) we fulfil the purpose of this stage of our journey. Thus it follows that length of days, fame, power, and outward achievement are all misleading evaluations of an earthly life, and that alone is important, which none of us can estimate without spiritual discernment. A short life which meets some ordeal with courage and undefeated cheerfulness, a spirit which meets frustration without embitterment, and loss without self-pity, a life lived in some commonplace or sordid setting whose kindness and helpfulness are known as dependable by all around—these are great achievements in the soul's progress. Challenge and response, which Professor Toynbee saw as a clue to the rise and fall of the world's civilisations, is the clue also to the soul's life on earth, whatever the setting.

There is an intuitive wisdom in some people by which these things are known without any need of analysis. Most of us in this age of scientific thought are more satisfied with the kind of truth which, having analysed as far as possible, we can see is reasonably based. I shall suggest, therefore, three forms of activity of the soul which appear to encompass wisdom for living.

(1) *The cultivation of spiritual sensitivity.* This comes more easily

to the old soul than to the young one. So far as terrestrial existence is concerned, it is to the latter perhaps the least important of the three. Most of us have known some admirable people, essentially practical and extraverted, generous and philanthropic, happiest when there is fun and fellowship, to whom however a few hours of solitude would be a trial. Meditation, to such, is not understood. Silence is the absence of activity and noise. Worship does not come naturally. Religion is "doing good". Their appreciation of the beautiful is frequently linked with what is useful. If they appreciate music it must have rhythm, colour, and intensity. The reader will recognise the type to which I am referring: the particular illustrations are unessential. Frequently these attitudes are normal in youth, but in the older soul they pass in later years when the inherent maturity can reveal itself through the developed personality.

Man participates, as we know, in different levels of reality, and in the older soul a greater measure of irreflective consciring in the higher bodies gives rise to a more marked sensitivity towards beauty and towards its subtler manifestations in art, music, poetry, and Nature. It is generally recognised that what we "see" in these things depends on what we bring to them, and they, to the sensitive person, can open doors on to wider views and profounder insights. It should be clearly understood that here is no ground whatever for criticism of those to whom these things do not appeal. It would be as foolish to criticise the first-form schoolboy because he is not in the sixth form: the important thing is that he should be as good as possible at subjects relevant to that stage of his development. There is no merit in greater maturity *per se*, as there is no merit in being older or younger: if there is any merit, it is relative to the use made of opportunity. I fear that all too often the generalisations of moralists show little recognition of this truth. I am tempted to quote to them the words of a sage,[1] "Sin is a form of childishness. . . . All sins are nothing but a searching for happiness in the wrong direction; and all sinners are but children who will eventually grow up. Tolerance is the recognition of this fact."

Where the beautiful makes some appeal, whether through the endless processes of Nature, as it has done to many of the English poets, or through music or art, it is a glimpse along that dimension of reality which can lead to our growth. It need not be a mark of other-worldliness to cultivate this sensitivity. Here is the confession of R. L. Nettleship[2]:

[1] From *The Initiate*, by "His Pupil". (George Routlege & Sons Ltd.)
[2] Richard Lewis Nettleship, *Lectures and Memories*, Vol. I, p. 72. (Macmillan & Co. Ltd., 1897.)

"The only strength for me is to be found in the sense of a personal presence everywhere, it scarcely matters whether it be called human or divine; a presence which only makes itself felt at first in this and that particular form and feature. . . . Into this presence we come, not by leaving behind what are usually called earthly things, or by loving them less, but by living more intensely in them, and loving more what is really lovable in them; for it is literally true that this world *is* everything to us, if only we choose to make it so, if only we live in the present *because* it is eternity."

(2) *The cultivation of an alert and open mind for Truth.* This is one of the great needs of our day. If somewhere along the endless road of our soul's evolution we must make all Truth our own, there is every reason at the earliest stages of our journey for cultivating the right attitude of mind. When I speak of Truth here, I mean right knowledge, which is the foundation of Wisdom. It is one of the settled traits of human nature that, on the whole, it fears new truth. This is itself an aspect of a more fundamental characteristic: human nature dislikes change and insecurity, preferring to move in the settled ruts and grooves of tradition. Men like to continue in the ways to which they are accustomed rather than face the disturbance of novelty, even though reason may support the change. This attitude is usually overthrown in the end, but soon the accepted novelty becomes familiar and creates a new conservatism. There is therefore generally a weight of inertia to be overcome before any progress can be made. At this point we seem to learn nothing from history, and we make the same mistakes as our forefathers. The heresy of yesterday has become the orthodoxy of today, but this does not disturb the implicit confidence of people that today's orthodoxy is final, and that only minor changes, if any, are conceivable. I draw the reader's attention again to the courageous words of the late Principal John Oman which precede Chapter 6, and to the words of Lord Balfour on p. 149. If these things are true, and they are very clear to me—is it not time that we fought against our psychological prejudices? With fearfulness the commonest of human traits, we may not always be able to *welcome* new truth, but at least we may adopt the wisdom which Gamaliel[1] expressed nineteen hundred years ago, and in which, incidentally, history proved him to be right.

We are really discussing the operation of the imaginal dynamic which constantly disturbs our equilibria with the introduction of novelty. It impels us along the rough road of history, which, in spite of ups and downs, is still, I venture to believe, a rising road. When I reflect on the universe in which we live and in which we conscire so feebly, many of the certainties and dogmas which men defend with so

---

[1] Acts v. 38-9.

great an air of assurance must, I think, make the gods laugh. I do not equate a becoming humility with reluctance to believe anything: far from it. Such an intellectual attitude, if it were possible, would waste the great opportunity of a reasonable venture of faith which our present life is designed to provide. It is surely, however, a true humility, in the light of our humble place in the universe, to pray with great sincerity an ancient prayer: "Lighten our darkness, we beseech Thee, O Lord", and then keep our eyes wide open.

(3) *The practice of self-forgetful goodwill which is Love in Action.* The two attitudes of which I have written are not living issues for everyone. Their practice is dependent upon a certain measure of exemption from the immediate pressure of physical existence—from what may be called the mechanics of living. Their very existence as possible attitudes presupposes a certain background of educational opportunity and cultural interest. To many people in our civilised society these privileges have not come, nor perhaps, where available, has the ability to profit by them always been present. How shall these our brothers and sisters fulfil the purpose of terrestrial life? Can the very material pressures and demands, the routines and monotonies which press upon them, become the means of the soul's progress? Most assuredly.

Personal relationships are the lot of everyone. We live with people; we have to work with them. We meet them on the streets, in shops and offices, factories and universities. There must be few indeed whose lives do not bring them into contact with other people, some intimately, some more remotely. The problems and opportunities of inter-personal relationships are therefore present to everyone. Such activities as affect higher levels of the self, those which stimulate spiritual sensitivity and add wide intellectual understanding, are doubtless activities which we shall have the opportunity to pursue to equal or greater advantage on higher levels than the physical one. This cannot, however, be said of personal relationships, which are at the very centre of our present kind of life. To fail in showing love and goodwill is to fail at a point where the remedy afterwards cannot be easy, and to pass at death on to the next level, a beggar in spirit.

Every great teacher of mankind has in a different way, and with his own emphasis, taught the supreme law of Love. In His own teaching, and by His own living, the supreme Master of Galilee emphasised the importance of human relationships. He was himself happier to suffer within the human family than retain His own life outside it. If we separate ourselves from our fellows and fail in friendship, through any self-esteem or self-interest however well-justified we may think it to be, we obviously do not follow Him. It is interesting to observe that in the only parable of judgment ascribed to Him (admittedly a parable), everything turns on the one virtue—compassion. Those who were turned away were condemned, because in a world of need they couldn't see it, or seeing it, cared only for themselves. If I had only one prayer to pray, it would be that at the end of this phase of my life, looking back, I should know that I had not failed in loving.

INDEX

72 73 74   12 11 10 9 8 7 6 5 4 3 2 1

COLOPHON BOOKS ON PHILOSOPHY AND RELIGION

*In Preparation